The Industrial Revolution 1750–1850

ROBIN M. REEVE M.A.

UNIVERSITY OF LONDON PRESS LTD

ISBN 0 340 06852 3

University of London Press Ltd
St Paul's House, Warwick Lane, London EC4P 4AH

Printed and bound in Great Britain by
Hazell Watson and Viney Ltd, Aylesbury, Bucks

THE LONDON HISTORY STUDIES

1. The French Revolution
   R. BEN JONES B.LITT. M.A.

ISBN 0 340 06759 4 Boards
ISBN 0 340 06760 8 Paper

2. T
   I

3. T
   i

4.

5.

6.

7.

8.

EDITOR'S INTRODUCTION

THE LONDON HISTORY STUDIES are designed expressly for students. They examine those events and personalities of the last five hundred years which continue to attract the attention of historians and arouse argument among them.

The books in the series are intended to be succinct and concentrated. Short quotations from contemporary sources are used both to enliven the text and to produce evidence to support particular arguments, while differing views of the principal historians are fairly represented. In addition to the facts, students should find a clear statement of the problems involved in each subject, presented in such a way as to ensure understanding and to stimulate thought. Short bibliographies give direction to further research.

The authors are practising teachers who have been asked to write on the subjects in which they are especially interested. They are naturally familiar with the current research in their chosen fields but they can in addition draw on the knowledge and experience of the scholars and leading historians who compose the Advisory Panel. Thus the books contain the fruits of modern scholarship and are written from a close acquaintance with the questions that occur to students and the difficulties that face them.

It is hoped that this series will provide not only vigorous and effective treatment of the topics under discussion, but also an aid to a clear understanding of the methods of the historian.

R. B. J.

CONTENTS

PLATES

between pages 240 *and* 241

FIGURES

ACKNOWLEDGMENTS

This book owes an obvious debt of gratitude to the many historians who have written on the Industrial Revolution. I also wish to record my appreciation of the help and encouragement I have received from Christopher Storm-Clark and Ted Maidment.

I wish to thank Allied Ironfounders Ltd (plates 1 and II), Thomas Wragg & Sons (Sheffield) Ltd (plate 4), The Council for the Preservation of Sheffield Antiquities (plates 5 and 6), The National Trust (plate 7), and Young & Co, The Ram Brewery, Wandsworth (plate 13) for permission to take photographs on their property.

I wish to thank the following publishers and authors for their permission to use copyright material: George Allen and Unwin Ltd for an extract from *The Age of Equipoise* by W. L. Burn and *Capital* by Karl Marx, and for extracts from *The Human Documents of the Industrial Revolution* by E. Royston Pike; The Athlone Press of the University of London for an extract from an essay by J. D. Chambers on 'Population Change in a Provincial Town: Nottingham 1700–1800' in *Studies in the Industrial Revolution* edited by L. S. Pressnell; Basil Blackwell for extracts from *The Condition of the Working Class in England* by F. Engels, translated and edited by W. O. Henderson and W. H. Chaloner; Cambridge University Press for extracts from *The Abstract of British Historical Statistics* by B. R. Mitchell and W. A. Cole, *British Economic Growth 1688–1959* by Phyllis Deane and W. A. Cole, *The Economic History of Modern Britain* by Sir John Clapham, and for an extract from *The Wheelwright's Shop* by George Sturt; Jonathan Cape Ltd for extracts from *The Industrial Revolution in the Eighteenth Century* by Paul Mantoux; J. M. Dent & Sons Ltd for an extract from *Rural Rides* by William Cobbett and extracts from *A New View of Society* by Robert Owen, both in the Everyman Library; The

Economic History Society for extracts from an essay by J. B. Brebner, 'Laissez-faire and State Intervention in Nineteenth-century Britain' and from T. S. Ashton, 'Some Statistics of the Industrial Revolution', both in *Essays in Economic History*, Vol. 1, edited by E. M. Carus-Wilson; Eyre and Spottiswoode (Publishers) Ltd for extracts from *English Historical Documents* Vol. XI, edited by A. Aspinall, and Vol. XII (I), edited by G. M. Young and W. D. Handcock; Victor Gollancz Ltd for an extract from *The Making of the English Working Class* by E. P. Thompson; Longmans Green & Co Ltd for an extract from *The Rise of Industrial Society in England*, by S. G. Checkland and for extracts from *The Town Labourer* by J. L. and Barbara Hammond; Macmillan & Co Ltd for extracts from *British Working-class Movements, Select Documents 1789–1875*, edited by G. D. H. Cole and A. W. Filson, an extract from *Building Cycles and Britain's Growth* by J. Parry Lewis, and from *The Fabric of Freedom* by Esmond Wright; Manchester University Press for an extract from *The Family Economy of the Working Classes in the Cotton Industry 1784–1833* by Frances Collier; Methuen & Co Ltd for an extract from *The Economic History of Modern Britain: The Eighteenth Century* by T. S. Ashton; The Clarendon Press, Oxford, for an extract from *Country Banking in the Industrial Revolution* by L. S. Pressnell and Oxford University Press for extracts from *The Industrial Revolution 1760–1830* by T. S. Ashton; George Weidenfeld and Nicolson Ltd for extracts from *Labouring Men* by E. J. Hobsbawm.

PREFACE

This book does not set out to be a narrative history of the Industrial Revolution. It centres on the causes and consequences of the historic transition to an industrial economy: these were social as well as economic and they were necessarily diverse. But the Industrial Revolution cannot be studied without reference to the well defined phases through which it passed. Part I summarizes the achievements of the British Industrial Revolution as they appeared by 1850. It discusses the major causes of economic growth during the preceding century. A list of key events appears at the end of this part. Any such list must be highly selective; this one tries to place as much emphasis upon the foundation of important firms as upon the more familiar technical innovations. The progress of the Industrial Revolution can also be followed in the statistics assembled in Part V. The statistics of industrial production (Part V) provide more detailed information about the performance of the British economy during the century 1750–1850. A careful study of the statistics of production, combined with reference to the list of key events, should enable the reader to begin to make his own analysis of the various phases of industrial expansion.

As a form of historical evidence statistics are sometimes thought to be unreliable and tedious. All statistics for this period have their limitations and anyone who uses them should recognize what these are. This admitted, statistics have the great merit of being concise and of forcing our attention on to the problems. Statistics are vital to achieving a degree of precision in economic history. But the study of the Industrial Revolution is a study in history as well as economics and it makes demands upon the imagination. That is one reason why this book contains photographs of industrial sites and buildings.

Part II examines the social changes underlying the Industrial Revolution. The starting point here is a description of the British labour force in 1851 and an analysis of the way in which it reflected the industrial progress of the preceding century. The diversion of men into industry is essential to any industrial revolution. The industrial routine is not that of the land and the early industrial worker often resented the discipline imposed by his new masters. This was particularly a problem for the factory industries and it is significant that it was here that anger against long hours of work and the systematic exploitation of children first made itself felt. Changes in conditions of work have to be set against those in the standard of living. These are notoriously difficult to assess. That improvements in living standards did occur is undoubted but the benefit was unevenly distributed. Industrial workers gained more than agricultural labourers, the skilled more than the unskilled, the middle class more than the working class. Even when living standards rose they were subject to the inroads made by periodic depression and unemployment. Government had no answer to contemporary distress and its taxation policies actually increased the burden of working-class families. It was under these circumstances that people experienced the Industrial Revolution.

The Industrial Revolution is sometimes thought to be synony-mous with the rise of the industrial town. The relationship between the two is the subject of Part III. In the eighteenth century urbanization was a phenomenon distinct from that of industrial revolution. Its causes lay in the remarkable and unimpeded rise of population in Britain after the 1740s. But just as population growth was interlocked with industrial expansion so the growth of towns had specific economic consequences. By the mid-nineteenth century industry was being increasingly drawn towards the towns. Even so much industry remained rural or semi-rural and this did not apply only to the surviving domestic industries. In the relationship between the town and the industrial revolution London occupies an exceptional place; not only was this the greatest town in Britain and the most important single market, it was also a manufacturing centre and the major port. The industrial towns provided the context for a revolution in the social system and the relations between class and class. While the issue of class in the Industrial Revolution cannot be restricted to the towns, it was certainly here that the threat of social conflict was most apparent. Just as the towns often lay outside traditional society so their migrant population was exposed to new problems and uncertainties. Both the decline of church attendance and the growth of Nonconformity indicated the disturbing effects of industrialization and migration into towns.

For an industrial revolution to become established and take root any community must adapt and 'modernize' its institutions. Before the late nineteenth and twentieth centuries it was impossible for government to be the agent of industrial revolution but it could well inhibit and perhaps prevent its accomplishment. The function of government during the British Industrial Revolution is the subject of Part IV. This period is one in which the prevailing attitude towards government was summed up in the familiar concept of laissez-faire. The chapter begins by examining the origins of laissez-faire. The discussion is extended by an account of the traditional policy of trade regulation and its replacement by Free Trade in the nineteenth century. Despite the increasingly non-interventionist character of government in this period the fact that it had to fight a major war made government expenditure an important factor in economic development. And while government abandoned some powers it acquired others. It could scarcely avoid some supervision of banking and business organization. The social problems which arose in the new industry and the towns likewise called for government action. At the same time the Industrial Revolution created a demand for more efficient government and a more objective basis for policy. Laissez-faire was not then the only guide to policy and much that government did in this period was not entirely consistent – which might be said of government at any time.

The statistics in Part V provide further background for the argument of Parts II, III, and IV. Part V should also be used by itself. The statistics sometimes suggest approaches to the subject which it has not proved possible to explore in the text. A book of this kind is only an introduction to what has now become a major field of historical enquiry. Like the statistics the photographs in Part VI are selective and cannot pretend to be comprehensive. The short commentary on the photographs links them to points made in the main chapters.

PART I

1750–1850: An Outline of the Industrial Revolution

[1] THE IDEA AND ITS USES

Much is implied by the now familiar phrase 'the Industrial Revolution'. The term gained popularity as a convenient label to identify the technical changes which led to the modern factory system of production. Since then it has become a shorthand summary for that period of unique transformation in the history of modern societies when the ancient reliance upon agriculture and craft industries was exchanged for a modern industrial structure and a largely urban way of life. The phase of 'industrialization' is now seen to involve much more than a technical or simply (if there is such a thing) economic revolution. It includes, as part of the same experience, changes in social outlook and structure, in cultural patterns, and in political life. So it can be argued that the Industrial Revolution is the central event of modern history. As a result we are inclined more and more to view all history in terms of 'before' and 'after' and to emphasize the discontinuity with the past which the Industrial Revolution has imposed upon modern times. However hackneyed the term itself may have become it is still a powerful reminder of the revolutionary origins of the modern world.

The significance of the British Industrial Revolution is that it was the first. For this reason it must always exert a peculiar historical fascination. Unlike later industrial revolutions in other countries that in Britain emerged spontaneously within what is sometimes called a 'traditional economy'. This has made it difficult to fix precise dates for the Industrial Revolution. Of course there is general agreement about its approximate location in the eighteenth and early nineteenth centuries. Not surprisingly historians want to be more precise than this. Doesn't the use of the word 'revolution' demand a fairly exact chronology? Unfortunately the origin of economic change in any period before the appearance of modern statistics is a wispy and elusive thing. The great French historian, Paul Mantoux, who ended his own account of the Industrial Revolution at the beginning of the nineteenth century, rightly warned his readers that

Economic movements are more confused [than religious and political movements]. Their progress is like the slow growth of seeds scattered over a vast area. Endless obscure facts, in themselves almost insignificant, form great confused wholes and mutually modify one another indefinitely. No one can hope to grasp them all, and when we pick out a few for description it is obvious that we must give up, together with some of the truth, the rather vain ambition of arriving at rigorous definitions and final explanations. (*The Industrial Revolution in the Eighteenth Century*, 1961 ed., p. 42.)

It was because he defined the Industrial Revolution as the appearance of the factory system that Mantoux was able to end in 1800. Although he did not regard the Industrial Revolution as complete by that date it could be argued that once this essential feature of an industrial society has been securely established then everything which follows can be seen as a process of 'in-filling'. But there is a danger in concentrating on the obviously 'revolutionary' features of the economy during the period: it is the danger of producing a very one-sided account of what was, after all, a period of massive economic change. If what stands out in the period is the growth of industry, it does not necessarily follow that this was everywhere the result of revolutionary changes in either the methods of production or the organization of industry.

There are at least two ways of guarding against this particular source of lopsidedness. The first is to treat the Industrial Revolution primarily as a period of exceptional economic growth and to look at each industry within the framework of the economy as a whole. This approach derives from the preoccupation of modern economists, since Keynes, with the structure of the national income and the gross national product. A national income table is an attempt to express, in monetary terms, the total value of goods and services produced in the nation during one year. Despite the deficiencies of eighteenth and nineteenth-century statistics it has been shown to be possible to apply this approach to the British economy during the period of the Industrial Revolution (see Phyllis Deane and W. A. Cole, *British Economic Growth 1688–1959*). The most useful result of this work is that it makes for a more exact assessment of the role of specific industries during the Industrial Revolution and, equally, for closer comparison between the British and other industrial revolutions. The second antidote to an overdramatization of the Industrial Revolution, or of certain features of it, comes from placing its events in an understood perspective. It is clearly legitimate to see in the Industrial Revolution a culmination of the economic history of Britain and Europe since the Middle Ages or, more narrowly, since the sixteenth and seventeenth centuries. Another perspective altogether is given by looking back from a point, say the mid-nineteenth century, by which Britain is generally recognized to have completed the first stage of its Industrial Revolution. This is largely the approach adopted in this chapter and throughout the book.

The popular history of the phrase 'Industrial Revolution' began with the publication in 1884 of Arnold Toynbee's *Lectures on the Industrial Revolution of the Eighteenth Century in England*. The lectures were as much protest as history. For the more socially conscious late Victorians Toynbee's lectures provided historical justification for an attack upon an individualist, laissez-faire society. He argued that the 'essence' of the Industrial Revolution was the triumph of the spirit of competition:

at the period we are considering it [competition] came to be believed in as a gospel, and, the idea of necessity being superadded, economic laws deduced from the assumption of universal unrestricted competition were converted into practical precepts, from which it was regarded as little short of immoral to depart.

This was a cultural interpretation of the Industrial Revolution, but Toynbee did not omit the importance of 'mechanical discoveries' to its accomplishment – what Victorian could, brought up as they were under the shadow of Samuel Smiles's *Self-Help* and *Lives of the Engineers*? Yet Toynbee was not the first to try to understand the Industrial Revolution nor even the first to use the phrase itself. Both Friedrich Engels in *The Condition of the Working Class in England* (1845) and his friend Karl Marx in *Capital* (1865) had already done this. Toynbee's interpretation of the phrase was, however, a wider one. Although he had no doubt about the thoroughgoing nature of the social changes of the period Marx used the phrase to refer to the rise of large-scale industry, the replacement, as he put it, of 'manufacture' by 'machinofacture'. It was in power-driven machinery that Marx saw the cause of the Industrial Revolution,

the machine that gives rise to the Industrial Revolution is one which replaces the single worker handling a single tool, by a mechanism operating simultaneously a number of identical or similar tools, and driven by a single motive power, whatever the form of that power may be.

But it was the outcome of this revolution which mainly interested Marx. He believed that the rise of 'machinofacture' had been accompanied by an even greater concentration of capital (the nation's productive resources) in the hands of the few than had been the case in the past. Marx could see the gains in productivity which this had brought about. Ironically the *Communist Manifesto* (1848) is most eloquent when it describes the great achievements of the nineteenth century business class. But the cost had been to undermine the value of labour and to reduce the worker to the position of a slave.

Marx's writings made it impossible to discuss the Industrial Revolution simply in terms of its causes. He himself was only able to consider the short-term consequences and, of course, he believed that they led towards social revolution. In a recent attempt to answer Marx an American economic historian, W. Rostow, has argued that the logic of the Industrial Revolution leads towards twentieth-century abundance, on the American pattern, and not, as Marx thought, towards greater and greater misery for the majority (*The Stages of Economic Growth*, 1960). Rostow isolated five distinct phases of economic development; 'the traditional society', the 'pre-conditions for take-off', 'the take-off', 'the drive to maturity', and 'the age of high mass-consumption'. The purpose of these categories is to allow comparison between the varying experiences of the industrial nations up to, and including, the twentieth century. Rostow has certainly aroused fresh interest in the timetable of the British Industrial Revolution. From the standpoint of economic growth the concept of 'stages' is clearly valuable: for the moment 'the take-off' is almost as familiar a phrase as the 'industrial revolution' itself. But, as Rostow confines the take-off to 1783–1802, while placing the rest of the nineteenth century in the stage of 'the drive to maturity', it is unlikely that his terms will have much use for British economic history. The earliest point from which it seems possible to assess the Industrial Revolution, either as a phase of economic growth or of social change, is 1850. By then, as Sir John Clapham has written,

Britain had turned her face towards the new industry – the wheels of iron and the shriek of escaping steam. In them lay for the future not only her power and wealth but her very existence. (*An Economic History of Modern Britain*, Vol. II, 1932)

[2] BRITAIN IN 1851

By 1851 Britain had been transformed by the progress of industry into a new type of society. In the map prepared for the Census Report of 1851 to show the distribution of occupations, four industrial regions, Lancashire and the West Riding of Yorkshire, Glasgow, Newcastle, and Birmingham, contained such a concentration and variety of industry as to require inset maps on a larger scale than the national map. South Wales, the

Derby–Nottingham complex, and the Potteries, were almost equally heavily industrialized. The familiar regional pattern of British industry was already an established fact. But there were, evidently, large areas where the economy was completely rural and where industrial crafts met only local needs, producing nothing, as Clapham has put it, for export. Yet there can have been few villages that had not experienced changes which were complementary to industrial growth elsewhere. During the three generations before 1850 the countryman had had to adapt himself to the successive impact of enclosure, the introduction of new practices on the farm, rural migration, and the intrusions of the turnpiked roads, the canals, and, finally, the railways.

These changes destroyed the old 'rural society'. No society can, of course, be completely agricultural in the sense that everyone is at work on the land. Craftsmen, merchants, priests and lawyers, as well as a military nobility, had existed at every stage of medieval and early modern history. This understood, a rural society is one which has a massive proportion of its population dependent upon agriculture. Only a tiny minority will live in towns or gain their livelihood by some other means than farming. When statistics first became available for the more backward areas of Eastern Europe towards the end of the nineteenth century, they usually revealed a rural population of about 80 per cent. In Britain in 1851 just under 50 per cent lived in rural districts and under 22 per cent of the labour force worked in agriculture. By contrast Ireland was indisputably a rural society in 1851. Britain was a uniquely urban and industrial society by the same date. Somehow or another the means had been found to build and equip the new towns and cities, to switch manpower from the land into industry, and to mobilize the resources required by industry and the new transport services.

The achievements of British industry were displayed to the world by the Great Exhibition of 1851. Under the clear light of Paxton's Crystal Palace the products of British industry seemed to enjoy effortless superiority. If anyone had tried to explain how this superiority had come about they would probably have referred to native ingenuity, perhaps to the blessings enjoyed by property under the British constitution. The origins of the Industrial Revolution in the eighteenth century were obscure. Later historians have suggested many causes for the Industrial Revolution but, as this chapter tries to show, the real challenge is how to relate a series of revolutions, in different industries, in such a way that the inevitable uncertainty of economic change acquires coherence. One issue can be put aside quite quickly. Subsequent industrial revolutions have had the advantage of outside aid. Foreign investment played virtually no part in the British Industrial Revolution. In the mid-eighteenth century the Dutch had held a quantity of government stock (in 1783 this amounted to £30 million, about 14 per cent of the funded National Debt). But during the nineteenth century Britain became an exporter of capital; £93 million was invested abroad in the period 1816–25 alone, and by 1851 overseas investment earnings amounted to £10 million a year. This must not be understood to mean that the British Industrial Revolution was achieved in economic isolation. It certainly required the existence of a rudimentary world market. To take only one example, the cotton industry not only needed to find export markets but its very existence depended upon an imported raw material.

[3] THE COTTON INDUSTRY: A PACE-SETTER?

Eighteenth-century Britain was a society with well-established craft industries, an active international commerce which increased its exports fivefold over the century, and an enterprising community of landowners and farmers. Even so it is difficult to measure the distance, in these varying respects, between Britain and other European nations. The Englishman certainly seems to have lived better than his European counterpart in the eighteenth century. His wages were higher, he was better clothed and shod, better fed, and better housed. Technical skill was probably more widely distributed in Britain than elsewhere. Even before 1776, the year in which James Watt's first engines began to work, steam power was well known in Britain. Smeaton noticed fifty-seven engines at work in the Newcastle area in 1767. It was the inadequacy of these existing engines which led Watt to the first of his great improvements, the development of the condenser. A recent estimate has put the number of steam engines built in Britain in the eighteenth century as about 1,200 (J. R. Harris, *History*, Vol. LII, p. 147). Yet steam technology was still in its infancy in 1800: it was in the textile industries that British machine makers showed really marked superiority in the eighteenth century.

If the Industrial Revolution was to begin in Britain it had to be expected that the textile trades would play a large part in it. English wool had been the nation's staple export in the early Middle Ages and its successor had been the famous English white cloth. In the eighteenth century Britain was still the largest European producer of wool. Clothes are a necessity and cloth, for this reason, had been the basis of European commerce for centuries. But the type of cloth worn is a matter of taste and fashion. As it happened English wool was the ideal raw material for the lighter cloths, the worsteds, which became so popular in Europe after the seventeenth century. When home and overseas demand began to rise quickly from 1740 the English industry responded by expanding its labour force and output. By 1800 the annual consumption of raw wool was about 46 million kilos (100 million lb), more than double that of the early eighteenth century. This would have been remarkable had it not been for the astonishing growth of the cotton industry in the last quarter of the century. From the mid-1770s to 1815–17 the value of British cotton products leapt from £900,000 in a year to £30 million. Who could blame contemporaries for hailing the progress of cotton manufacture as the wonder of the age? The consequences of the revolution in the cotton industry were evident enough, both for the national economy and the cotton districts, but the extent to which an Industrial Revolution relies upon a 'primary growth sector' (Rostow's phrase), and whether cotton fulfilled this role in Britain, are still open issues. Cotton bewitched not simply because of its production statistics, but because it set up a new, and enduring, method of production – the factory system.

Cotton was an attractive material with a wide range of uses. It washed easily and was pleasant to wear, especially as underwear and it quickly supplanted the body linen which, in any case, had been worn only by the rich. Cotton calicoes, 'print goods', became the standard material for working-class women, and their menfolk wore cotton shirts, and fustian trousers and jackets. 'Fustian' was pre-eminently the working man's dress and Feargus O'Connor was said to have made a great impact upon Chartist audiences in Manchester in 1842 by appearing in a fustian suit. The middle classes preferred wool and silk, but ladies wore muslin gowns in the summer and servants were dressed in the cheaper calicoes. The standard of clothing may not have been high, yet it may be wondered how the population of 1851 could have been clothed at all without the revolution in cotton manufacture. The stimulus of domestic demand was a needful incentive to change in the industry. There were nearly three times as many people in Britain in 1851 as there had been in 1751.

Domestic demand was only one factor operating on the cotton industry. At the opening of the eighteenth century woollen goods had accounted for more than two-thirds of British exports. This primacy survived the century, but only just. In the 1790s (with the exception of 1799) woollen exports were still more than double the value of exported cottons. Cotton edged ahead in 1802–3, and by 1830 50 per cent of British exports consisted of cotton yarn and manufactures. Throughout the first half of the nineteenth century at least half the output of the cotton industry had been exported. The industry's origins lay in the colonial trade; its raw material came from the West Indies, where the plantations were worked by African slaves. After 1793, when Eli Whitney invented a gin which successfully drew out the seeds from the cotton boll of the short staple plant of mainland

America, the southern States quickly became major producers of cotton. By 1815 50 per cent of Britain's cotton imports came from the U.S.A. and by the end of the 1820s this share had grown to 70 per cent. Thus, in the words of a modern historian, 'the cotton industry was launched, like a glider, by the pull of the colonial trade to which it was attached'. The re-orientation of British overseas trade towards the Mediterranean, the Americas, Africa and Asia, had been growing throughout the eighteenth century. By 1797–8 Europe was absorbing only 30 per cent of Britain's domestic exports, although it took most of Britain's re-exports of non-European products. Cotton exports were easily promoted within this pattern. North America, which had its own industry, was not a good market, but the West Indies, South America, India and Africa were ready customers for the cheap products of machine industry. By 1840 Europe bought some 180 million metres (200 million yards) of cotton goods in a year, compared with the 484 million metres (529 million yards) of South America (nearly 275 million metres [300 million yards]), India and Asia, and Africa.

In pioneering the first mass market cotton had a number of important advantages over wool. Because cotton was a plant fibre it was easier to expand the supply of raw material, especially as the area of supply was the virgin land of the American South. Further, as cultivation intensified, the price of raw cotton fell; at 5d or 6d a pound in the 1850s raw cotton cost between a half and a third what it had at the beginning of the century. By contrast the supply of wool was not easily increased. The domestic wool clip amounted to 36 million kilos (80 million lb) in 1770 and reached a peak of 73–7 million kilos (160–70 million lb) in the 1860s. Imports from Australia did not exceed the domestic clip until 1870 and significant price reductions did not occur until the 1880s. Of course there is no strict comparison between wool and cotton, but it is observable that the period of most rapid expansion in the woollen industry, 1850–70, coincided with both the climax of mechanization and the coming of dependence upon imported wool. With cotton it was clearly of great importance that the era of mechanical innovation in cotton spinning was not impeded by shortages of the raw material.

The pull of demand at home, the awareness of overseas markets, and the availability of raw cotton, constitute the context in which the Industrial Revolution in cotton manufacture took place. The history of technical progress in the cotton industry is well known. The great leaps in productivity attained by the water-frame and the mule thrust the spinning wheel into almost instantaneous obsolescence. The frame needed power, at first water, then – after a successful installation of a Boulton and Watt engine at a mill in Papplewick (Nottinghamshire) in 1785 – steam. Economies of scale were now added to those in production. The power loom, first applied in 1791, made slower progress. Its ultimate success was clear by 1820 but it took another generation to force the hand loom out of use. Once again cotton was fortunate; its tougher, more predictable fibres withstood the jerkiness of the early machines remarkably well. Nevertheless much patience and skill was required to make the best of the early machines and in the progress of the industry as much credit should go to the anonymous, piecemeal improvers as to the initial innovators. Many of the early wooden machines lasted well on into the nineteenth century and no doubt prolonged the age of improvisation. The self-acting mule (1825, improved 1830) was an all-metal machine. By the 1830s there were not only Manchester firms which specialized in spindle or roller-making, but, like Fairbairn and Lillie or T. C. Herves, in building and equipping a complete mill.

Technological progress was not a new phenomenon, but its pace from the late eighteenth century was unprecedented. By the 1850s technical advance was a self-sustaining process: there were some who saw in 'invention' the essential activity within an Industrial Revolution but, as Samuel Smiles noticed in his biographies of the industrial pioneers (published in the 1860s), successful application (innovation) by the resourceful businessman was quite as important as invention itself. It has not proved easy to explain the increased flow of invention and innovation during the Industrial Revolution. The study of individual industries has thrown light on the mechanics of change by revealing specific problems of, for example, labour supply, transport, and raw material costs. In the case of cotton the limitations of the domestic system, in the distribution of the raw material and collection of the finished product, and in the supervision of the worker, were plain enough by the second half of the eighteenth century. Yet these problems were not new; they were inseparable from an outworking system and they grew worse as it expanded. These difficulties were not peculiar to Britain although their solution was; even after the success of machine industry had been established beyond doubt continental nations often found themselves incapable of emulating it without the aid of British technicians. There is enough evidence here to suggest that, in addition to the setting up of cycles of innovation in the major industries, there were some features of British society which fostered innovation as a general response. The wider issues have been well defined by a recent writer.

Inventive activity is closely related to the general condition of society; whether its members are of an inquiring frame of mind, whether it has the means and the will to retain and disseminate knowledge, and whether it permits the adoption of new modes of production, with the inevitable threat to established positions and incomes. (S. G. Checkland, *The Rise of Industrial Society in England 1815–1885*, p. 73)

The technical revolution in the cotton industry was not, then, an isolated phenomenon. Had this been the case the history of the Industrial Revolution would have had to be written in terms of how growth in one industry was transferred to others, an operation so difficult one might well wonder if it could have been accomplished at all. A sense of proportion begins to intrude as soon as cotton's contribution to the national income, or its share of the total labour force, is contrasted with its predominant role in the export economy. In the two decades 1820–40 cotton's share of the national income was about $4\frac{1}{2}$ per cent. Its labour force was 331,000 in 1850, compared with 572,000 (1851) in metal manufacture and machine making, trades which had,

perhaps, an equivalent history of innovation and technical progress, and with 394,000 in mining, 497,000 in building and
construction, 1·3 million in domestic service, and 2 million in
agriculture, industries in which technical progress had been of
little (or no) significance. Moreover the cotton industry employed
only 142,000 adult men; 24,000 workers were children under 13,
and 37,000 young persons under 18. The cotton workers were,
of course, an important group of consumers whose purchasing
power added to the growth of domestic demand in other fields.
As their wages stagnated after the first decade of the nineteenth
century (the *general* movement of prices was downwards) their
purchases can seldom have stretched beyond the necessities, food
and drink, clothing, rent, and fuel. But perhaps what matters
here was that they *had* purchasing power and were in productive
employment. The cotton masters were better placed. While the
value of cotton products rose by £16 million between 1819/21
and 1849/51, and the value added to the raw material by £7
million, wages and salaries rose by only £1·2 million. A high
proportion of this rising profit was re-invested, a lesser proportion on maintaining a more elaborate way of life. Clearly by 1850
the cotton industry was making considerable demands on other
industries through the purchasing power of masters and 'hands'
and its own demands for 'capital goods' – machinery, steam
engines, materials for the construction of mills. The importance
of these 'multiplier effects' was definite, but limited. If cotton
converted the economy to the habits of an industrial revolution,
it was more by persuasion than force. What the cotton masters
had achieved instructed others.

In my humble opinion [wrote a manufacturer in 1804] the woollen
cannot too closely follow the steps of the cotton trade: that nation
which brings forth its goods the best and the cheapest will always
have a preference, and it is only by means of the adoption of every
possible improvement that pre-eminence can be secured.

[4] IRON, COAL AND STEAM

If the cotton industry was, chronologically, in the forefront of the Industrial Revolution the expansion of the iron and coal industries, and the improvement of the steam engine as a source of industrial power, were indispensable to widespread industrialization. Like cotton, iron was a commodity with an immense potential. Even before the boost in production in the 1780s Britain made greater use of iron than her neighbours; by the end of the eighteenth century the disparity was more marked – Britain used four or five times as much iron per head of population as France. Although the eighteenth-century iron industry was familiar with large-scale operation it suffered from severe problems of raw material supply, both of fuel and ore. Timber for charcoal was costly and its location restricted the use that could be made of British ore. British forgemasters came to rely more on imported Swedish bar iron. Escape came through the substitution of coal for charcoal, first for smelting and the production of pig iron (the moulds into which the molten metal was poured were called 'pigs') and then for forging and the production of wrought iron. The first known use of coke for smelting was by Abraham Darby at Coalbrookdale (Shropshire) in 1709 but the adoption of the new process was slow; although no new charcoal furnaces were built after 1750, there were only 17 coke furnaces in 1760, and even by 1790, when there were 81 coke furnaces, there were still 25 charcoal furnaces in operation.

The explanation for this delay was a basic failure to understand the chemistry of iron manufacture. The problem was not an easy one to solve by empirical methods. Coke had been used in a variety of industries since the seventeenth century, but not every coal made a coke suitable for smelting iron ore. Coke smelting needed a stronger blast and the pig which it produced was often impossible to work into wrought iron. For many years the forges continued to use charcoal. The problem of the blast was overcome in 1776 when John Wilkinson installed a

steam engine (with rotary action, and making use of the cast
ron blowing cylinder developed in 1760) in his works at Willey
in Shropshire. Eighteenth-century blast furnaces were always
extravagant with fuel. Where the main advantage derived from
them was in the use of coke rather than charcoal this scarcely
mattered. But fuel economies had become important by the
nineteenth century. The Scottish iron industry was certainly
impeded by the high fuel costs of the old furnaces and the
breakthrough here came in the form of Neilson's hot-air blast of
1828–9. By 1830 it was possible to obtain a ton of pig iron with
$3\frac{1}{2}$ tons of coal: in the 1790s the ratio had been more like 1 to 8.

In forging the decisive advances followed Henry Cort's success
with the puddling and rolling process which he patented in 1783
and 1784. In the puddling furnace the molten iron was subjected
to variations in temperature, and stirred until free of impurities:
it was then drawn out of the furnace and, after hammering out
the slag, the iron was finally passed through rollers. Rolling has
been described (by Mantoux) as 'perhaps the most original part
of Cort's invention'. It cut down the need for lengthy hammering
and, as a result, it greatly accelerated production. Hammering
and rolling were powered operations, but puddling remained a
manual task. This was arduous, punishing work, possibly 'the
heaviest regular task ever accepted by man' (T. K. Derry and
Trevor I. Williams, *A Short History of Technology*, p. 478). With
the adoption of Nasmyth's steam hammer in the 1840s both
the scale and precision of iron forging were further enhanced. In
cast iron the industrial revolution had produced what was
virtually a new material: the improved quality of wrought iron
was hardly less important.

'The partnership thus contracted between coal and iron
opened the most brilliant prospects to the English metal industry' (Mantoux). The output of the iron industry rose spectacu-
larly. By 1788 the output of pig iron had increased fourfold
since the 1740s, by about 1805 it quadrupled to reach 250,000
tons, and by 1850–4 stood at 2.7 million tons. Imports of bar
iron dropped from over 50,000 tons in the 1790s to under 20,000
in the 1820s; by the 1850s exports of iron were over a million

tons a year, some 38 per cent of the total product. The uses of
iron multiplied as the great John Wilkinson foresaw that they
would. He himself made forty miles of cast iron piping for the
water supply of Paris, projected, with Abraham Darby III, the
first iron bridge, and with a gesture of almost Napoleonic self-
aggrandizement, planned to be buried in an iron coffin. By the
nineteenth century the use of iron seemed almost prodigal;
foreigners were astounded at the iron rollers used in English
gardens. The skill of an ironmaster, Matthew Boulton, and his
craftsmen had made possible Watt's development of the steam
engine, and the launching of the railways created an appetite
for iron which, by the mid-nineteenth century, seemed in-
satiable. Inextricable from this pattern was the growth of the
coal industry. The output of coal rose from 11 to 49 million tons
between 1800 and 1850 and of this the iron industry's share rose
from 10–15 per cent to over 25 per cent.

The interdependence of iron, coal, and steam now seems one
of the most predictable features of the Industrial Revolution in
Britain. Its very familiarity can, however, distort the historical
perspective. For Mantoux steam locked together what had previously been unrelated:

The use of a common motive power, and especially of an artificial
one, thenceforward imposed general laws upon the development of
all industries. The successive improvements in the steam engine
reacted equally on the working of mines and of metals, on weaving
and on transport. The industrial world came to resemble one huge
factory, in which the acceleration, the slowing down and stoppage of
the main engine determines the activities of the workers and regu-
lates the rates of production.

Yet it is possible to exaggerate the importance of steam in the
early nineteenth century and before 1850. By that date industry
employed 500,000 h.p. derived from steam engines, and railway
locomotives accounted for another 750,000+ h.p. Cotton mills
were using 71,000 h.p. of steam, and 11,000 h.p. of water power;
in 1838 the share of water power had been larger, at 12,000 h.p.
it had provided 26 per cent of the power used in the mills. At
sea, in 1850, steam tonnage was a tiny fraction of the total

tonnage; 168,000 tons out of 3·56 million tons. Not until 1883 did steam tonnage exceed sail. It was, in fact, in the second half of the nineteenth century that the potentialities of steam were realized. In 1870 the capacity of Britain's steam engines was 4 million h.p. and since 1850 capacity had grown at over five times the rate for the first half of the century. One recent estimate suggests that it would have required 6 million horses to equal the capacity of steam horse power in 1870. Quite apart from the inefficiency of the horse, the strain that this number of horses (i.e. *additional* horses) would have placed upon agricultural resources is not difficult to imagine. Yet if the accumulation of steam power now appears to have proceeded slowly during the Industrial Revolution its ultimate significance was never in doubt. Power derived from a mineral fuel had none of the familiar limitations of wind and water. The building and maintenance of steam engines was, of course, a highly skilled task but to utilize steam power entailed none of the great problems of organization which had arisen from the employment of massed labour in earlier centuries. Ebenezer Elliott, the Corn-Law Rhymer, in his poem 'Steam at Sheffield', written in the 1830s, expresses popular confidence and pride in the new source of power, and clearly regards it as the ally of Liberalism.

> Engine of Watt! unrivall'd is thy sway.
> Compared with thine, what is the tyrant's power?
> His might destroys, while thine creates and saves.
> Thy triumphs live and grow, like fruit and flower;
> But his are writ in blood, and read on graves!
> Let him yoke all his regimented slaves,
> And bid them strive to wield thy tireless fly,
> As thou canst wield it. Soon his baffled bands
> Would yield to thee, despite his wrathful eye.

[5] THE TRANSPORT REVOLUTION

By the 1840s it was the turn of the railway locomotive to stir poetic imagination. 'The very lion among machines', as Samuel Smiles later described the locomotive, was the proud embodiment of a new system of transport. In 1850 there were 10,000 kilometres (6,000 miles) of railway in Britain, worked by some 2,500 locomotives. Mechanized travel is correctly regarded as the complement to the factory system. The railway timetable set new standards of punctuality. Aided by the electric telegraph the railways imposed Greenwich time upon the nation and made every Englishman march in step with the Londoner. The economic consequences of the railways were profound. Goods and passengers were conveyed with regularity and speed. By 1850 the best trains had schedules of 65 k.p.h. (40 m.p.h.). Railway expansion created massive demand for iron and provided a new means for the transport of coal. The pace of economic life accelerated; news and information spread more quickly, manufacturer and retailer were brought closer together and the necessity for stock piling eliminated, the food supply of towns was improved in quality and quantity and the townsmen acquired the means of escape into suburbs. The railway companies were pioneers of large-scale enterprise: to Smiles the railways 'exhibited the grandest organization of capital and labour that the world has yet seen'. Railway services, and the demands of railway construction and maintenance, were making an impressive contribution to the economy by 1850 and were to grow in importance in the ensuing decades. But however spectacular railway growth appears it was not an isolated event, nor should it be regarded as an unanticipated bonus conferred upon an economy which had successfully dragged itself through the preliminary phases of industrialization. The development of a successful railway was the culmination of a series of transport improvements which stretched back into the mid-eighteenth century, and which was related at almost every stage to needs of industry and of the growing towns.

In Britain the railway era was necessarily a secondary phase in the Industrial Revolution. The needs of railway construction could only be met by a developed iron industry; by 1850 nearly 2 million tons of iron had gone into railway track and this did not represent the railways' total demand for iron. For the community the railway effected cuts in transport costs of anything up to 50 per cent. This was comparable to the savings in cost achieved by canal construction in the eighteenth century. The opening of the Worsley Canal in 1761, which connected the Duke of Bridgewater's coal mines with Manchester, cut the average price of coal in the city by a half. The Duke believed that 'a navigation should have coals at the heel of it' and a majority of the canals authorized in the second half of the eighteenth century sought to facilitate the transport of coal. Industrialists and merchants were quick to seize the opportunities opened by canals. Liverpool and Manchester were joined by the Bridgewater Canal in 1767: even in the 1840s this waterway customarily carried twice the tonnage of the railway which connected the two cities. Josiah Wedgwood was particularly energetic on behalf of the Grand Trunk Canal, which linked the Potteries to the Mersey, the Midlands, and London, and rescued the region from the tyranny of its appalling roads. Wedgwood built his new works at Etruria on the bank of the Grand Trunk and brought the coal and china clay barges right into the factory. Canal investment was on an impressive scale; by 1825 eighty canal companies had a paid-up capital of £13 million. At this date Britain possessed a nation-wide network of canals and river navigations and the industrial districts, especially Lancashire and the Midlands, had a dense complex of canals. Canals, at least in the north (and where their engineering costs had not been excessive), were paying concerns. The ten most successful companies averaged a return of 27·6 per cent on their capital in 1825. In fact, by the third decade of the nineteenth century many canal companies were exploiting a monopoly and by doing so encouraged businessmen to look at railway projects seriously.

The canals were mainly responsible for the concentration of British industry, certainly more responsible than the steam engine. In their impact they foreshadowed the railways, just as the railways often followed their routes. 'If we think', wrote Mantoux (1927), 'of the influence which railways exert today on the development of industry we shall realize the great part played by canals, after centuries of strictly local economic life.' Canal transport was slow by railway standards but this comparison was, of course, irrelevant in the eighteenth century. Goods travelled more quickly and more efficiently by canal than by river or road. In his *Treatise on Inland Navigation* (1785) John Phillips noted the contrast in efficiency between river and canal which was observable at Barton Bridge, where the Bridgwater Canal was carried by aqueduct over the Irwell. There one could see 'seven or eight stout fellows labouring like slaves to drag a boat slowly up the Irwell, and one horse or mule, or sometimes two men at most, drawing five or six of the Duke's barges, linked together, at great rate upon the canal'. On the canal towpath a horse could be expected to pull a load of 50 tons: on a well surfaced road 2 tons was a maximum. Yet it should not be thought that road improvement under the turnpike trusts was of no significance. Road surfaces and maintenance were better at the end of the eighteenth century than ever before and with the introduction of Macadam's technique of providing roads with an impervious surface and side drains standards improved still further in the early nineteenth century. The new roads greatly reduced the journey time of long-distance coach travel and even after coaching had died (accompanied by an outburst of nostalgia which compares with modern nostalgia for the steam locomotive) the trusts could be seen to have left a valuable legacy of serviceable roads. A horse-drawn vehicle could not only move faster on the new 'metalled' road, but the horse could pull three times as much as before. The trusts themselves were rarely profitable and, for them, the coming of the railways was calamitous. Yet, as Clapham has commented: 'Calamity to the turnpike trusts, it need hardly be said, was not calamity to the horse-drawn traffic of the country'. More and more vehicles went onto the roads in the early nineteenth century. By 1850 much of the ensuing traffic fed the railways.

Collection and delivery services centred on railway goodsyards and warehouses. In the cities and towns traffic multiplied; along London's main thoroughfares the heavy drays, the horse omnibuses, carriages and hansom cabs were locked in what seemed continuous conflict.

[6] CAPITAL ACCUMULATION AND THE FLOW OF INVESTMENT

By the middle of the nineteenth century Britain's position as 'the workshop of the world' was unique. At this date the most arresting feature of the Industrial Revolution was the capital accumulation which it had generated and which made Britain the most productive community in the world. Because the population had been rising for at least a century, and work, homes, and services had had to be provided for the additional population, the nation's 'capital' (its assets, like industrial buildings, machinery, and transport installations) could be expected to grow. It was the range of capital equipment in Britain in 1850 which gave most eloquent testimony to the achievements of the Industrial Revolution. The prodigious investment in railways indicated both the reserves of funds available for investment in Britain and the willingness of those who held funds to place their savings in stock of this kind (the distinction between *investment* in railways and the creation of a new species of property, railway stock, is worth noticing). In 1848 the economist Thomas Tooke noted the coming of a new era in which 'in every street of every town persons were to be found who were holders of railway stock'. Railway investment was accomplished in a society which not only had the resources to finance investment, but also the means and incentive to put funds at the disposal of businessmen of imagination and energy. Money for investment was mobilized through the stock exchange and the banks, both of which had at least originated in the century before the Industrial Revolution. The railway companies were able to create stock, and to employ these institutions, because they were 'incorporated' under Act of Parliament. This was not the case with ordinary industrial enterprise until after the Limited Liability Acts of 1855 and 1862 and, even then, the number of industrial undertakings which became public companies was small. In the mid-1880s *The Times* could report under twenty manufacturing companies regularly quoted on the London Stock Exchange. 'Stock' in the mid-nineteenth century meant holdings in government (Bank of England) securities, in incorporated trading companies and public utilities, in banks and insurance companies, and in railways. How then had capital accumulation in the industrial sector been financed during the Industrial Revolution?

An answer to this question requires some further definition of capital itself and an account of the sources available for investment over this period. What distinguishes an 'industrial' from a 'pre-industrial' community is, amongst other things, its very much greater stock of capital goods. The stock of machines and tools in use during the eighteenth and nineteenth century in the *domestic* industries was impressive by contrast with an earlier period and in the same period capital accumulation extended to the acquisition of new, more sophisticated and elaborate industrial buildings and plant. The result was not only to increase production but to accelerate it. Increased capital in the form of transport facilities further stimulated this process. One consequence of capital accumulation was thus to reduce the funds (money) tied up in what is sometimes called 'circulating capital', for example, the raw materials of the textile trades. The financing of circulating capital had played, historically, an important part in the evolution of credit mechanisms in Western Europe and thus in the origin of what historians have called 'capitalism'. The need to bridge the gap between the purchase of raw materials and the sale of the finished, manufactured article had called for a high degree of financial ingenuity since the Middle Ages. Around it there developed the system of dealing in bills of exchange (see Part IV, pp. 168–9) which remained a vital part of the financial system during the Industrial Revolution.

If 'capital accumulation' represented the *physical* assets acquired during the century of Industrial Revolution what had, in turn, made it possible was the accumulation of funds and so the means of investment. In eighteenth-century England funds were concentrated in a few hands. Most important, in a collective sense, were the landowners and farmers and, closely linked to them, the largely dependent community of professional men, like the clergy, the lawyers, and the doctors. There was then a small, but important, commercial and financial élite, especially evident in London but present in all large towns. Lastly there was the assorted group of 'industrialists' themselves, a group which extended from the small master, like the smith, the saddler, or the tailor, to the miller and the brewer and, at the other end of the scale, the large-scale employer in a 'developing' industry, like, for example, one of the great ironmasters. Taken together these groups formed only a small percentage of the total population in the eighteenth century and, of course, both between and within them there existed great diversity in family income. Nevertheless their incomes all reached a level high enough to permit saving, that is to say their income was not totally absorbed by the cost of the basic needs, food, clothing, shelter, and a few pleasures. The possibility of deciding to reduce, or stabilize, what was spent on the household in order to use their money for another purpose was at least open to them. How far this possibility extended down the social scale it is difficult to say with precision. The propertyless labourer, even the small farmer, whose cottage contained little but the bed, table, chairs and few utensils necessary for mere existence, certainly had little chance of accumulating any surplus and was unlikely to 'invest' it if he did. The windfalls which sometimes enriched the agricultural community went, for the most part, to the farmers and landowners and not to the labourers. The position of skilled craftsmen in town or village might be different and general expectations might alter with the spread of domestic industry. For the wealthy investable funds could be held in a variety of 'liquid' or semi-liquid forms, cash, bullion (like jewels and plate), bank deposits, or existing investments in stock. Even in the lower levels of society the bag of coins hidden in the mattress, or up the chimney in a crock of gold, was not unknown! In the nineteenth century the savings bank appeared to serve the small saver (not necessarily the same thing as 'the working man'): deposits in savings banks rose from under £1 million after 1815 to nearly £29 million in 1850 (see Part II, p. 89).

Those who controlled investable funds in the eighteenth century were primarily engaged in maintaining their traditional status as landowners. Extravagance was their way of life. Country houses became larger, more splendid, even more comfortable as the century advanced. The greater families (and the desperate!) expected to possess, or rent, a town house for the London season. Social life and family prestige was made possible only by keeping large households and offering generous entertainment. The number of servants employed was always as much an index of status, or status seeking, as of necessity. Landownership was a prerequisite for sharing in political life (and what wealthy man doesn't sooner or later develop some political interests?), fortunes made in trade and in the plantations were naturally used to found landed families. But the great landowner did not live in a world of economic innocence. To live generously without impoverishing one's successor was an art which required expertise as well as the assistance of a reliable steward and a good attorney. The landowner's worries usually arose within his family; they ranged from inherited debts and mortgages, to settling dowries upon his daughters and providing maintenance for his sons. And as often as not he was the cause of his own worries, especially when he built or entertained, or gambled, beyond his means. But whatever his situation or ability the landowner's first object was to obtain the best living he could from his estates. It was for this reason that many landowners had always been interested in the improvement of their estates. From the mid-eighteenth century they gave increasing attention to the advantages of enclosure as a means of exploiting more efficiently the rising national demand for food. Some two million hectares (six million acres) of open field and common land was enclosed in the eighteenth and early nineteenth centuries; the periods of most intense activity were the two decades after 1760, and the war years from 1793 to 1800. Enclosure was expensive. On the Fitzwilliam estates in Northamptonshire and Huntingdonshire £37,658 was spent on twelve enclosure schemes between 1790 and 1815: on seven of these estates the return averaged 16 per cent. It has been suggested that an enclosure could be expected to yield a return of 15–20 per cent on the initial outlay. The growth of agricultural output to which enclosure contributed was the basic cause of rising national income in the eighteenth century and was thus closely linked to the supply of resources for industrial investment. But the landowner was rarely a direct agent of this investment. He had good reason to be most interested in the land. The exceptions included those landowners who drew large revenues from coal. Even so these revenues took the form of royalties: landowners seldom took a direct hand in the development of the mining industry and where they did so, as in the North East in the eighteenth century, they often reverted to leasing at a later stage.

Landowners did not, then, scorn profit. Yet this was more likely to be from projects that lay within their conventional interests: their own estates, the Funds (government stock, or 'consols'), and canals and turnpike trusts and other transport improvements. Some great landowners, like the Earl of Lonsdale at Whitehaven, or the Duke of Devonshire at Barrow-in-Furness, invested in the laying out of towns as well as in exploiting their coalfields. All over the country the gentry were able to raise their rent income by becoming urban speculators (the building was usually left to others) and in doing so they played a not unimportant part in shaping the new society. Beyond this it may be difficult to trace the landowner's direct contribution to industrial investment and growth. Only a fraction of the 40–50 per cent increase in rents marked up between 1760 and 1790 went directly into industry. But the community did gain from cheap food and quicker and more efficient communications. Whatever it was on which the gentry spent their money it created employment and increased the potential market for industrial goods. Even if a great deal of the expenditure by the gentry was somewhat unproductive (although any increase in consumption creates employment and, thus, further consumption and demand), it remains true that no other section of the community was so well situated to invest in projects which necessarily carried an uncertain and long-term yield.

Merchant enterprise was clearly another sector within the eighteenth-century economy which could result in the accumulation of funds for investment and thus of industrial capital. There were certainly examples of this taking place, but the links between merchants and industrialists were fewer than might be supposed. After a life of risk taking the trader was likely to seek rural contentment, or the fashionable ease of the city. What happened to merchant profits is not easy to discover. Much of it remained in commerce to finance further trade, some went into the purchase of country estates and to other traditional forms of property like the Funds, and some, no doubt, directly into industry. The role of merchants was to act as brokers between Britain and the rest of the world: insofar as Britain bought more overseas than she sold merchants were responsible for an outflow of resources. But, like landowners, they were interested in the improvement of transport and related facilities, like docks. Liverpool and Bristol merchants in the nineteenth century both took leading roles in floating of railway companies to serve their cities. The history of both cities in this period is inseparable from that of the increasingly active Atlantic trade which, in turn, was of the greatest importance to the growth of British industry. Expanding trade and manufacture caused the further development of Britain's already precocious banking system. Eighteenth-century Britain was remarkably familiar with 'paper instruments'; promissory notes and bills of exchange were in regular use throughout commerce. As more country banks were founded after 1750 credit transactions spread far beyond London and the main merchanting centres. The Industrial Revolution was not financed by the banks, but their contribution was more than marginal. Even in the nineteenth century the banks were extremely cautious about financing industrial capital: in the 1880s one banker still shuddered at the thought of putting money 'into works of any description' (Clapham, Vol. II, p. 355). But the banks were an important source of short-term credit to industry. By the end of the eighteenth century the deposits of the country banks with their London agents or 'correspondents' were being used by these London bankers to discount bills sent to them by contacts in the manufacturing districts. In this way the profits of agriculture were being made available to industry and, with low interest rates, the cost of this service was very reasonable. The benefits of this exchange have been well described by Professor Ashton: 'The marriage between the thrift of the South and East and the enterprise of the Midlands and North was both happy and fertile. It meant in effect that rural England was providing foodstuffs for the growing urban communities without requiring an immediate return...'.

The Industrial Revolution drew some of its momentum from the investments of landowners and merchants and, perhaps as important, from the machinery of credit which enabled the savings of other sections of the community to be put at the service of industry. But to a considerable extent industry supplied, through its profits, the finance for further investment. Transport improvements and centralized production in a factory made it possible, as Professor Ashton has written, 'to transmute circulating into fixed capital', a process he places 'at the centre of what is called the Industrial Revolution'. Further, the requirements of early industry were not large. Arkwright's first mill at Cromford (1771), including machinery and stock, was insured for only £1,500, and the second mill (1777) for £3,000. By the 1790s some inflation, as well as the need for more elaborate buildings, and the introduction of steam power, had pushed up the cost of a mill to between £10,000 and £15,000. Forty years later the large mills in the Glasgow area cost between £40,000 and £80,000. By this date the scale of operations in the textile industries could be considerable, but it was not altogether unique. A Tyneside colliery might cost between £10,000 and £150,000 to put into production; in 1838–43 more than £250,000 was spent on opening the Murton Colliery in Durham. Large plant of this kind could be found at many points in the economy

by 1850. The iron industry required particularly heavy investment. In 1812 the ten iron works in the Midlands were said to
have cost over £50,000 each to erect: forty years later this would
have seemed a very modest sum. The cost of capital equipment
in the iron industry was so great that, in the eighteenth century,
some ironmasters actually doubled the role with that of banker.
Similar problems of financing large-scale enterprise could be
found in the brewing industry, in flour milling, and in the newly
born gas industry. In the last case the investment needs of the
industry were most commonly met by the formation of a public
company with limited liability (this needed an Act of Parliament). The smaller gas works were often built by 'contractors'
on short-term loans from banks or by generous credit from the
firms which supplied their equipment: once established the plant
then sold, for a profit, to a typical cross-section of landed, or
middle-class 'rentiers' (M. E. Falkus 'The British Gas Industry
before 1850', *Economic History Review*, Vol. XX, pp. 494–508).

In most industries, however, even in 1850 the works and
workshops were small, and this was true even of the textile
trades. In 1853 five Yorkshire artisans joined in a partnership to
establish a silk mill. Their investment, saved out of wages,
amounted to £127. The small mill which they rented cost £40 a
year and the four combing machines which it housed were built
by the least affluent and most skilful of the five partners. As it
happened this tiny venture did not survive more than a few
months. Its resources were too slender. Yet many successful
businesses began in a very similar way and, surviving the initial
crises, were able to accumulate capital from the profits of
technical progress and the low cost of raw materials and labour.
Important, too, were movements of capital within an industry,
or from one industry to another. An analysis of the early cotton-
spinning firms in the Midlands has shown all types of textile
manufacturers and traders moving into this progressive trade
between 1769 and 1800 in conjunction, and this seems significant,
with other industrialists, potters, ironmasters, millers, and
retailers. In the nineteenth century, as power-loom weaving
began its advance from the 1820s, prominent cotton spinners

moved into this branch of the industry. The giant concern, which straddled across the whole industry from spinning to finishing, remained a rarity and so, too, did a firm like Ashton's of Hyde which acquired its own coalmine to provide fuel for the mills. Nevertheless there was no doubt that within the textile industries circulating capital had been almost completely overshadowed by fixed capital by the mid-century; in the 1840s the spinners of Bolton could claim that four-fifths of their capital consisted of buildings and machinery.

[7] LABOUR SUPPLY

However approached, the methods of capital supply in the Industrial Revolution reveal an avid sense of economic opportunity running through the community. To an extent this was the obvious response of enterprising landowners and businessmen to the challenge of rising population. Provided that it could avoid starvation, and disastrous epidemic disease, an increased population meant the chance to utilize a large labour force. The basis for success throughout the economy was higher agricultural productivity; this enabled the non-agricultural work-force to continue to grow and, ultimately, to transfer men from agricultural to industrial employment. Some such redistribution of the labour force was essential to the Industrial Revolution. How far this was achieved by driving families from the land was a matter of controversy even in the nineteenth century and has remained so ever since. To an extent enclosure deprived the labourer of the use of common land, and the opportunity to work a plot of his own. How important, and how widespread these rights had been it is difficult to estimate. Certainly later in the nineteenth century radicals came to believe that the labourers' prosperity and self-respect could only be recovered (though this begged the question of what had been 'lost') by the acquisition of a smallholding. Whatever the injustice of enclosure its immediate consequence was not to add to the rural unemployed; the number working on the land continued to rise until the mid-century, although agriculture's share of the labour force did, of course, decline. The headlong exodus from the countryside did not begin until the 1840s. Of course the movement of population did not begin then. It is now thought that migration was a regular feature of life even in the pre-industrial period. Certainly in the eighteenth century there were pronounced patterns of regional migration, into London from the south-eastern counties and, by the end of the century, into the manufacturing districts from nearby rural areas. Until the beginnings of Irish immigration the migrant had not usually made a long journey. Movement from the agricultural south to Lancashire was, for example, comparatively rare; when poor law officials moved families from the south to the cotton towns after 1834 they encountered a resistance from the northern operatives which, although understandable in terms of a threat to prevailing wage rates, suggests that long-distance migration was looked upon as unusual.

In the countryside itself a rising population forced an increasing number of labourers into dependence on casual work. 'Underemployment' was a permanent feature of the agricultural economy; the seasonal demands for a large labour force, at threshing and at harvest, could only be met by a reserve 'army' of labour (the phrase is Marx's, but he applied it differently) which eked out a living at other times by a day or so of work for a neighbour, by using the commons, or by 'industrial' employment. It was to take advantage of this underemployed labour force that domestic outworking had been organized; outwork had the virtue of being able to provide work for every member of the family, except the very youngest. Regional concentration of the domestic industries in the eighteenth century created populations that were almost completely reliant on industrial occupation and, within this context, it was not difficult to recruit a factory work-force. The early Industrial Revolution led to a greater use of the domestic system, not its disappearance. In the textile districts, as the established workers moved into the mills,

domestic hand-loom weaving often gave employment to the
immigrant. In the 1830s and 1840s, when hand-loom weaving in
cotton was being brought into direct competition with the power-
loom, the domestic weavers, many of them Irish immigrants,
were compelled to accept desperately low wages. An abundance
of domestic weavers may have delayed the development of the
loom in the early decades of the nineteenth century. The power-
loom quickly made the position of large numbers of hand-loom
weavers untenable, but they did not easily find factory work and
their experience should, perhaps, provide a warning that 're-
deployment' was not a simple process, even in the nineteenth
century. The weaving mills depended heavily upon the labour of
women and children; adult men often found work difficult to
obtain. The domestic outworker survived longer in the other
textile trades and in other industries. In the woollen industry
hand-loom weaving survived well into the 1870s; one manufacturer, from Calverley near Leeds, recalled in 1902, 'I went out
of business in 1876, and our firm never had a single piece woven
by power'. In the hosiery industry, in cutlery, in the Midlands
metal trades, in shoe-making, domestic outwork continued to
prevail in 1850 and for some decades afterwards.

The domestic system implied a small outlay on fixed capital:
it also brought a higher proportion of the population into industrial employment, and thus increased productivity. Rising
population, as well as persistent rural underemployment, meant
that the Industrial Revolution took place in a context of labour
abundance. This was particularly true of the thirty years after
1815. Although industrial wages kept well ahead of those for
agricultural work they dropped back quickly after the end of the
war and of the comparative labour shortage which had accompanied it. Even so it was not always easy to recruit labour for
industry. In the eighteenth century when the early mills had
relied on water power (early steam engines were not all that
reliable either) the manufacturers had had to provide houses if
they were to bring workers into remote districts, like the Derwent Valley. As improved transport and the use of steam power
began to encourage industrial concentration in towns it became

unnecessary for the manufacturer to think of providing houses, although some realized that to do so might enable them to attach the worker's loyalty to their business. By the 1840s masters needed to offer few inducements to the workman; only the man who possessed a marketable skill was in any position to bargain with an employer. Not surprisingly the trades unions of the 1850s and 1860s were essentially combinations of skilled men seeking both to enhance their bargaining power with the employers and to raise their own standard of living well above that of the semi-skilled and manual workers. Skilled men were also more adept at moving in search of work and in this way they could use their superior organization and education to escape from localities affected by depression, or a glut in the labour market for their particular trade. As well as helping the men themselves this kind of organization also assisted employers by providing labour where it was needed: but for most of the nineteenth century the majority were held in the grip of a labour market which operated, jerkily, on the crudest principles of supply and demand. The most that an advancing industrial revolution offered was that more men could enter the skilled (and white collar) jobs and thus pass into the 'labour aristocracy'.

[8] THE CONTEXT OF INDUSTRIAL PROGRESS: POPULATION AND DEMAND

A supply of cheap labour was thus a central feature of the Industrial Revolution. The danger here was that low incomes might check demand. This was avoided partly because of the rise of population and, with it, of *total* demand and partly because of the growing size of Britain's export trade. A plentiful labour supply meant that manufacturers were able to keep labour costs at a minimum while experiencing few problems of supply. The sharp edge of necessity drove the more resourceful worker to learn the new skills which in a modern society might come from education or formal retraining. The importance of cheap and abundant labour is clear enough in the early and mid-nineteenth century. It is less easy to define the role of labour supply for an earlier period. How fast does a population have to grow in order to accelerate the mobility of its labour force? At what point does the additional demand created by rising population provide a unique stimulus to enterprise and innovation? These may or may not be the right questions to ask. But one thing is certain: both nineteenth and twentieth-century experience should warn us against thinking that there is any *automatic* relationship between an industrial revolution and an upsurge in population. Yet it is unlikely that an industrial revolution could have emerged within a society whose population was declining. A shortage of labour may stimulate technical innovation as it did in nineteenth-century America and seems to have done in the third and fourth decades of the eighteenth century in England. Even during the Industrial Revolution – particularly in the eighteenth century – there were often local shortages of labour. But a declining population is most unlikely to provide that growth in demand which is so essential to industrial progress. Technical innovation itself only makes sense where the market is potentially large.

The beneficial results of rising population in the eighteenth century are to be explained largely in terms of improved agriculture. The crucial changes here came in the early eighteenth century. They had the effect of enabling labour to be released from the land and of preventing the erosion of incomes by soaring food prices (these had fallen in the early eighteenth century). Had food prices mounted uncontrollably the result must have been to curtail demand for industrial goods.

The second half of the eighteenth century was also blessed by the disappearance of epidemic disaster on the scale to which people had become accustomed in the previous century. Population now rose in town and country alike. In the past towns had grown by absorbing the surplus population of the villages but, during the late eighteenth century, they probably began to grow by natural increase, an excess of births over deaths. From

1745 to 1750 the population of Nottingham began to rise steadily by natural increase: by the 1790s the city was growing as much by natural increase as by immigration. The death-rate in Nottingham in this period rarely fell below 35 per thousand except in the 'recovery' period after the savage epidemics of 1725–40. The crucial factor after 1770 seems to have been the town's very high birth-rate but, perhaps, the introduction of vaccination at the turn of the century made a contribution as well. In commenting on these findings Professor Chambers is confident that Nottingham had passed a turning point in its history by the end of the eighteenth century:

The power of epidemic disease was now definitely tamed; the death-rate might rise under the influence of overcrowding and falling health standards, but it could never again run amok; the town had broken through the demographic barrier that had formerly kept its population in check, and was now launched on the uncharted path of continuous growth. (*Studies in the Industrial Revolution*, ed. L. S. Pressnell, London 1960)

A similar rise in birth-rate and population took place in the industrial villages of Nottinghamshire in the eighteenth century. These changes were independent of the Industrial Revolution in their origin: but by the beginning of the nineteenth century they were an important incentive to further industrial progress. The towns now increasingly served to focus demand (which, in *per capita* terms, was rising only slowly if at all).

[9] ONE CAUSE OR MANY?

The Industrial Revolution is too complex an event to have a single cause. A tidy explanation is almost certain to be incomplete. This said, the causes may be summarized as follows:

1 Agricultural incomes rose in the eighteenth century first as a result of greater efficiency ('improvement') and then as a

consequence of rising demand exerted by the growth of population. Increased consumption by landowners, farmers, and labourers led to a related rise in industrial employment, incomes, and investment.

2 The ready response of agriculture *and* industry to rising demand after 1750 had been prepared for by the attraction of the London market in the previous century. Not only did the pull of the London market continue but the benefits of concentrated demand spread further afield as other towns began to grow rapidly in the wake of the general increase in population.

3 As rising population began to be reflected in rising food prices, the expansion of industry and industrial employment (in the first place a consequence of 1) imparted a continuing buoyancy to wages. The progressive 're-deployment' of the rural population into industrial, or semi-industrial employment was facilitated by the comparatively straightforward expansion of domestic outwork.

4 1, backed by 2, created the opportunity and need for new investment in transport improvements. This in turn created new incomes and a rise in consumer demand. It also called for an increased output of 'producer' goods like iron (i.e. goods which formed the plant of other industries). This cycle of investment, followed by a growth in consumption as new incomes are spent (=expansion of demand), which then results in further investment and demand, is central to all economic progress. It had begun on the land (see 1). Improved transport cut industrial costs by feeding raw materials into industry more rapidly and by distributing the finished goods more quickly. Coal now became widely and cheaply available as an industrial fuel while its domestic use also increased (see 2).

5 Under the combined effect of 1–4 a number of key industries approached and then passed the point at which innovation became both practical and progressive. The result was a revolution in output. This was achieved either by changes in organization or in production techniques (and sometimes by both: in any case one may stimulate the other). In some industries (cotton, iron, pottery, brewing) this stage was characterized by

successful experiment in large-scale production. Businessmen now became increasingly aware of possible economies of scale, i.e. the competitive advantages of the large firm began to out-weigh the disadvantages attached to the management of a large work-force and the burden of a heavy initial investment in plant. This process, that of the Industrial Revolution in its most familiar sense, was extremely patchy: it took a generation or more to transform a single industry and when the revolution was approaching completion in one industry (like cotton) it was often only in its preliminary stages in another (woollen).

6 A buoyant export trade offset any lengthy faltering in demand which might occur as food prices rose in response to population pressure. 4 and 5 ensured that British goods were competitive in world markets and profits (the source of most explicitly *industrial* investment) remained high even when the prices of industrial goods fell. It is difficult to see how the Industrial Revolution, especially in the textile industries, could have been based simply upon domestic demand.

7 Nothing occurred to interrupt 1–6. Either civil war or arbitrary interventionist government could have checked 1, as it did in the seventeenth century. Eighteenth-century wars were fought overseas and they seldom disturbed important markets more than temporarily. There was no recurrence of the severe epidemics of the seventeenth and earlier eighteenth-century type which might have caused population growth to slow down or halt.

8 Britain was an 'open' society in which wealth did give access to status and position. Further wealth was lightly taxed and private property was more than adequately protected at law.

Under these circumstances Britain achieved a more efficient use of her resources than had ever been possible before. The land was more fully exploited for its mineral wealth and the yields of agriculture were markedly improved (itself a rare event in history). Labour became more productive. Savings were drawn into more productive uses and industrial plant of all kinds was more intensively operated. But the language of economics does less than justice to the human endeavour on which the Industrial Revolution was built. The British were pioneering a new society. The Industrial Revolution belongs after all to the era of the Romantic Movement and the Victorians were surely right to bring out its own romantic qualities. Behind all the efforts of economic historians to offer a general explanation of the Industrial Revolution there lies something which is at once too simple and too complex for any explanation to box in; the individual's decision to take his opportunity. A precious glimpse into such a decision is given in this description of his early career by the great ironfounder, Isaac Wilkinson (father of John):

I worked at a forge in the north. My master gave me 12s a week – I was content. They raised me to 14s – I did not ask them for it. They went on to 16s–18s. I never asked them for the advances! They gave me a *guinea* a week. I said to myself, if I am worth a guinea a week to you, I am worth more to myself. I left them. (quoted by W. H. Chaloner in 'Isaac Wilkinson, Potfounder', in *Studies in the Industrial Revolution*, ed. L. S. Pressnell, 1960)

Further Reading

An immense amount has been written on the Industrial Revolution. An extensive recent bibliography of the subject can be found in *The Cambridge Economic History of Europe*, Vol. VI, Part II, pp. 952–67. There are also full bibliographies in Phyllis Deane and W. A. Cole's *British Economic Growth 1688–1959*, 2nd ed. (Cambridge University Press, 1968), and in B. R. Mitchell and Phyllis Deane's *The Abstract of British Historical Statistics* (Cambridge University Press, 1962) where the references are listed at the end of each section.

The most succinct and lucid account of the Industrial Revolution is that of T. S. Ashton, *The Industrial Revolution 1760–1830* (Oxford University Press, 1948). Where Ashton is brief, Paul Mantoux's *The Industrial Revolution in the Eighteenth Century*, revised ed. (Methuen University Paperbacks, 1961) is a fascinatingly full account which concentrates on the rise of the factory system. A penetrating recent survey of the Industrial Revolution from the technological standpoint is David S. Landes's 'Technological Change and Development in Western Europe 1750–1914', *Cambridge Economic History of Europe*,

Vol. VI, Part I, Chapter V, I, ed. H. J. Habakkuk and M. Postan (Cambridge University Press, 1965). A modern economist's approach to the Industrial Revolution is Phyllis Deane's *The First Industrial Revolution* (Cambridge University Press, 1965); this book takes a longer view than earlier accounts and covers the century 1750–1850. Sir John Clapham's 'The Early Railway Age', *An Economic History of Modern Britain*, Vol. I, 2nd ed. (Cambridge University Press, 1930) disclaims any attempt to analyse the Industrial Revolution as such but is still the most illuminating historical description of the early nineteenth-century economy. A shorter general economic history is W. H. B. Court's *A Concise Economic History of Britain, 1750 to Recent Times* (Cambridge University Press, 1954); Book I deals with 1750–1837. P. Mathias's *The First Industrial Nation* (Methuen University Paperbacks, 1969) divides its account of the economy from 1700 to 1914 in the early nineteenth century; it is strong on the eighteenth century. The consolidation of the Industrial Revolution in the nineteenth is the subject of S. G. Checkland's *The Rise of Industrial Society in England* (Longmans, 1964), a book which rivals Clapham in its comprehensiveness. Checkland covers the years 1815–85 and this is also the period of J. D. Chambers's *The Workshop of the World* (Oxford University Press, 1961) which has a very clear and concise introduction.

The phasing of the Industrial Revolution has attracted more attention since the publication of W. W. Rostow's *The Stages of Economic Growth* (Cambridge University Press, 1960). The importance of more exact phasing is strongly emphasized in M. W. Flinn's *Origins of the Industrial Revolution* (Longmans, 1966). A number of important articles are included in *Causes of the Industrial Revolution* (ed. R. M. Hartwell, Methuen University Paperback, 1967); the editor's introduction is a valuable survey of recent writing on the subject and his *The Industrial Revolution in England* (Historical Association pamphlet, 1965) is a preliminary guide and contains a useful short bibliography.

The role of the businessman or entrepreneur is covered in Checkland, Chapter 4, and there is also a stimulating introduction to this important subject in Charles Wilson's 'The Entrepreneur in the Industrial Revolution in Britain', *History*, Vol. XLII, pp. 101–17, 1957. The problems of management in the Industrial Revolution, especially as business grew in size, is the subject of Sidney Pollard's *The Genesis of Modern Management* (Pelican, 1968).

Principal Events, 1750-1850

1750   Samuel Whitbread (d.1796) bought King's Head brewery

1751   Benjamin Huntsman (1704–76) began production of crucible steel at Sheffield

1753   Isaac and John Wilkinson (1728–1808) leased furnace at Bersham, Denbighshire

1755   Sankey Navigation

1756–63   *Seven Years' War*

1759   Josiah Wedgwood (1730–95) opened works at Burslem, Staffordshire

1759–65   Matthew Boulton (1728–1804) began to build and operate first Soho Foundry, Birmingham

1760   Dr John Roebuck (1718–94) opened Carron Iron Works, Falkirk

1761   James Brindley (1716–72) completed first stage of Bridgewater Canal, Worsley–Manchester

1761–2   John Wilkinson became owner of Bersham and opened new iron works at Broseley, Shropshire

c.1764   James Hargreaves (d.1778) invented spinning jenny (patented 1770). Robert Peel established calico printing firm at Blackburn

1765   Anthony Bacon leased coal and iron rights around Merthyr Tydfil, Glamorgan

1766–77   Grand Trunk Canal (Trent and Mersey)

1769   Jedediah Strutt (1726–97) ribbed hosiery patent
Richard Arkwright (1732–92) water frame patent

1769–82   Strutt and Arkwright partnership
Wedgwood opened new works at Etruria
James Watt (1736–1819) first patent for steam engine

1771   Arkwright and Strutt opened cotton spinning mill at Cromford, Derbyshire

1773   Turnpike Act. Completion of Runcorn locks (Bridgewater Canal)

1774   Boulton and Watt partnership
Wilkinson boring mill patent

1775–83   *American War of Independence*

1775   Boulton and Watt patent extended to 1800

1776   Wilkinson installed B & W engine for blast at Broseley
        Whitbread installed engine at brewery
        Manufacture of plate glass begun at Ravenhead, St Helens,
        Lancashire
        Adam Smith, *Wealth of Nations*
1779   Samuel Crompton (1753–1827) completed development of
        the 'mule'
        Abraham Darby III (1750–91) cast iron bridge for River
        Severn at Coalbrookdale
1780   James Keir (1735–1820) set up alkali works at Tipton, near
        Dudley
1781   Watt patented rotary motion
1782   Lord Dundonald opened works to extract tar from coal at
        Culross, Fife
1783   Anthony Bacon sold Cyfartha Ironworks to Richard Craw-
        shay (d.1810)
        Thomas Bell invented (cylinder) calico printing
        Arkwright invited to visit Scotland
1784   Henry Cort (1740–1800) patented 'puddling' process: works
        at Fareham, Hampshire
        David Dale (1739–1806) and Arkwright opened mill at New
        Lanark
        Samuel Greg (d.1834) opened Quarry Bank Mill
        John Palmer (1742–1818) ran first mail coaches
1785   First steam driven cotton mill at Papplewick, Derbyshire
1786   John Horrocks (1768–1804) opened cotton mill at Preston
1787   Edmund Cartwright (1743–1823) patented power loom
1788   Watt patented *governor* which made steam engine adapt-
        able for general industrial use
1790   Joseph Bramah (1748–1814) and Henry Maudslay (1771–
        1831) mechanized production of Bramah's patent lock of 1784
        William Jessup and Benjamin Outram (1764–1805) opened
        Butterley Ironworks
        Humber–Severn, Mersey–Thames canal link completed
1791–4 Canal 'Mania', 81 Acts passed
1792–3 William Gott established Bean Ing Mill
        Leeds (scribbling, carding, fulling)
1793–1815 *Revolutionary and Napoleonic Wars*
1794   Commercial Society (Chamber of Commerce) founded at
        Manchester

1796   New Soho Foundry for specialized construction of steam engines

1797   Suspension of cash payments by the Bank of England

1797–1802 Matthew Murray (1765–1826) set up Round Foundry, Holbeck, Leeds

1798   Forth and Clyde Canal completed

1799   Robert Owen (1771–1858) took over at New Lanark

1799–1802 West India Docks, London

1800   Charles Tennant (1768–1838) set up St Rollox works for manufacture of bleach by passing chlorine over lime

1800–9   Maudslay and Marc Isambard Brunel (1769–1849) partnership for manufacture of block-making machines for Admiralty

1801   General Enclosure Act
          First Census

1803–6   East India Docks, London
          Richard Trevithick built and ran a locomotive to run on rails at Coalbrookdale
          William Symington (1763–1831) built steamship *Charlotte Dundas*

1805   Surrey Iron Railway, Croydon–Wandsworth
          Grand Junction Canal completed

1806–7   William Murdock (1754–1839), who had lit Soho Foundry by gas in 1800, completed first commercial installation of gas lighting at a Salford cotton mill

1806–13   *Napoleon's Continental System*

1809   John Heathcoat (1783–1861) introduced first successful lace-making machine

1810   Maudslay opened Lambeth works

1812–17   Luddite Riots
          Parliament awarded Crompton £5,000 for development of the 'mule'

1814   *The Times* began printing by steam
          Parish of St Margaret's, Westminster, lit by gas
          George Stephenson (1781–1848) built his first locomotive, *Blucher*

1815   Corn Law

1816   Richard Roberts (1789–1864) opened machine tool works at Deansgate, Manchester

1817	Joseph Clement (1779–1844) opened machine tool works at Newington Butts, London
1818	Institute of Civil Engineers founded
1819	First Factory Act
1821	Resumption of cash payments by the Bank of England
1822	Aaron Manby (1776–1850) built iron steamship at his Horseley Ironworks, Tipton
	Manby entered consortium for lighting Paris by gas
	James Akroyd, Old Lane, near Halifax, introduced power looms into his worsted mill
1823	Robert Napier (1791–1876) began manufacture of marine engines on the Clyde
	James Muspratt (1793–1886) began manufacture of soda by Leblanc process at Liverpool
	Roberts developed power loom
1825	Stephenson completed Stockton and Darlington Railway
1826	Thomas Telford (1757–1834) completed Menai Suspension Bridge
	Joint stock banks permitted outside London area
1827	Clement perfected constant speed facing lathe
	Pilkington glass works opened at St Helens
1828	Muspratt and Josias Gamble (1776–1848) opened soda works at St Helens
1829	Stephenson's locomotive with tubular boiler, *The Rocket*, successful at Rainhill trials
	Liverpool and Manchester Railway
	James Neilson (1792–1865) began use of hot blast at Clyde Ironworks
1830	Liverpool and Manchester Railway opened
	Roberts constructed self-acting mule
	Richard Oastler (1789–1861), letter on *Yorkshire Slavery* published in *Leeds Mercury*
1830–2	Vulcan Foundry, Newton-le-Willows (Lancashire), founded by Charles Tayleur
1831–2	Cholera epidemic
1832	Reform Act
1833	Factory Act established factory inspectorate
	Joseph Whitworth (1803–87) opened Manchester works
1834	New Poor Law
1835	Samuel Morse (1791–1872), electric telegraph

1836   James Nasmyth (1808–90) opened Bridgewater
            Foundry, Patricroft, Manchester
            Registration Act
1837–48   Chartist Movement
1838–46   Anti-Corn Law League founded in Manchester
            London and Birmingham Railway opened
            London and Southampton Railway opened
            Great Western Railway installed electric telegraph
            Paddington–West Drayton
            Isambard Kingdom Brunel (1806–59), engineer of the
            Great Western Railway, completed *Great Western*, the first
            steamship designed for a regular Atlantic run
1839   Napier began to build iron ships
            Nasmyth built first steam hammer
1840   Penny Post
            Railway Department of the Board of Trade
1841   Great Western Railway completed
            Whitworth lectured to Institute of Civil Engineers on his
            proposals for the standardization of screws
1842   'Plug Plot' Riots
            Edwin Chadwick (1800–90), *Report on the Sanitary Condi-
            tion of the Labouring Population*
1842–4   Friedrich Engels in England
            Southampton Outer Dock
            Sir Robert Peel (1788–1850) restored Income Tax
1843   Brunel's *Great Britain*, first screw-driven steamship for
            Atlantic run
1844–7   Railway 'Mania' promotions
            George Hudson (1800–71) negotiated
            Midland Railway amalgamation
            Railway Act introduced 'parliamentary trains'
1846   Repeal of the Corn Laws
            Albert Dock, Liverpool
            William Cooke (1806–79) and Charles Wheatstone (1802–75)
            formed Electric Telegraph Company
1847   Institute of Mechanical Engineers founded
            Factory Act, '10 hours' Act
            First docks opened at Birkenhead
1848–9   Cholera epidemic
            Public Health Act

1851   Great Exhibition
        G. E. Donisthorpe and S. C. Lister (1815–1906) produced
        wool combing machine (worsted industry)

PART II
Work and Life in the
Industrial Revolution

[10] THE SOCIAL ISSUES

Did the people of Britain suffer as a result of the Industrial
Revolution? This was a question asked with insistence from the
late 1830s. By then a large enough proportion of the population
was at work in industry for what Carlyle called 'the condition of
England question' to be thought of as a problem primarily about
industry. Although there had been industrial discontent before
the 1830s – the Luddite movement was only one example – if
men had thought of a 'condition of England question' they
would have done so in terms of the agricultural labourer and the
land. Parliament conceived of the New Poor Law of 1834 almost
solely in relation to the rural community; poverty seemed to be
a rural problem. The Poor Law officials quickly experimented
with a scheme to 'redeploy' village paupers in the industrial
areas. All this altered with the onset of depression and distress
in industry in the late 1830s. The severity of this crisis provoked
a flood of criticism against both industrial living standards and
the general conditions of life and work which existed in many of
the industrial areas.

The debate about living standards in the Industrial Revolution continues as lively, and sometimes as bitter, as ever. Several
issues are raised by it. Living standards were (and are?) usually
determined by food supply and food prices. Cheap food would
mean higher purchases of goods other than food and these, in

turn, led to industrial investment and employment. For most of
of this period Britain's food supply was adequate and only in
the nineteenth century did Britain begin to need regular imports
of foreign grain. For much of the period food was cheap (this
was the achievement of eighteenth-century agriculture) but
there was a marked tendency for it to become dearer under the
pressure of sustained population growth. Cheap food creates the
possibility of rising living standards (real incomes). But so would
a drop in the prices of industrial goods, provided that they were
goods which were, or might be, bought by the majority. The other
side of this equation is, of course, the level of wages. Wage rates,
as Adam Smith noticed, are not determined solely by economic
factors: they are also a matter of convention. As income is also
an index of status it would be surprising if the conventional view
of the labourer's wage had been overturned in the eighteenth
century. But there was a differential between the wages of
agriculture and industry and the Industrial Revolution increased
its importance. Again rising population can be *expected* to depress
wage rates. But it by no means always did so because the labour
market was local rather than national and families had to be
attracted into industry. In addition to these considerations are
those of wage variations between trades, the difficulty of know-
ing how to calculate *family* incomes and of assessing the importance of non-money income (the vegetables in the labourer's
garden).

If this economic framework began to squeeze working-class
incomes what could be done about it? Working men could
attempt to combine to reduce hours of work, to increase wages,
or to prevent the 'dilution' of their trade by outsiders. But it
must be admitted that their attempts to do this during the
Industrial Revolution were ineffectual because both their employers and the law were extremely hostile to anything like
trade union action. In any case the best organized sections of the
working class were often the better paid skilled workers whose
bargaining position with their employers was naturally stronger.
Other 'benefits' for working people might derive from charity,
from the Poor Law, and from changes in the government's

taxation policy. But any real improvement in their living standards could only be expected as a result of favourable economic
conditions. Obviously they were best off in times of rapid
expansion and full employment.

As important as living standards were the conditions of work
during the Industrial Revolution. This is sometimes inseparable
from the wider question of the general environment of life in the
industrial areas and, particularly, in the industrial towns. This is
discussed in the next part. Changes in the conditions of work are
difficult to describe or assess. Initially change is often resented
although, within a generation, it comes to be taken for granted.
Unfavourable comparisons between the work of the field or the
craftsman's shop and that of the new industry were common in
the nineteenth century. They cannot be discounted: nor, of
course, can the evident suffering which existed in this period.
But the shadow of those 'dark, satanic mills' should not be
allowed to fall across the whole of the Industrial Revolution.
The mills were often grimly reminiscent of the prison or the
workhouse. Yet they could sometimes look more like the centrepiece of a country estate, set in attractive country, surrounded
by comfortable cottages, like Samuel Greg's mill at Styal in
Cheshire which is now the property of the National Trust.

[11] A DIVERSITY OF MEN AND TRADES: THE LABOUR FORCE IN 1851

The worker's circumstances were determined by the circumstances of his trade. A sharp division had always existed between
the artisan and journeyman, who had served his apprenticeship
(he was sometimes known as a 'society-man', a term which
referred to the organization of artisans in trade clubs or societies),
and the unskilled, general labourer. In the surviving traditional
trades – and the majority not only survived, but grew – the
position of the artisan often continued unchanged. And by

creating new skills the Industrial Revolution encouraged the growth of new élites. The emergence of a class of managers, foremen, overseers, and mechanics or technicians was an important, if gradual process; it was, of course, largely the outcome of an expansion of large-scale industry. The revolution in the textile industry caused the appearance of the most familiar figure of the Industrial Revolution, the factory operative. The factory was by no means always as grand and imposing as it is envisaged but it is true that the operatives came to stand out as a distinct group whose way of life was very different from that which prevailed in the older trades. The large class of domestic outworkers had existed before the Industrial Revolution and they were certainly not confined to the textile trades. For much of this period industrial expansion meant a growth in the number of domestic outworkers. In Clapham's opinion outwork

was still the predominant form of capitalist organization in Britain in the reign of George IV; for, though it was losing ground on one side to the great works and factories, it was always gaining on the other at the expense of household production and handicraft.

In the eighteenth century the status of the outworker had often approximated to that of the artisan. As the Industrial Revolution progressed few outworkers were able to safeguard their position. Technical advance brought some outworkers into direct competition with machine industry while others, and this could be a complementary process, found their trade inundated by fresh recruits.

Industry always requires skill, but it does not necessarily have a use for old skills. A number of the artisans' trades experienced a dilution of their skilled labour force by unskilled 'cheap-men'. A traditional structure of independent master, journeymen, and apprentices could find itself challenged by the growth of subcontracting and outwork. This transition was aided by the repeal, in 1814, of the apprenticeship regulations of the 1563 Statute of Artificers which largely deprived the artisans of their control of their trade. Where conditions were suitable, as they were in the consumer trades, the end product was a sweated industry, marked by horrifying exploitation of its workers. The artisans did not disappear altogether, but they no longer dominated their trades. In 1851 Henry Mayhew drew attention, in his *London Labour and the London Poor*, to the existence of two 'distinct classes' among the working people. The cabinet-makers were made up of between 600 and 700 society-men, and a much larger group of nearly 5,000 'cheap-men' or 'competitive men', among whom were included the struggling 'garret-masters' who sold their work to a new race of employers, grimly known as the 'slaughter-house men'. A similar structure had appeared in the much larger tailoring trade. Here Mayhew estimated that there were just under 6,000 independent masters and society-men, and a further 18,000 in the 'slop' trade (where the clothes were ready-made). In both cases the changed structure of the trade, and the situation of the men within it, was ultimately dictated by the growth of London itself and the emergence of a new class of consumers. The sweated trades clearly depended upon the existence of a ready supply of cheap labour. Improvement in their conditions was slow, even after 1850, and was associated with the transition to factory production. The conquests of the sewing-machine (Isaac Singer's was patented in 1851) did not stop at alleviating drudgery in the home. By encouraging employers in the clothing trade to set up larger workshops – although this was more true of Leeds than London – the machine did something to improve life for the seamstresses (73,068 of them were enumerated in the 1851 Census) whose plight had been described by Thomas Hood in his poem 'The Song of the Shirt' (1843):

> Oh, Men, with Sisters dear!
> Oh, Men, with Mothers and Wives!
> It is not linen you're wearing out,
> But human creatures' lives!
> Stitch – stitch – stitch,
> In poverty, hunger and dirt,
> Sewing at once, with a double thread,
> A Shroud as well as a Shirt.

Competition for work was naturally keenest among the unskilled labourers. As a group the unskilled were as diverse as the artisans or outworkers. The largest group, if they are to be included, were the agricultural labourers, some of whom, with their families, had experience of domestic outwork. In 1851 there were nearly a million and a half working on the land. At that Census 376,000 were described as 'undefined' labourers, but more than 70,000 appear as attached to specific branches of industry. The Census of 1831, which did not attempt an elaborate breakdown of the labour force, recorded 500,000 labourers 'employed in labour not agricultural'. To these should, perhaps, be added the domestic servants who, in 1851, numbered more than a million. Difficult to trap within any category was the army of 'street people' described by Mayhew in his account of London. The ways of earning a living in the streets of the capital were various and bizarre: in the late 1840s Mayhew specifically noticed that the number of costermongers increased whenever there was unemployment in the regular trades. For Mayhew the situation of the unskilled, manual worker was well illustrated by the London dock-labourers: 'they are', he wrote, 'a striking instance of mere brute force with brute appetites. This class of labour is as unskilled as the hurricane. Mere muscle is all that is needed; hence every human locomotive is capable of working there.'

Whether artisan or labourer most men worked for what would now be regarded as a very small employer. Even in the cotton textile industry only 411 employers, out of a total of 1,670 in 1851, employed more than a hundred men. Only in the worsted and silk industries did the large master figure on anything like the same scale. In a 'new' industry, like 'engine and machine making', four out of five employers had less than ten men, and only one in twenty-five had more than a hundred. There were great employers in almost every industry, but they were the exception. Fifty-two building contractors employed more than a hundred, and the large business was quite usual in the Potteries. In the older trades masters commonly employed no more than a handful of men. The figures collected for the Census of 1851 were incomplete (a summary of the returns appears in J. H. Clapham, op. cit. Vol. II, p. 35) but they demonstrate once again how dangerous it is to give undue prominence to the factory, or the factory worker, in an overall account of working conditions in the Industrial Revolution. As yet few men worked with machines: a majority continued to use the tools and implements which their grandfathers had known. Rather more women were at work in 1851 than we should expect in the twentieth century. Most employed women worked either in domestic service, where they numbered well over a million, or in the textile and clothing industries which together employed a similar total; these three categories accounted for 2·25 million of the 2·83 million women in work in 1851. Agriculture employed another 229,000. Outside the textile industry women and girls did not form an important proportion of the industrial labour force, but some could be found at almost every type of industrial work. Although the employment of women underground was prohibited by the Mines Act of 1842, there were 11,000 working above ground at coal mines and quarries in 1851. In the workshops of the Black Country women workers were not uncommon; altogether 36,000 were employed in the metal trades.

Despite the undoubted importance of women most industrial work was performed by men and boys: only in the textile industry was their position challenged by women. Boys continued to be trained through an apprentice system. In the craft trades this was to be expected. Elsewhere the child 'apprentice' was exposed to varying degrees of exploitation. In some cases the element of training was both scanty and worthless. Worst off, in the eighteenth century, were the pauper apprentices bound to the mill owners by the poor law authorities. This practice died out in the nineteenth century when the town mills were able to recruit 'free' child labour at will. Nevertheless, the scandals associated with apprentice labour in the early textile industry were the cause of the first attempt to regulate modern industry, the Health and Morals of Apprentices Act, 1802. In other industries it was more difficult to control the conditions under which pauper apprentices served, and were bound to, their masters;

like Oliver Twist they could only try to escape. The lot of the pauper apprentice was unenviable. Other boys had to work just as hard. Across the span of at least two generations Arnold Bennett described, at the opening of his novel *Clayhanger* (1910), the life of a young apprentice potter in the mid 1830s: Bennett probably drew his sketch from local knowledge, but he could have come to a very similar result by using the evidence on the pottery industry contained in the Report of the Royal Commission on Childrens' Employment, 1843. Darius Clayhanger began work at seven as 'mould-runner' to a 'muffin [plate]-maker':

The business of Darius was to run as hard as he could with the mould, and a newly created plate adhering thereto, into the drying-stove. This 'stove' was a room lined with shelves, and having a red hot stove in the middle. As no man of seven could reach the upper shelves, a pair of steps was provided for Darius, and up these he had to scamper. Each mould with its plate had to be leaned carefully against the wall, and if the soft clay of a new-born plate was damaged, Darius was knocked down. The atmosphere outside the stove was chill, but owing to the heat of the stove, Darius was obliged to work half naked. His sweat ran down his cheeks, and down his chest, and down his back, making white channels, and lastly it soaked his hair.

Seventy years earlier the evidence of the Royal Commission on Childrens' Employment was used by Disraeli in his novel *Sybil*, (1845) to provide the background for the account of the Midland metal trade village of 'Wodgate'. Here the business was 'carried on by master workmen in their own houses, each of whom possesses an unlimited number of what they call apprentices, by whom their affairs are principally conducted, and whom they treat as the Mamelukes treated the Egyptians'.

[12] 'A NEW & UNFORESEEN CREATION': MANAGEMENT, THE FACTORY SYSTEM AND LABOUR DISCIPLINE

The organization of the first industrial labour force was an immense undertaking. Not surprisingly early management was often crude and insensitive: its major incentive, perhaps its only incentive, to considerate handling of the work-people was local labour shortage. Management was made necessary by large-scale enterprise: in the craftsman's workshop it had had no place. In the traditional crafts the master had been, and remained, close to his men in every sense. His training and apprenticeship meant that he shared an inheritance of skill and traditional methods with his men. He often had only the haziest notion of the economics of his business. Wages and prices were as much part of tradition as the rules of the craft itself. Even where the scale of enterprise was still small the intrusion of machines fractured the ties between master and man. In his *Wheelright's Shop* (Cambridge, 1923) George Sturt described the change which came over his relations with his men when, in 1889, he set up machinery – 'a gas engine, with saws, lathe, drill, and grindstone' – in his shop at Farnham.

And from the first day the machines began running, the use of axes and adzes disappeared from the well-known place, the saws and saw pit became obsolete ... There in that one little spot, the ancient provincial life of England was put into a back seat. It made a differ-ence to me personally, little as I dreamt of such a thing. 'The Men,' though still my friends, as I fancied, became machine 'hands'. Unintentionally, I had made them servants waiting upon gas com-bustion. (*The Wheelwright's Shop*, p. 201)

Sturt's analysis is convincing because it sprang from experience, and has all the sharpness of valid regret. His machines undoubt-edly saved time and toil – men no longer had to spend days in the saw pit – but they threatened the craftsman's intimate knowledge of his materials and, with that, the position of (ancient) craftsmanship itself. It was this threat to which William Blake, the London engraver, referred in his prophetic poem 'The Four Zoas' (1795–1804): he saw,

The hour glass contemn'd because its simple workmanship
Was as the workmanship of the plowman, and the water wheel
That raises water into Cisterns broken and burn'd in fire
Because its workmanship was like the workmanship of the Shepherd:
And in their stead, intricate wheels invented, Wheel without wheel

In the future Blake saw men spending the 'days of wisdom in sorrowful drudgery': for him the machine seemed more an end than a beginning.

The truth was that satisfaction in work was no more easy to discover during the Industrial Revolution than at other times, before or since. The old 'trades' had, perhaps, been more successful in this respect: it is difficult to explain the sense of loss, of lowered standards, without admitting this. Although work had been hard (this was just as much true for the craftsman as the labourer) it was often absorbing, its lore intricate and its standards a challenge. These were not attitudes which could survive in new, expanding industries whether organized on a factory or outwork basis. Had the transfer of men and women into industry depended upon the rate at which they could be absorbed into the craft structure it is clear that progress would have been slow and the century from 1750 to 1850 would not appear to be the era of revolutionary change which it seemed to be at the time, and ever since. In the new industries, in the textile mills, in the mines and ironworks, and on the contractors' sites, the standards of the 'shop' were (sadly?) inapplicable. The mills were certainly untraditional; those who worked in them underwent no gradual initiation into a craft but had to learn, quickly, how to adjust their work and their lives to the machine. The methods by which the first factory workers were 'disciplined' aroused the interest and, often, the condemnation of contemporaries. This discussion is itself evidence of the novelty of the factory system.

Neither from contemporary accounts nor from later historical analysis is it easy to reach an impartial assessment of the effects of the factory system. Even when extreme judgments, on either side, have been excluded it may be that everyone who studies the question is bound to choose between the economic advantages of the factory system and the social loss, or tension, which it also entailed. The divergence of opinion among modern historians has been considerable. In their book *The Town Labourer, 1760–1832* (London, 1917) J. L. and Barbara Hammond emphasized the destructive impact of the factory system upon the early textile workers:

The men and women of Lancashire and Yorkshire felt of this new power that it was inhuman, that it disregarded all their instincts and sensibilities, that it brought into their lives an inexorable force, destroying and scattering their customs, their traditions, their freedoms, their ties of family and home, their dignity and character as men and women. (p. 31)

By contrast T. S. Ashton in *An Economic History of England: The Eighteenth Century* (London, 1955) chose to draw attention to the force of economic necessity behind the factory system and discipline:

Yet it is obvious that if the workers of the eighteenth century had refused to conform to some code of conduct when at work, there could have been no factory system, and no such rise of output, and hence the standard of life, as was, in fact, attained in the nineteenth century. (p. 212)

How great is the distance between these interpretations?

The answer is that much depends upon what is taken to be the correct 'vantage point' from which to survey the Industrial Revolution. The Hammonds opted to look backwards into the eighteenth century. Further, they were concerned to contrast not simply the physical character of work but also the context in which it was performed. They admit that 'scarcely any evil associated with the factory system was entirely a new evil in kind': in the domestic industries the home worker 'worked long hours, but they were his own hours . . . his house was stifling, but he could slip into his garden; he had spells of unemployment, but he could use them sometimes for cultivating his cabbages'. Against this background it is quite legitimate to argue in terms of retrogression and 'loss'. Such an account may have particular relevance for the understanding of first-generation factory workers, and for those that *experienced* the transition which the Hammonds describe so poignantly. But what of the second and third generation of factory workers? Their life was certainly no less arduous than their grandparents', but the experience of domestic outwork will have been more remote and factory discipline will have taken on more of the character of familiar routine. It is important to recognize that the process of adaptation to new conditions of work was not complete by 1850: equally that by this date a 'trained' industrial labour force had come into existence, that the age of the pioneers had, to an extent, passed. Professor Ashton, by looking away from the early Industrial Revolution into the nineteenth century, inevitably stresses the progressive, positive achievement of the Industrial Revolution. Yet he does not, of course, say that the process of adaptation was easy; on the contrary it 'was long and can hardly have been pleasant'. From this position it becomes necessary to move the discussion on to the question of living standards and the rewards of work; factory discipline – no matter how 'unpleasant'? – has to be accepted as the twin of technical progress, as indispensable to Industrial Revolution.

How great a change in the methods and habits of work was effected by the Industrial Revolution? As a method of organizing and employing labour, what were the advantages of the factory system? The limitations of the outwork structure for an expanding industry, like cotton textiles, were well understood in the late eighteenth century (see Part I, p. 26). Outwork provided additional employment for country people who often had all too little regular work on the land or who, like the women and children, were more easily employed at home. Not surprisingly there was little inclination to move into the early mills. The mills themselves had a resemblance to the workhouse which heightened a natural distaste among those used to working at home, in a 'shop', or in the fields (the loss of contact with Nature is a constant theme in criticism of the factories and it would be a mistake to ignore its importance). The mills were noisy and, no doubt, frightening; it took time to overcome the shock they gave the senses. Thus in the eighteenth century the mill owner often had to scour the countryside for his work-force and, once assembled, it gave him many headaches. In *A New View of Society* (1813) Robert Owen described the problems that faced David Dale in establishing his spinning mill at New Lanark in 1784. Accommodation had to be provided for the apprentices, most of whom were paupers from the cities of Edinburgh and Glasgow: in 1799, when Owen arrived at New Lanark, the works was employing about five hundred children. They were not easy to manage. Many left as soon as their term of apprenticeship was completed – in Owen's view because the discipline to which they had been subjected proved too much for them. The adult workers were equally difficult to manage. The suspicion of factory work was such that 'only persons destitute of friends, employment, and character, were found willing to try the experiment'. Once at New Lanark 'they grew so valuable to the establishment, that they became agents not to be governed contrary to their own inclinations' (*A New View of Society*, Everyman ed., London, 1927, p. 27). Owen attributed the mounting crisis at the New Lanark mills to Dale's inability to give his full attention to direct personal management of the mills at New Lanark. Robert Owen's 'reform' of this early factory community showed unusual managerial flair and insight. He ceased to employ pauper children and thus freed New Lanark of the pauper stigma. He improved the housing and amenities of the town and made remarkable efforts to educate the operatives in self-reliance. He saw this as sound business practice: 'the proprietors derived services from their (the workpeople's) attachment, almost without inspection, far beyond those which could be obtained by any other means than those of mutual confidence and kindness' (Owen, op. cit., p. 33).

The conditions which governed the management of the early,

water-driven, spinning mills did not always apply to the later, steam-powered urban mills. The first millowners tried, and often succeeded, to mould the whole life of the communities which grew up around their concerns. In the nineteenth century Richard Arkwright was most admired for the way in which he had trained his operatives: 'so admirable were his plans of management', said his late nineteenth-century biographer (*Dictionary of National Biography*, 1890 ed.), 'that they cannot be said to have yet been in any degree superseded'. The most extravagant praise of Arkwright came from Dr Andrew Ure in his *Philosophy of Manufactures* (1835): 'To devise and administer a successful code of factory discipline, suited to the necessities of factory diligence, was the Herculean enterprise, the noble achievement of Arkwright'. Ure was, perhaps, a naïvely enthusiastic observer of the factory system. Whereas he could see happiness in the factory, his indignant critics, like Engels and, later, Marx, saw only a form of slavery and a regime of almost military harshness. The manufacturers had a powerful incentive to control their workers strictly; they had often a large, and increasing, capital sum invested in their machinery and buildings. To suffer from negligence, lateness, absenteeism and other 'desultory habits of work' (Ure) could mean business disaster. The standards of work suited to domestic and craft industries, where little fixed capital was at stake, had necessarily to be discarded within the factory.

The most novel feature of factory work was its continuity and regularity: the machines had to be kept running. The pace of work was set by the water-wheel or steam engine, not by man's physical endurance or dexterity. While the tasks themselves were monotonous, and often simple, the factory worker had to be alert and reliable. It was for this, rather than skill, that he was paid. To punish lateness, absenteeism, casualness and inattention, the factory owners applied a series of scaled fines and wage reductions. Friedrich Engels commented severely upon the factory rules that had come to his attention:

I have before me another set of factory rules, which state that a worker who is three minutes late loses a quarter of an hour's pay, while anyone who is 20 minutes late loses a quarter of a day's pay. An operative who does not arrive at the factory until after breakfast is fined 1s on Monday and 6d on other days. These regulations are in force at the Phoenix Mill, Jersey Street, Manchester. It will be argued that such rules are necessary to ensure the smooth coordination of the various processes carried on in a big, well-run factory. It will be said that stern discipline of this kind is just as necessary in the factory as in the army. That may be true enough, but how can one defend a state of society which can only survive by exercise of such shameful tyranny? (*The Condition of the Working Classes in England*, ed. W. O. Henderson and W. H. Chaloner, Oxford, 1958, p. 202)

Engels at least admitted the force of the arguments which supported the policies of the factory masters. Leisurely work habits were one of the characteristics of an older society which the early industrialists were bound to question. The heavy fine for absence on Mondays at the Phoenix Mill is explained by the persistence, well into the nineteenth century, of the ancient practice of declining work on the second day of the week. In the Potteries the observance of 'Saint Monday' long inhibited the development of regular hours of work. Darius Clayhanger was made to recall how, 'after three days of debauch', his master expected him to begin work at 3 a.m. on Tuesday mornings.

By the early nineteenth century the working day was carefully measured by the clock and punctuated by the factory bell and the whistle. Even on the land work became more regular. Like other changes this one met with resistance. Not surprisingly some employers tampered with the clock to their own advantage and workpeople began to watch it with a disturbing intentness. In the early factories employers had relied upon regulations to recast older attitudes to work and to control the casualness (as distinct from idleness) which had been so much a feature of the old world. But rules alone were insufficient. In a society where there was scanty provision for the unemployed the fear of dismissal was always a powerful aid to discipline. Important too was the mounting emphasis placed upon work and endeavour within a framework of Christian morality. The role of the Protestant 'ethic' in the growth of capitalist enterprise was first

expounded by the German sociologist Max Weber. Weber, in
The Protestant Ethic and the Spirit of Capitalism, argued that
Calvinist theology deprived man of all the traditional assurances
of salvation. Left alone with their faith as the only guarantee of
salvation the Calvinists (i.e. the Puritans) were vulnerable to
doubt and despair. To escape they threw themselves into a
frenzy of activity. Weber noticed the significance of Bunyan's
question:

It will not be said: did you believe? but: were you Doers, or Talkers
only?

The Puritan tradition laid great emphasis too upon the careful
use of time. That this tradition remained alive in the eighteenth
and nineteenth centuries is undoubted and it was particularly
active, as one might expect, among those Nonconformist groups
from which so many of the early industrialists were recruited.
For these employers the training of the industrial labour force
could take on the character of a moral crusade. The religious
basis for what has been called the 'economic virtues' (by R. H.
Tawney) is well illustrated by this notice to employees put up
by Samuel Oldknow in his mill at Mellor in 1797:

WHEREAS The horrid and impious Vice of profane CURSING and
SWEARING, – and the Habits of Losing Time – and DRUNKENNESS –
are becoming so frequent and notorious; that unless speedily checked,
they may justly provoke the Divine Vengeance to increase the
Calamities these Nations now labour under.
NOTICE is hereby given, That all the Hands in the service of SAMUEL
OLDKNOW working in his mill, or elsewhere, must be subject to the
following RULE: That when any person, either Man, Woman, or
Child, is heard to CURSE or SWEAR, the same shall forfeit One Shilling.
And when any Hand is absent from Work (unless leave obtained),
the same shall forfeit as many Hours of Work as have been lost.

Clearly if the Protestant 'ethic' played any part in the emergence of modern business attitudes it also had the further function of shaping the working class into a tractable labour force.
In the eighteenth century Methodism specifically encouraged
responsible and moral conduct: respectability and good work-

manship were made to appear close allies. The same belief was precious to the early temperance campaigners in the nineteenth century. Periodic bouts of drunkenness were very much a feature of the world of casual and undisciplined work. Nineteenth-century beer drinking was arguably less damaging than the orgies of the Gin Age but it was still a cause of poverty and violence. The consumption of alcohol rose after the government removed the beer duty in 1830. Of course the need for drink, and even more for the pub, is easily understandable given the scant amenities of both towns and homes; a visit to the pub was a social act and those who thought it a sin necessarily pointed a lurid moral. Still it is possible to see what Samuel Smiles meant when he wrote that 'drinking was incompatible with economy, decency, health, and honest living'. Even when most heavy drinking was done on a Saturday night – it was then that Engels remembered that he 'seldom went home without seeing many drunkards staggering in the road or lying helpless in the gutter' – there is little doubt that it often dislocated work. In the pottery manufactory where Darius Clayhanger worked as a boy 'the beer came [in] as steadily as though it had been laid on by a main pipe'. Self-control did not rely solely upon the force of religious teaching. In the work of Samuel Smiles the Puritan gospel of abstinence, thrift and punctuality was secularized into the familiar Victorian creed of 'Self-Help'. To the seventeenth-century Puritan, Richard Baxter, time spent unwisely necessarily curtailed the God-sanctioned pursuit of a life of useful work. Smiles's sermon on the irrevocable nature of lost time suggested a similar sense of urgency:

Some take no thought of the value of money until they have come to the end of it, and many do the same with their time. The hours are allowed to flow by unemployed, and then, when life is fast waning, they bethink themselves of the duty of making a wiser use of it. But the habit of listlessness and idleness may already have become confirmed, and they are unable to break the bonds. . . . Lost wealth may be replaced by industry, lost knowledge by study, lost health by temperance or medicine, but lost time is gone for ever. (*Self-Help*, 1859, ed. 1908, p. 323)

[13] THE FACTORY CHILDREN

Not all work discipline was as indirect as factory fines or the still
more uncertain technique of moral and religious persuasion.
When so many workers were either children or young adolescents
it was only to be expected that the impersonal discipline of
factory regulations would be supplemented by 'corporal punish-
ment'. Critics of the factory system frequently stressed the
cruelty to which children were subjected within the mills. There
can be little doubt that beating was common and that it could
be vindictive. The Reports of the Royal Commission on Child
Employment, 1842–5, make it clear that the conditions in the
factories were not exceptional: while few would accept Andrew
Ure's famous description of factory children as 'lively elves', it
seems that their lot was better than that of many children in
other industries. Informed contemporaries were convinced that
the major evil of the times was the length of the child's working
day. The second Report of the Royal Commission on Child
Employment, 1843, noted that 'in almost every instance the
Children work as long as the adults; being sometimes kept at
work sixteen, and even eighteen hours without any intermission'.
Worst off were those children who were employed, not by the
master, but by one of his men. These children suffered, even
more than the employers, from irregular habits of work among
the men and 'they are almost always roughly, very often
harshly, and sometimes cruelly used' (second Report of the
Royal Commission on Child Employment, 1843). There was, of
course, nothing novel about the employment of children during
the Industrial Revolution. While the need for better education
came increasingly to be recognized all classes of society accepted
that work would be expected of children into the foreseeable
future. What created a new situation was that children were
now to be found in industrial employment, both in factories and
elsewhere, and this certainly meant that they became subject to
more intensive and exhausting work than had been the case in

domestic and rural employments. It is quite understandable
that this should have become a matter for protest. The context
of childhood changed. The child's dependence upon its parents
altered (in the cotton industry the parents sometimes became
dependent upon their children). The demands of industry were
such that the child could not be trained for life in the home, nor
always work with his father: the Industrial Revolution required
a modern educational system which diminished the responsibility of parents, and introduced into the family the impersonal
demands of society. 'Education' at first meant work, but the
significance of the early factory schools is obvious enough. If
work was education, so most education, while only part-time
and supplementary, and provided by religious bodies, was
directed to fashioning children for work.

[14] FAMILY LIFE IN THE INDUSTRIAL REVOLUTION

That the Industrial Revolution bore heavily upon children is
well known. Its impact, more generally, upon family life has
received much less attention. Nevertheless complaints that the
factory system disrupted family life were a commonplace of the
early nineteenth century and reached something of a climax in
the 1830s. Just as the erosion of craftsmanship aroused regret,
so did the family economy of pre-industrial England arouse a
sense of nostalgia. In his *Manufacturing Population of England:
Its Moral, Social, and Physical Conditions, and the Changes which
have arisen from the Use of Steam Machinery* (1833), P. Gaskell
spoke of the domestic manufacturer (i.e. worker):

working under the eye of, and with the assistance of his family; his
children growing up under his immediate inspection and control . . .
engaged in pursuits similar to his own, and in a subordinate capacity;
and lastly, the same generation living age after age on the same spot,
and under the same thatched roof, which thus became a sort of heir-

loom, endeared to its occupier by a long series of happy memories
and home delights. (Quoted in E. Royston Pike's *Human Documents
of the Industrial Revolution*, London, 1966, p. 25)

In writing his well known introductory chapter in *The Condition
of the Working Class in England* Engels leant heavily upon
Gaskell. For him, too, the idyllic quality of pre-industrial life
was axiomatic:

The workers' children were brought up at home, where they learned
to fear God and obey their parents. This patriarchal relationship
between parents and children continued until the young people left
home to get married. (op. cit., p. 11)

The belief that the factory system destroyed parental authority
was strongly argued by its opponents; to Richard Oastler this
was 'the greatest curse ... the very acme of the evil, of the
factory system'. Related to this theme was the further objection
that girls sent to work in the mills later proved ill equipped to
run their own families. The fears that the mill fostered immorality
were, no doubt, more irrational (though there were examples of
millowners and overseers abusing their position) but belong to
the same general feeling that the factory undermined family
life and ties.

There was substance in this criticism. Some of the issues are,
indeed, familiar ones in an industrial society. The problem of
wives and mothers who work away from home can be a genuine
one even in the mid-twentieth century, yet there can be no
question of dispensing with their contribution to the home and
national economies. 'Domestic Science' is an accepted feature of
the school curriculum: no one imagines that the child must
learn everything from its parents. We accept that it is during
our leisure that family life has most meaning: we do not expect
for the most part, to work with other members of our family.
But the adaptation of the family to something like its modern
role was necessarily painful. In the domestic industries the
family remained, throughout this period, the normal working
unit. Only in a contracting domestic industry, like hand-loom
weaving from the 1830s, would children have to seek work

outside the home. In the earliest factories it proved possible to employ a whole family; recruitment was on this basis, and the advantages of using normal parental control of children were recognized by the mill owners. Into the 1820s it was usual for a child to enter a spinning mill as a 'scavenger' at eight or nine years old and to work with his father. Later he became a 'piecer' and, finally, at about eighteen, a spinner. From the 1820s it was difficult to maintain this pattern. Improved machines carried many more spindles – and thus required more children to act as piecers, while the demand for adult labour did not expand at the same rate. Mechanized weaving relied even more heavily upon children, and women. It was thus technical progress which finally ended the era of family employment in the mills: in retrospect this seems an inevitable development. The family unit could not survive as an *economic* entity in the industrial town which, by definition, offered a variety of employment (the impact of the Industrial Revolution on the family structure of cotton textile workers is analyzed in Neil J. Smelser's *Social Change in the Industrial Revolution*, London, 1959). But it must be remembered that the textile towns were a special case.

[15] WORK AND WAGE-RATES

To bring more of the nation's labour force into industry, where its work was more productive, was a primary function of the Industrial Revolution. The new generations of industrial workers had to be trained and had to an extent to abandon cherished habits. Necessity was perhaps the major pressure behind this transformation. But there were positive incentives, too. Opportunities were more numerous in the town and wages were generally higher. Labour was exploited more systematically in industry but, at least partially, by encouraging workpeople to participate in higher production: the device which achieved this was payment by piece or job. Piece work, and piece payment, were not new, but were practices which originated in the craft and domestic industries. During the Industrial Revolution piece work became more widespread and generally supplanted payment by time. Karl Marx saw in piece rates a characteristically capitalist means of increasing the intensity of labour:

Given the existence of piece-wages, it is, of course, to the personal interest of the worker that he should strain his labour power to the utmost, and this fact enables the capitalist all the more easily to increase the normal degree of intensity of labour. It is, moreover, to the personal interest of the worker that the length of the working day should be increased, since he will thereby be enabled to secure an increase in his daily or weekly wage. (*Capital*, Everyman ed., 1930 Vol. II, p. 605)

What Marx saw as a commonplace of the nineteenth century Adam Smith had already noticed in the previous century. Smith accepted the advantages of a high-wage economy:

The wages of labour are the encouragement of industry, which, like every other human quality, improves in proportion to the encouragement it receives. A plentiful subsistence increases the bodily strength of the labourer, and the comfortable hope of bettering his condition, and of ending his days perhaps in ease and plenty, animates him to exert that strength to the utmost. (*Wealth of Nations*, 1826, ed. p. 83)

Smith observed that men were generally paid by the piece in 'manufactures' and pointed out the disadvantages of the system:

Workmen . . . when they are liberally paid by the piece, are very apt to overwork themselves, and to ruin their health and constitution in a few years . . .Excessive application during four days of the week is frequently the real cause of the idleness of the other three, so much and so loudly complained of. (op. cit., pp. 83–4)

Piece rates certainly had the effect of lengthening the working day. It took time to convince masters that this was not to their advantage. The doubtful economy of long hours had impressed Robert Owen: he questioned 'whether any manufactory, so arranged as to occupy the hands employed in it twelve hours per day, will not produce its fabric . . . nearly if not altogether as cheap as those in which the exertions of the employed are continued to fourteen or fifteen hours per day'. The number of millowners who could recognize the argument for shorter hours had certainly grown by 1850: up till then, and no doubt for long afterwards, many employers had had only the crudest notions of how best to work their employees. The prevailing attitude among millowners towards working hours was criticized by the Preston manufacturer, Robert Gardiner, in 1845 in terms which well illustrate the pressures exerted on workpeople in the early Industrial Revolution:

All the arguments I have heard in favour of long time appear based on an arithmetical question – if 11 produce so much, what will 12, 13, or even 15 hours produce? This is correct, as far as the steam engine is concerned; whatever it will produce in 11 hours, it will produce double the quantity in 22. But try this on the animal horse, and you will soon find he cannot compete with the engine, as he requires both time to rest and feed.

[16] LIVING STANDARDS AND SOCIAL CLASSES

The position of the middle class

Early industrial life was a strain. It was more competitive. If it extended opportunity and choice, it offered, or seemed to offer, less security. After 1850 the flight from the villages gathered speed and it was clearly the higher living standards of the towns, and of industry, which attracted the migrants. So too, in the earlier Industrial Revolution, the recruitment of industrial workers had required some incentive from higher wages. An industrial society was a wealthier society, although this meant little to the agricultural labourer or to the poorest paid anywhere. Nevertheless more people were now engaged in regular, productive employment and a growing section of the community was thus divorced from the uneconomic, seasonal ebb and flow of agricultural labour. In industry, but especially in those industries where the revolutionary partnership of man and powered machinery was first concluded, productivity bounded upwards. For the first time Britain possessed a transport system which was not just adequate to its needs but was itself a stimulus to further growth. There are thus good reasons why an industrial revolution can be expected to raise living standards and why, in the long run, it transforms them. But before 1850 the benefits of industrialization had accrued mainly to a minority.

A recent estimate of the gross national product (i.e. the total value of goods and services: the estimate is that of Phyllis Deane and W. A. Cole, *British Economic Growth 1688–1959*, p. 283) in the first half of the nineteenth century suggests that it was growing at 2·9 per cent per year and by 1·5 per cent per head. This is not spectactular growth by modern standards but it should have made possible an increase in consumption. But the gains from the Industrial Revolution were always under pressure from the growth of population. Most labour was unskilled and its output low. The immigration of thousands of impoverished Irishmen and their families in the 1830s and 1840s did little to help here. There was thus room for only a slight increase in real incomes. Whether or not they were able to increase depended upon the distribution of incomes. This had, of course, been very uneven in the eighteenth century. The main contribution of the Industrial Revolution in this direction was to expand the middle class, the nation's business and professional community. Most middle-class families could afford a substantial expenditure on food and clothing; they moved inevitably towards a more spacious way of life, a larger house and a rising number of servants. By 1851 the middle class may have been three million strong and although it included commercial and professional families whose links with the industrial economy were tenuous it is reasonable to see this as the first community to owe its existence and prosperity to the Industrial Revolution. Within the middle class there was a wide range of incomes. The living standards enjoyed by clerks and teachers were not very different from those of the skilled labourer. The small middle-class income is as much a feature of the literature of this period as is the wealth and ostentation of the successful. The straightened circumstances of the good ladies of Mrs Gaskell's *Cranford* (1853), whose ingenuity consisted of stretching out tiny incomes by careful housekeeping, belong to one corner of the middle-class continent while the gloomy magnificence of the Dombey household belong to another (*Dombey and Son* was published in 1848).

The changing pattern of middle-class life is approached best by individual examples. The family of Joseph Chamberlain (*b.* 1836) was established in London by the politician's great-grandfather, William Chamberlain. William was apprenticed to a City shoemaker and set up his own business in Milk Street in the 1740s, becoming a member of the Cordwainers' Company. The six or seven hundred Cordwainers dominated the London shoe trade and it is not surprising that William became a wealthy man. Just before his death in 1788 the family moved out to a new suburban house at Islington and the business was then worth £11,800. Joseph's father moved with his bride to a house in Camberwell and then, in 1846, they moved back into a spacious Regency house in Islington. In 1854 Chamberlain's brother-in-law, John Nettlefold, decided to buy the American patent of a machine for making carpenters' screws. The two men raised £30,000 and with it revolutionized the production methods at Nettlefold's small screw factory in Birmingham. The young Joseph Chamberlain went to Birmingham to represent his father in the new venture. Under his father the Chamberlains had embarked upon a more expansive way of life and brought the savings accumulated in an old 'craft' business to a characteristically modern enterprise of the mid-century.

Perhaps a more typical family history was that described by the French journalist Hippolyte Taine in his *Notes on England* which were based on a visit he made in 1859. 'Mr W–' was the son of a shopkeeper who had seen to it that his son was trained as an engineer. Mr W was first successful in the design of two lighthouses and then of a tubular bridge. This had led to his appointment as a company secretary and, when Taine knew him, he was on a salary of £600 a year – and working at his office for nine or ten hours a day. Mr W belonged to the new professional salariat of the nineteenth century. His income, way of life, and family background had little in common with the Chamberlains. Taine, however, thought the Ws were a representative family, a 'very good specimen of English life' and he may have been right. The family rented a 'cottage in the environs of London for £200 a year'; a comfortable house was the first condition of both status and comfort. The Ws spent a higher proportion of their income upon their house than was usual among working people. Neither were they content with a day excursion to provide the high spot of the family's year; the Ws went on holiday. As a result they lived well up to their income. To Taine it was evident that 'they expend everything' and their savings, if any, took the form of life assurance (i.e. from the point of view of Part I their contribution to the economy was twofold, Mr W's expertise and the family consumption). Taine believed that this family illustrated some important features of English middle-class life:

to be thrown early upon one's resources, marry a woman without fortune, have plenty of children, expend one's income, save up nothing, work prodigiously, put one's children to the necessity of working also, lay in continuously stores of facts and positive information, recruit oneself by travel, always producing and always acquiring.

No doubt this family of the managerial middle class is more typical of the twentieth century than of the nineteenth, just as it was more metropolitan than provincial. But the example of the Ws certainly makes it clear that middle-class life in the Industrial Revolution was quite as competitive and precarious as it was substantial.

Social frontiers are notoriously imprecise. To define the middle class in this period is not at all easy. Pitt's income tax of 1798 began at incomes of £60 a year but it only reached a maximum rate at £200 a year and over. In 1801 there were 320,659 incomes of £60 a year and over. Unfortunately Peel's income tax of 1842 did not touch incomes under £150 a year. In some ways it is these lower middle-class incomes which are particularly interesting because the growth of this section of the community has a direct bearing on the wider issue of the movement of living standards during the Industrial Revolution. Contemporaries had the impression that the middle class was growing rapidly at its base. The evidence for an up-scaling of incomes was in the profusion of new suburban homes, many of them put up during the building booms of the 1790s and 1820s, and the emergence of new tastes and patterns of consumption. A writer of the late 1820s argued:

the middle classes are receiving recruits from the lower in much greater number than the latter do from the former. This state of things is clearly proved by the vast number of neat houses of the smaller class arising in every part of England, in exchange for the crowded and filthy dwellings formerly inhabited by artisans which are as rapidly in every county disappearing, this view is further strengthened by referring to the great increase in the consumption of all those articles which form the comforts of those a few steps above the indigent class. (W. Jacob, 1828, quoted in M. D. George, *London Life in the Eighteenth Century*, London, 1925, p. 402)

Observations like this leave no doubt that there were many thousands for whom the Industrial Revolution brought genuine improvement. On the other hand the distances between workmen and employers seemed to widen, especially in industries, like the textile industry, which required high capital outlay. Early mechanization enabled profits to grow faster than wages. An estimate of the labour cost per pound of final product suggests that in cotton spinning this fell from 4·2d in 1829–31 to 2·3d in 1844–6 and 2·1d in 1859–61, and in cotton weaving from 9d to 3·5d and 2·9d at the same dates. By contrast there was little on the demand side to enhance the value of labour. Not surprisingly could it be said of Manchester 'there is no town in the world where the distance between the rich and the poor is so great, or the barrier between them so difficult to be crossed' (Canon Parkinson of Manchester Collegiate Church in 1839, quoted in Asa Briggs, *Victorian Cities*, p. 110, London, 1963). The cotton operatives found little to comfort them in the know-

ledge that 'retained profits' were a vital instrument of progress
in their industry.

Working-class living standards

Controversy about living standards in the Industrial Revolution
has, of course, centred upon working-class incomes. Whatever
the general conclusions which are possible here, it must first be
understood that there was a striking variety of incomes within
the working class in both the eighteenth and nineteenth centuries. The 'aristocracy of labour', which consisted of the skilled
men of all trades, could always expect a standard of comfort
well above that of the labourer, whose wages were usually only
about two-thirds those of the journeyman. Outside the regular
trades earnings might fall even lower, while there were some
trades, like tailoring, which centred on a busy season when both
wages and employment were higher than in other times. Agricultural wages were everywhere lower than urban or industrial
wages, although the countryman might expect to use his garden
to good effect and his rent was invariably lower than it would
have been in the town. Apart from the differential between town
and country there were strong regional contrasts in wage rates.
Regional variation, except in agriculture, became less marked in
the nineteenth century when both labour market and wage rates
moved towards a more national structure. To Adam Smith
regional variation in wages was a conspicuous feature of the
eighteenth-century economy:

Eighteen pence a day may be reckoned the common price of labour
in London and its neighbourhood. At a few miles distance it falls to
fourteen and fifteen pence. Ten pence may be reckoned its price in
Edinburgh and its neighbourhood. At a few miles distance it falls to
eightpence, the usual price of common labour through the greater
part of the low country of Scotland, where it varies a good deal less
than in England.

Money wages remained stable during the eighteenth century
until they began to rise steeply in the 1790s. A pronounced
upward movement over the whole century has, however, been

established for Lancashire and may well have existed in other industrial districts. In 1700 the wages of both craftsmen and labourers in Lancashire were very much lower than in Oxfordshire, Kent, or, of course, London. By the 1770s wage rates in Lancashire had overhauled Oxfordshire rates and could compare with rates in Kent: in real terms there was probably little to choose between the remuneration of labourers in the capital and in industrial Lancashire. The Industrial Revolution imparted an upward swing to wages in Lancashire and brought its working population money incomes which, by the last quarter of the eighteenth century, could compare favourably with the traditionally more prosperous southern counties.

Money wages may be no guide to living standards. The best available index of eighteenth-century wages, by Elizabeth W. Gilboy, shows that, in London, money wages began to increase in the 1760s, fell back during 1775–8 to the level of the 1740s and 1750s, and then advanced further in the 1780s. This was a prelude to the rapid rise in wages which began in the 1790s and continued throughout the two decades of war, reaching a climax, in most trades, about 1812 (B. R. Mitchell and Phyllis Deane, *Abstract of British Historical Statistics*, Cambridge, 1962, pp. 348–9). It is unlikely that thirty years of rising wages brought any increase in real incomes because these were also years of soaring prices. For the most part wages did not keep pace with prices, although the worst years of 'lag' were possibly not until after 1810. The impact of this extraordinary period of inflation is not easy to assess. Yet its importance to an understanding of movements in the standards of living during the Industrial Revolution can scarcely be exaggerated. These were years of very rapid economic change. While Britain was maintaining larger armies than in any earlier war, it was also making more intensive use of its labour force. Many more families were now relying upon money wages, only slightly, if at all, supplemented by payments in kind. For them the war meant full and regular employment, but also long hours of work. The impact upon generations varied significantly. For those born in the 1740s, and the mid-century, the economic climate of the war years must have seemed hectic and arduous. For the following generation the war was the formative experience; its steady activity, marked by progress in both domestic and factory industry, contrasted favourably with the era of dislocation, technical upheaval, and vulnerability to the trade cycle, which followed the peace in 1815. On the other hand the war, by providing full employment, certainly put a brake on technical progress in the cotton industry; the number of hand-loom weavers grew rapidly and this was to be a cause of great misery in the postwar period as the new power looms forced down their wages.

If the early benefits of higher earnings were lost in the price inflation of the last years (1808–14) of the Napoleonic War, the ensuing years of peace saw prices fall faster, and perhaps further, than incomes. The various price indices which have been constructed for this period show a fall of something just over 40 per cent between 1815 and 1850. The fall was not, however, unbroken. 1817–19, 1824–5, 1836–40, and 1844–7 were years when the general trend was arrested (see *British Commodity Prices 1790–1850* by Gayer, Rostow, and Schwartz, and 'Price Indices 1800–1913' by P. Rousseaux, in *The Abstract of British Historical Statistics*, pp. 470–3). The price indices have not escaped criticism. One danger in using them is, clearly, to fail to distinguish between the prices of agricultural as distinct from industrial goods. Food prices did not fall as much as prices of industrial commodities and they continued to be subject to violent fluctuation. A recent index for money wages for 1790–1860, based on the wage statistics for select industries and districts assembled by G. H. Wood and A. L. Bowley in the 1890s, shows wages falling from a peak of *c.* 1810, when wages were perhaps 75 per cent higher than in 1790, to a plateau which extended from 1830 to 1850 during which wages settled at about 20 per cent *below* the level reached at the end of the war. Thus, over a comparable period after 1815 prices fell by 40 per cent and wages by approximately 20 per cent. The statistics point, then, to some improvement in real incomes in the early nineteenth century. If there *was* improvement it was unlikely to have been as substantial as that secured in the late eighteenth century.

To an extent the argument for improvement in the nineteenth century is at odds with the well (but perhaps too well) known social facts of the period. The prevalence of severe poverty, and a widespread contemporary insistence upon a retreat in living standards, both argue for only cautious generalization on the basis of the indices. In the long-term view the falling price of industrial commodities was to be of the utmost importance to living standards. But before 1850 not only was the range of industrial commodities in common consumption rather limited but the importance of industrial prices in the average family budget was overshadowed by that of food prices. In any case the indices themselves make it abundantly clear that the era 1815–50 was one in which good times alternated all too frequently with bad. In 1836–41 price levels returned to almost those of the 1820s while wages were some 10 per cent lower. The hardship of the late 1830s and early 1840s is certainly not minimized by the indices (which is, perhaps, one good reason to accept their conclusion of *overall* improvement 1815–50). What the indices do not measure is the impact of unemployment upon living standards. If a man was in work, if his wages were 'average', then the benefits suggested by the indices were, no doubt, real. With several members of a family at work the gains may have been larger still and it should certainly have been possible to counterbalance a fall in wages that was slightly greater than 'average'. The greatest gains clearly went to the aristocracy of skilled labour which, in many trades, kept earnings close to wartime levels and whose prosperity had much to do with the growth of savings banks. The total deposits of savings banks rose from £3–£4 million in 1820 to £28·9 million in 1850. Not all depositors belonged to the working class but neither were all those who did artisans; some were ordinary labourers. An estimate from Bristol in 1838 gave 15·7 per cent of heads of working-class families as depositors in savings banks, or members of benefit societies or trade clubs (E. J. Hobsbawm, *Labouring Men*, London, 1964, p. 278). Some working-class families had the resources to survive at least short periods of unemployment. The majority had no reserves at all, apart from their furniture and clothes and the limited generosity of relatives and neighbours.

Unemployment and distress

The statistics of unemployment in the early nineteenth century are scattered and incomplete. Periodic unemployment was as much a feature of industrial life as chronic underemployment had been of rural life (and, to an extent, remained). If unemployment was seen as a problem in the nineteenth century no solution to it seemed accessible: discussion of the recurrent crises of the time centred upon the mechanisms of international trade, or the banking and currency systems. The cause of industrial unemployment in this period was, generally, the collapse of an important overseas market (or markets). Business confidence at once began to subside, interest rates rose, investment was halted, or slowed down, and unemployment in one or more industrial sectors was soon reflected in a more general slackening in the demand for industrial goods. When, in addition, this characteristic 'downswing' in the trade cycle was associated with a poor harvest and rising food prices the impact upon consumption and employment was severe. Where the reliance upon money wages was complete, and particularly in towns dominated by a single industry, the slump could involve almost the whole working population. Figures from Bolton for the great slump of 1842 illustrate the far-reaching impact of unemployment in a really bad year:

Trade	Total employed in 1836	Total employed whole or part-time in 1842	Percentage unemployed
Mills	8124	3063 *full-time*	60
Ironworks	2110	1325 *short-time*	36
Carpenters	150	24	84
Bricklayers	120	16	87
Stonemasons	150	50	66
Tailors	500	250	50
Shoemakers	80	40	50

(quoted in E. J. Hobsbawm, op. cit., p. 74)

The factory industry of Bolton provided the bulk of the un-employed in 1842 while the ironworks, much of whose work may have been the result of long-term investment which was less affected by the crisis, was less badly hit. The building industry had come to a virtual standstill. The consumer trades had suffered severely. The seriousness of this depression is well brought out by contrasting the turnover of 50 Salford shop-keepers in 1839 and 1841:

	1839	1841
13 provision dealers	£70,700	£47,300
14 butchers	27,800	17,200
10 grocers	63,800	43,300
13 drapers, etc.	35,400	22,300

(quoted in E. J. Hobsbawm, op. cit., p. 76)

Engels believed that 'practically every English worker can recall considerable vicissitudes in his own personal fortunes'. His impression (formed 1842–4) was that:

the condition of all workers is liable to fluctuate so violently that every single worker is faced with the possibility of passing through the stages that lead from relative comfort to extreme poverty and even death from starvation. (op. cit p. 87)

How great a percentage of the working class of this period was, in fact, accustomed to poverty in its bitterest forms it is im-possible to know. Engels's view that poverty was something which might overtake any working-class family is somewhat similar to the conclusions reached, late in the nineteenth century, by two pioneer social surveys, that of Charles Booth in London, and of Seebohm Rowntree in York. Booth and Rowntree believed that perhaps a third of working-class families were, at any one time, living in poverty. If progress had been made towards better living standards in the early Industrial Revolu-tion it must be recognized how limited this progress was.

The pressure of unemployment varied, but in some trades 'distress' became permanent. Cotton hand-loom weaving was the worst example of such a trade in the nineteenth century. The number of weavers grew rapidly in the late eighteenth century in response to the progress of mechanization in the spinning sector of the industry. The work was attractively easy to learn, and could engage whole families: even by the end of the eighteenth century there may have been too many weavers. Unemployment struck hard during the Napoleonic War. After the war the labour force continued to grow and, as demand increased, there was some prosperity for the weavers. From the mid-1820s the power loom began its conquest of weaving and the slow agony of the hand-loom weavers commenced. In 1834 the Select Committee of the Commons reporting on the weavers' petitions expressed 'deep regret at finding the sufferings of that large and valuable body of men, not only not exaggerated, but that they have for years continued to an extent and intensity scarcely to be credited or conceived'. In 1834 16/– was discovered to be a good wage for a family of weavers and 7/6–9/6 was not unknown. At this date a Manchester iron worker earned 34/– a week, a mule spinner about £1, and a woman throstle spinner between 7/– and 10/6. Even without competition from machines the inundation of a trade with new recruits could thrust onto a downward course and preclude all but the most modest improvement in living standards. The Midland frame-work knitters had reached this situation by the 1840s. They, like the hand-loom weavers, were largely excluded from the benefits of the new society, such as they were.

[17] GOVERNMENT POLICY AND ITS EFFECTS

Government, in the early nineteenth century, took notice of distress but had no solution to it. After the Poor Law Amendment Act of 1834 expenditure on poor relief fell (both absolutely and, more dramatically, in per capita terms), although the new poor law authorities were never able to abolish completely the much criticized practice of 'outdoor relief'. As Radicals con-

sistently pointed out, the working class carried a dispropor-
tionately heavy share of the cost of government, especially in
the immediate postwar period. Wartime expenditure had at
least brought, or helped to bring, full employment: after the
peace returning soldiers greatly intensified the competition for
work. Further, the costs of war had been met, to an extent, by
an increase in direct taxation on incomes: even so government
had had to borrow very heavily. After the war government faced
an era of greatly inflated debt charges and, almost at once, in
1816, it was forced to abandon the income tax. The result was
that a great proportion of revenue had to be raised through taxes
on articles of common consumption: no wonder that resentment
was felt against 'fundholders'. The burden of the excise taxes
began to ease in the 1820s and the next decade brought substantial alleviation for the working-class taxpayer. The repeal of
the beer duty in 1830, though no aid to provident housekeeping,
constituted a gift, as Clapham pointed out, 'of something like a
£1 a year to the average labouring household' (*Economic History
of Modern Britain*, Vol. I, p. 560). Under Peel, after 1842, came
further evidence that government was prepared to distribute the
cost of its own services more fairly (it should, perhaps, be noted
that, apart from ordinary soldiers and sailors, those who lived
on government incomes did not belong to the working class).
Faced with a deficit inherited from the Whigs Peel chose to
reintroduce income tax in 1842. He also continued to lift both
customs and excise dues. The repeal of the Corn Laws (1846)
may not have produced an immediate drop in wheat prices but
it did lessen the likelihood of violent fluctuation in prices and
ensured that they did not return to the high levels of the early
eighteenth century. Peel was aware of the social benefits which
his policy could bring and there can be little doubt that government was making a more substantial contribution to wellbeing
in 1850 than at any earlier stage in the Industrial Revolution.

[18] A NEW LIFE?

Whatever the family income, much obviously depended upon skilful housekeeping. The transition to money incomes, and to town life, created some new problems for the housewife. Neither hedgerow nor garden was (often) available to supplement diet: country crafts did not readily transplant in the town. A working mother had, in any case, all too little time to practise domestic crafts. She had now to 'budget' and to calculate. Careful shopping was essential, a vital art. Mayhew, as alert as always, knew good shopping when he saw it (in a London street market on a Saturday night):

The housewife in her thick shawl, with the market-basket on her arm, walks slowly on, stopping now to look at the stall of caps, and now to cheapen a bunch of greens.

Good food was not always easy to find and the value of money was reduced by the widespread adulteration and fraud practised both in shops and markets. The week's earnings did not always reach the housewife intact, as again Mayhew noticed:

The system of paying the mechanic late on Saturday night – and particularly of paying a man his wages in a public house – when he is tired out with his day's work, lures him to the tavern, and there the hours fly quickly enough beside the warm taproom fire, so that by the time the wife comes for her husband's wages, she finds a large portion of them gone in drink, and the streets half cleared, so that the Sunday market is the only chance of getting the Sunday's dinner. (*Mayhew's London*, ed. P. Quennell, London, 1951, p. 34)

In the factory districts girls sent out to work were said to make poor housewives. Robert Owen's view was that parents who sent their children out too young:

deprive their children of the opportunity of acquiring the habits of domestic life, without a knowledge of which high nominal wages can procure them but few comforts, and without which among the working classes very little domestic happiness can be enjoyed. (*Observations on the Effect of the Manufacturing System, 1815*, op. cit., p. 125)

Owen's answer to this problem, which troubled observers for much of the nineteenth century, was both better education and a longer period of training in the home. Little opportunity for either had appeared by the 1830s and 1840s, although it is here that factory legislation may have been particularly beneficial. Engels believed:

all the factory girls are wholly ignorant of housewifery and are quite unfitted to become wives and mothers. They do not know how to sew, knit, cook or wash. They are ignorant of the most elementary accomplishments of the housewife and, as for looking after babies, they have the vaguest notion of how to set about it. (op. cit., pp.165–6)

Perhaps Engels should not be taken too seriously, but his was not a lone voice. What is certain is that household skills could be quite as relevant to living standards as the movement of prices and incomes. The Industrial Revolution changed the running of the home as it changed everything else.

For the working classes the Industrial Revolution brought with it wider, and widening choice counterbalanced by periodic and unpredictable misery. Some glimpse into the intricate profit and loss account of industrialization is provided in the opening chapters of Mrs Gaskell's novel *Mary Barton*, published in 1848. John Barton and his wife, together with their friends, Jem Wilson and his wife, return from a holiday stroll in the fields on the outskirts of Manchester. Once home the Bartons prepare tea for their visitors:

'Run, Mary [Barton's daughter] dear, just round the corner, and get some fresh eggs at Tipping's (you may get one apiece, that will be fivepence), and see if he has any nice ham cut, that he would let us have a pound of.'

'Say two pounds, missis, and don't be stingy', chimed in the husband.

'Well, a pound and a half Mary . . . and Mary . . . you must get a pennyworth of milk and a loaf of bread – mind you get it fresh and new – and, and – that's all, Mary.'

'No, it's not at all', said her husband. 'Thou must get sixpennyworth of rum, to warm the tea: thou'll get it at the 'Grapes'.

Barton then sends his wife out to invite in a relation of the
Wilson's to join the family for tea. The scene that Mrs Gaskell
created has the stamp of authenticity: it suggests that operatives
could sometimes live well. As a picture of domestic happiness it
is quickly followed by tragedy, the death of Mrs Barton in
childbed, and misfortune, the beginning of unemployment for
John. The rapid change of fortune is understandable in a novel,
but Mrs Gaskell's licence was legitimate. Whatever gains the
Industrial Revolution had carried with it security was not yet
one.

Further Reading

Many of the books mentioned at the end of Part I are also relevant
reading for this chapter. Harold Perkin's *The Origins of Modern
English Society* 1780–1880 (Routledge, 1969) is perhaps the first
attempt at a full social history of the Industrial Revolution. Clapham,
Vol. I, Chapter XIV, is indispensable and Checkland, Chapter 7 is
also important. E. P. Thompson's 'Standards and Experiences', *The
Making of the English Working Class*, Chapter X (Pelican Books,
1968) is a powerful and sympathetic analysis of the predicament of
working people during the early Industrial Revolution. The same
author's essay 'Time, Work-Discipline, and Industrial Capitalism',
Past and Present, No. 38, December 1967, is an important survey of a
neglected subject. N. J. Smelser's *Social Change in the Industrial
Revolution* (Routledge, 1959) is a sociological study of the Lancashire
Cotton Industry and its conclusions would not apply to other indus-
tries. A great deal has been written on the standard of living during
the period. The most important recent articles are E. J. Hobsbawm's
'The British Standard of Living 1790–1850', *Economic History
Review*, Vol. X, 1957 (reprinted in the author's collection of essays,
Labouring Men, Weidenfeld, 1964), R. M. Hartwell's 'The Rising
Standard of Living in England 1800–50', *Economic History Review*,
Vol. XIII, 1961, E. J. Hobsbawm and R. M. Hartwell's 'The Standard
of Living during the Industrial Revolution: A discussion', *Economic
History Review*, Vol. XVI, 1963, J. E. Williams's 'The British Stan-
dard of Living 1750–1850', *Economic History Review*, Vol. XIX, 1966.
A. J. Taylor's 'Progress and Poverty in Britain 1780–1850, *History*,
Vol. XLV, 1960 tries to resolve the conflicting views on this subject.

Useful contemporary sources are reprinted in *English Historical Documents*, Vol. XI, ed. A. Aspinall (Eyre and Spottiswoode, 1959) and Vol. XII, Chapter I, ed. G. M. Young and W. D. Handcock (1956). Engels's *The Condition of the Working Class in England*, edited and translated by W. O. Henderson and W. H. Chaloner (Blackwell, 1958) is still the best contemporary text for an understanding of the social impact of industry in the nineteenth century and any temptation to accept everything that Engels said is more than offset by the sharply critical approach of his modern editors. E. Royston Pike's *The Human Documents of the Industrial Revolution* (Allen and Unwin, 1966) contains selections from most of the better known contemporary accounts of the industrial scene; it has little editorial comment or explanation but is extremely useful as a sourcebook.

PART III
The Industrial Town: the Experience of an Urban Civilization

[19] THE INDUSTRIAL TOWN AND THE INDUSTRIAL REVOLUTION

The rise of the industrial town is sometimes thought to be inseparable from the Industrial Revolution: to be, in fact, as much a feature of it as cotton machinery or the steam engine. Certainly by 1850 both technical change in industry and the effect of transport improvements were causing industry to move irresistibly into the towns. Although this transition had begun in some industries, notably cotton, long before 1850, it was still, in general, a new departure. The great works of the eighteenth century had been situated in the countryside, sometimes to be close to their raw materials and always to have access to water to supply them with power. The domestic outwork industries took a rural context for granted. By the nineteenth century many of these sites had become well established and there was no question of abandoning them. Steam was not always a better or more reliable source of power than water and, in any case, it was often possible to get coal to the site. The concentration of industry had, of course, great advantages and nineteenth-century conditions very much encouraged it. But it should, perhaps, be remembered that a town does not always offer the industrialist a good, or large enough, site. When Titus Salt of

Bradford came to develop his gigantic alpaca works in the 1860s he chose a country, or at least, suburban site well outside the town.

The towns had begun to grow rapidly as soon as population began its upward spiral in the eighteenth century. Their growth interlocked with the Industrial Revolution; the towns provided easily accessible markets and their expansion increased the demand for the products of many trades and industries. By 1850 people were almost as concerned with the problems of the new towns (or of old towns grown larger) as they were with those of industry. In the large cities the impersonal quality of urban life, now an everyday experience, came as a disturbing discovery. Even a Londoner, like Disraeli's Coningsby, was shocked into reflection by the sight of Manchester:

The feeling of melancholy, even of uneasiness, attends our first entrance into a great town, especially at night. Is it that the sense of all this vast existence with which we have no connection, where we are utterly unknown, oppresses us with our insignificance? (*Coningsby*, 1844, Bk. IV, Ch. 2)

Disraeli was no doubt unusually sensitive. Some of his contemporaries were unusually callous. Walking into Manchester with a fellow businessman Engels spoke with warmth on the town's social conditions: he had a very cool response:

I spoke to him about the disgraceful unhealthy slums and drew his attention to the disgusting condition of that part of the town in which the factory workers lived. I declared that I had never seen so badly a built town in all my life. He listened patiently and at the corner of the street at which we parted company he remarked: 'And yet there is a great deal of money made here. Good morning, Sir.' (Engels, op. cit., p. 312)

In the 1840s the towns were very much on the nation's mind; this itself was an indication that Britain was beginning to recognize itself as a nation of townsmen.

The 1851 Census showed that what it referred to as 'the vast system of towns' (there were 580 of them) contained 10·5 million out of a total population of nearly 21 million (i.e. in England

and Wales, and Scotland). The towns were not easy to classify.
A good number were industrial towns but 'Coketown' (the town
in Dicken's novel *Hard Times*, 1854) was certainly not typical of
them. Many townspeople had been born in the country; the
'natives' usually only just outnumbered the 'settlers' but a high
proportion of the natives were children. Among the adult population the migrants were usually in a majority. This was not a
new development. It was true of eighteenth-century towns.
High death rates gave the towns the grim role of consuming the
surplus population of the countryside. What struck the 1851
Census Commissioners as remarkable was not the number of
migrants in the towns but the fact that Britain would soon
possess an immense, self-recruiting urban population:

it is evident that henceforward the great cities will not be like camps –
or the fields on which the people of other places exercise their energies
and industry – but the Birth-place of a large part of the British race.

The tides of urbanization and industrialization were now running
together.

The concentration of population, like that of industry, had
been encouraged by better communications. The pull of the
London market had long controlled the agricultural economy of
the surrounding countryside. Something like this now happened
around other towns. These were not all industrial towns although,
of course, there were trades in every town. In the eighteenth
century the growth of the Atlantic seaports, especially of
Liverpool, and of the commercial and merchanting centres
linked to the domestic industries, had been quickened by the
Industrial Revolution but not caused by it. The turn of the
century also saw the appearance of a cluster of new entertainment towns like Bath, Cheltenham, and Brighton, where landowners, 'fundholders', and the professional classes could enjoy
'Society', take the waters or bathe in the sea, and reproduce in
miniature something of the gaiety and ostentation of London
itself. These towns were as much part of their age, and its
economic history, as the industrial towns: ironically enough
nineteenth-century social surveys were to reveal in them living

conditions for the poor quite as horrifying as anything to be found in 'Coketown'. William Cobbett was always particularly bitter about the spas and resorts, perhaps because they served people whom he thought exploited the farm labourer:

Cheltenham is a nasty, ill-looking place, half clown and half cockney. The town is one street about half a mile long; but then, at some distance from the street, there are rows of white tenements, with green balconies, like those inhabited by the tax-eaters around London. Indeed this place appears to be the residence of an assemblage of tax-eaters. These vermin shift around between London, Cheltenham, Bath, Bognor, Brighton, Tunbridge, Ramsgate, Margate, Worthing, and other spots, in England . . .' (*Rural Rides*, for 1821, Everyman ed. I, pp. 33–4)

From the viewpoint of the Industrial Revolution these centres of extravagant consumption had their importance: their spendthrift inhabitants helped to generate incomes elsewhere. The green balconies, to which Cobbett referred with such distaste, were of iron and their supply fattened the order books of the ironmasters.

[20] LONDON: CAPITAL OF AN INDUSTRIAL NATION?

Until the last quarter of the eighteenth century the overwhelming bulk of internal migration in England and Wales was towards London. Even in 1700 London was twice as large as any provincial city was to be in 1851. The capital grew by under 10,000 between 1700 and 1750, yet to do so it drew 500,000 migrants from the rest of the country. Some industrial counties – Lancashire is the leading example – grew by heavy migration as well as by natural increase for most of the eighteenth century. Some, like Staffordshire, were even exporters of manpower until the beginning of the nineteenth century. From 1801 to 1831 London continued to attract the majority of the nation's migrants:

Gains by migration 1801–31

Middlesex   396,790
Surrey   115,357
Lancashire   183,500

There was, of course, a shift in the distribution of population between 1750 and 1831: but it told against the South rather than against London.

Percentage of total population of England and Wales living in the South, London, and the North-West in 1750 and 1831

	1750	1831
South	37·8	28·3
London	17·5	19·0
North-West	21·5	31·1

What these figures immediately suggest is the enormous significance of London to the economy both before and during the Industrial Revolution. Once the importance to the Industrial Revolution of rising demand, imparted by the growth of population from 1750 onwards, is clearly understood then the existence of this uniquely large, and uniquely concentrated market, must be given a place among the causes of the Industrial Revolution (there is an important discussion of London's role 1650–1750 by E. A. Wrigley in *Past and Present*, 37, July 1967). London's economic importance did not decline after 1750. In this vital period London actually increased its relative share of the total population. Yet very few of the standard accounts of the Industrial Revolution give the capital more than passing attention.

The growth of London almost defies explanation. London has almost invariably seemed too large to be understood. A correspondent of the weekly journal, *The Builder*, who had an address on what was then the city's suburban frontier, Norton Street, off Roman Road, put his finger on this problem in 1844:

So rapid is the growth of this queen of cities, that a population equal to that of Salisbury is added to its numbers every three months, but so overwhelmingly large is this Leviathan of towns, that this constant and progressive increase is scarcely perceived, for it is almost like throwing a bucket of water into the Ocean. Such is London – the city of the world. (*The Builder*, Vol. 2, p. 11)

William Cobbett was typically scathing about London; to him it was the 'Great Wen', the worst of Britain's parasitic towns. With a population of nearly 1 million in 1801, and 2½ million in 1851, there were many who thought, with the American, J. Fennimore Cooper, that London was 'already too large for the kingdom' (1837). The less sophisticated saw London as the simple expression of national progress. Early Victorian worship of size and scale was quaintly expressed by a popular guide to the capital issued for the Great Exhibition:

Stress is frequently laid upon the impressive signification of a particular word; perhaps there is no word more comprehensive in its character, more interesting in its development, and more indicative of the progress of national power and national industry than the dissyllable, London. The hieroglyphic inscriptions on the pyramids are said to record the territorial greatness, and the pre-eminence in learning and art, for which, in ancient days, Egypt was renowned; but what pyramid – were there no other means of communicating with posterity – would be sufficiently expansive tablet whereon to perpetuate the wonders of London in 1850? (W. Gaspey, *Illustrated London*, Tallis, 1851)

The full impact of modern city life had long been felt in London. In 'The Prelude' (1799–1805) Wordsworth recalled his own 'shock of that huge town's first presence' and noticed the loneliness which surrounded its inhabitants,

> Above all, one thought
> Baffled my understanding: how men lived
> Even next-door neighbours, as we say, yet still
> Strangers, not knowing each others' name.
>   Book VII

In his first book, *Sketches by Boz* (1836), Dickens made much the same point;

It is strange with how little notice, good, bad, or indifferent, a man may live and die in London . . . his existence a matter of interest to no one save himself.

Where life in a great city was to be the pattern laid down by the Industrial Revolution London already provided a clear guide to the future.

The American writer Fennimore Cooper imagined that London's size was explained by its role as the capital of an empire. He was convinced that Britain's Empire would not endure: at its collapse 'London's suburbs will probably recede quite as fast as they now grow' (*England, With Sketches of Society in the Metropolis*, 1837). What escaped Fennimore Cooper was that London was the greatest *industrial town* in Britain and in the world. Of course it was not a single industry town. Nor was it a centre for those great industries which were the basis of the industrial revolution in the North. Yet London had its large firms, like the breweries, which could make a good claim to be 'revolutionary'. Into the 1830s London set the pace in the small but crucially important machine tool industry; Henry Maudslay opened his works at Lambeth in 1810 and Joseph Clements at Newington Butts in 1817. From the 1830s the makers of machine tools were irresistibly drawn to the major centres of the textile and engineering trades in the North. London had had within it a textile town, the ancient suburb of Spitalfields where silk weaving was well established in the eighteenth century. By the 1820s the Spitalfields silk industry was in a state of pronounced decline. Even so there were still some 7,000 silk weavers in the district in the 1840s. By 1861 London's labour force amounted to 1½ million and of these 468,000 were working in manufacturing industry. The London Directory of 1837 had listed 16,500 employers of industrial workers in the capital.

It was the consumer industries which dominated in London. In 1861 a quarter of the nation's workers in the clothing trades were employed in London: over a third of the furniture makers and half the printers were employed there too (P. G. Hall, *The Industries of London since 1861*, London, 1962, pp. 39, 72, and 97: the figures are for Greater London).

It is easy to forget the importance of the consumer trades to the Industrial Revolution and, in doing so, to underestimate the London industries. The history of the northern textile industries must surely have been very different if they had not had access to this uniquely large and uniquely concentrated market where so many of their fabrics went to be made up and put on sale.

Successive improvements in the transport system, from turnpike and canal to railway and telegraph, did as much to strengthen the historically powerful position of London as they did to forge more efficient links between manufacturing industry and its raw materials and fuel. Londoners did not cease to buy silk when the Spitalfields industry declined; the trade was put out to Macclesfield and Coventry. New manufacturing industries, like chemicals and rubber, moved into London while older trades declined. The majority of Londoners, however, worked in the service trades. Most of these were shopworkers, street traders, and domestic servants. These had their links with the industrial revolution but they were not perhaps as close as those which bound London's banks and business houses to the nation's industrialists and merchants. London's clerks – and it had over 30,000 in 1841 – hurrying into the City from the northern suburbs or across London Bridge, and its businessmen, jammed into Oxford Street to Bank omnibuses, have as much claim to be regarded as the pacesetters of the Industrial Revolution as the mill hands and factory masters of Lancashire.

[21] PATTERNS OF INDUSTRIAL SETTLEMENT

Industrial city and industrial village

Although its growth became interlocked with the Industrial Revolution London remained a special example of urbanization. Elsewhere the Industrial Revolution did not immediately thrust millions into town life. Urbanization acted progressively upon a growing population: at the beginning of the nineteenth century it was still very much in its infancy. The townsman of 1851 belonged to a community that was different in both size and character from that of fifty years earlier. Of the principal British towns (i.e. either 10,000 inhabitants by 1801, or to reach 100,000 by 1951) 34 had populations 10–20,000 in 1801, while only 6 remained in this category in 1851 and only three towns, Blackpool, Middlesbrough, and Wallasey, were then under 10,000 but were to grow to 100,000 by 1951. Significant changes in the urban pattern appeared in the first half of the nineteenth century:

Population

	Towns: 1801	1831	1851
10–40,000	44	37	34
40–80,000	7	15	18
80–100,000	2	1	4
100,000 and over	—	7	9

(London excluded)

(Based on figures in *The Abstract of British Historical Statistics*, Ch. I, Table 8.)

Not only were there far fewer townsmen in 1801 but they lived in much smaller towns which retained, for the most part, close contact with the countryside. Further, the prevalence of domestic and small-scale industry meant that a high proportion of industrial workers lived, not in towns, but in industrial *villages*. Only gradually, as the towns pushed out their frontiers, and the countryside, economically, and in walking distance, became more remote, did the sense of separation from a rural heritage became at all acute. By the 1840s the need to provide townspeople with formal open spaces had at least been recognized and, characteristically, in arguing the case for the provision of picture-galleries, Charles Kingsley (in 1848) envisaged the townsman taking his country walk in a single room:

his hard-worn heart wandering out free, beyond the grim city-world of stone and iron, smoky chimneys, and roaring wheels, into the world of beautiful things. (quoted in W. E. Houghton, *The Victorian Frame of Mind*, Yale University Press, p. 80)

The Britain of 1850 possessed a number of contrasted types of 'industrial urbanization', from the industrial village, belonging, perhaps, to a complex of similar small communities, to the compact industrial town and the great regional capitals, like Glasgow, Manchester, Birmingham, Leeds, Sheffield, and New-castle. Even within the cotton textile industry the industrial village (or small town), which originated in the reliance of the first powered spinning mills upon water, continued to flourish. Those who were disturbed by cotton towns believed that the industrial village, dominated by a single employer, was, in many ways, an ideal community – a compromise struck between the machine age and Nature. In *Coningsby* Disraeli's description of Millbank indicates the basis for this approval:

In a green valley of Lancaster . . . a clear and powerful stream flows through a broad meadow land. Upon its margin, adorned, rather than shadowed, by some old elm trees, for they are too distant to serve except for ornament, rises a vast deep red brick pile which, though formal and monotonous in its general character, is not without a certain beauty of proportion. . . . The front [of the mill] . . . is flanked by two projecting wings in the same style, which forms a large court.

About a quarter of a mile further on, appeared a village of not inconsiderable size, and remarkable for the neatness and even picturesque character of its architecture, and the gay gardens that surrounded it. On a sunny knoll in the background rose a church . . . and near it was a clerical residence and a school house of similar design. The village, too, could boast another public building; an Institute where there were a library and a lecture-room . . . about half-a-mile up the valley, surrounded by beautiful meadows, and built on an agreeable and well-wooded elevation was the mansion of the mill-owner. (Book IV, Chapter 3)

The political advantages of such arrangements were not lost upon Disraeli. In his next novel, *Sybil*, he described the solid resistance of a similar community to the appeals of the Chartists.

The West Riding

Industrial villages of this type were more characteristic of the eighteenth than the nineteenth century. They existed primarily because of the employer's need to recruit and hold his labour force. In the industrial towns of the nineteenth century this was a less important consideration. The concept of enlightened and humane management, and fundamentally better labour relations, made little progress in this period. Even so the activities of the Akroyd family in the West Riding, and a little later of Titus Salt, show that the wider benefits of the self-contained community were not ignored in this period of rapid urbanization. In the West Riding the smaller community, the successor either of ancient villages or market towns, and sometimes of the earlier decades of industrialization, survived the growth of the great towns like Leeds, Bradford, Halifax, and Huddersfield. Engels found the West Riding 'a very pleasant part of the country' and admired the houses 'built of grey stone, which look so clean and charming in comparison with the smoke-blackened brick buildings of Lancashire'. This may have been due to the still extensive use of water power in the West Riding in the early nineteenth century. But Engels could have discovered Lancashire grime in the West Riding. In 1831 a Miss Lister significantly complimented Halifax, where many of the mills were still water powered, on its 'fine clear air' but regretted that she had never seen a 'more smoky place than Bradford'. By the 1840s the once rural industry of the West Riding, in which communities of domestic outworkers and clothiers were dependent upon the towns only as merchanting and market centres, had had to accommodate itself to the rise of industrial giants like Bradford and Leeds. Bradford's population which had been 16,000 in 1811 was 104,000 by 1851, and Leeds grew from 63,000 to 172,000 over the same period. These great towns were more than important centres of the worsted or woollen industries. Coal, iron, and engineering were as much part of their economies as the textile trades and, where once they had served these trades as commercial centres, they were now developing specialized new industries, like the manufacture of steam engines or textile machinery, without which the continued growth of the West Riding would have been impossible. If the textile trades of the West Riding clung to its old centres the rise of the great towns was, even here, the most remarkable feature of nineteenth-century expansion.

The Black Country

In the West Midlands industry was similarly characterized by dispersal over an 'industrialized countryside' (the phrase is Professor Court's). By the beginning of the eighteenth century a majority of the people of this region were dependent upon the metal trades. Once again transport improvements strengthened an existing regional concentration. In the nineteenth century the 'capital' of the West Midlands had grown to a city of 233,000 by 1851: Wolverhampton grew from 13,000 to 50,000 between 1801 and 1851. Despite this only a bare majority of the total population of the area, 350,000 out of 650,000, were, in 1851, living in communities which the Census recognized as 'towns' (see T. W. Freeman, *The Conurbations of Great Britain*, p. 81). Yet however one cares to describe the 'Black Country' in the early nineteenth century it is very doubtful if it can, or could, be thought of as 'rural'. Certainly this was not the impression it made on Little Nell as she trudged through its drear landscape:

'Two days and nights!' thought the child. 'He said two days and nights we should have to spend among such scenes as these. Oh! if we live to reach the country again, if we get clear of these dreadful places, though it is only to lie down and die, with a grateful heart I shall thank God for so much mercy.'

To leave the town itself was only to enter a 'cheerless region, where:

On every side, and as far as the eye could see into the heavy distance, tall chimneys, crowding on each other . . . poured out their plague of smoke, obscured the light, and made foul the melancholy air. On mounds of ashes by the wayside, sheltered only by a few rough boards, or rotten pent-house roofs, strange engines spun and writhed like tortured creatures . . . making the ground tremble with their agonies. (*Old Curiosity Shop*, Ch. 45: 1841)

This was a stranger's view, the horror romanticized: the desolation was real enough.

The colliery districts

Both the West Riding and the Black Country lay on coalfields which were exploited in this period. In established industrial districts colliery villages contributed, sometimes extensively, to that 'infilling' of population and activities which did so much to make these areas classic examples of the indiscriminate exploitation of resources. In the specialized mining districts the communities of pit villages were often scattered and remote: they were, perhaps, less brutalized communities than they had been in the past. At least one writer of the 1850s believed that 'the march of the intellect has found its way into pit villages' with the result that 'the queer and questionable things one hears of pit-folk belong mainly to the past'. The same writer described a new colliery village at South Hetton, near Durham:

It is not only one of the largest . . . [but] is an example of most rapid growth. Some five years before it was commenced, the locality was a barren spot of ground, from which the nearest habitation was two miles distant. Now it is covered with buildings – a colliery village of new houses for miners, and a population of 2,000 persons [528 worked at the colliery itself], who are exclusively connected with the colliery. (*Our Coal and Our Coal Pits*, by a Traveller Underground, London, 1853, p. 181)

Even more isolated industrial settlements were to be found in the Merthyr Tydfil district of South Wales. Here, where the collieries rarely employed more than 150, the miners still lived among the surviving agricultural workers. Around the iron works however:

The people are for the most part collected together in masses of from 4,000 to 10,000. Their houses are ranged round the work in rows, sometimes two to five deep, sometimes three stories high. . . . Volumes of smoke from the furnaces, the rolling-mills, and the coke-hearths, are driven past, according to the direction of the wind. Gardens are few, and almost entirely neglected. (Seymour Tremenheere's account of the miners and iron workers of Bedwelty and Merthyr Tydfil, 1839, *English Historical Documents*, Vol. XII(I), p. 964)

The metropolis of these 'colonies in the desert' was Merthyr, a raw, formless, and straggling frontier town. Nine years later another visitor noticed,

The interior of the houses is, on the whole, clean. Food, clothing, furniture – those wants the supply of which depends upon the exertions of each individual – are tolerably well supplied. It is only those which only a governing body can bestow that are here totally absent. (C. Wilkins, *History of the Iron, Steel and Tinplate Trades of Wales*)

[22] THE FACTORY TOWN

Despite the variety of urban forms created by the Industrial Revolution it is the factory town which has commanded most attention. Contemporary commentators were equally fascinated by it. For Engels Lancashire and Manchester were 'the masterpiece of the Industrial Revolution'. The factory town was a forceful and convenient symbol of an age of urban growth. To many the factory town was the epitome of ugliness, the most glaring expression of an ignorant and insensitive misuse of men and Nature. While the factory seemed to impose a new code of work the town mechanized and regimented life itself. Like the factory too it was described in contemptuous military metaphors; the town was a barracks – although its muddled layout reminded one more, as Chadwick noticed, of a nomadic encampment. Something of the claustrophobia and nostalgic regret engendered by the factory town was expressed in a poem by the Chartist leader, Ernest Jones, in 1855:

> Thinner wanes the rural village,
>   Smokier lies the fallow plain –
> Shrinks the cornfields' pleasant tillage,
>   Fades the orchards' rich domain;
>
> And a banished population
>   Festers in the fetid street –
> Give us, God, to save our nation,
>   Less of *cotton*, more of *wheat*.

> Take us back to lea and wild wood,
>   Back to nature and to Thee!
> To the child restore his childhood –
>   To the man his dignity!

Victorian criticism of the factory town culminated in a brilliant chapter, entitled 'The New Town', in J. L. and Barbara Hammond's *The Town Labourer* (1917). The medieval town, they argued here, was a satisfying environment because it was the 'home of the race, with all the traditions and pieties and heirlooms of a home' (Longmans, 1966, p. 49). By contrast the industrial town did nothing to counteract the evils of industrialism:

Life in such a town brought no alleviation of the tyranny of the industrial system; it only made it more real and sombre to the mind. There was no change of scene or colour, no delight of form or design to break its brooding atmosphere. Town, street, buildings, sky, all had become part of the same unrelieved picture . . . the town was so constructed and so governed as to enforce rather than modify, to reiterate rather than to soften the impressions of an alien and unaccommodating power (p. 56).

From the additional retrospect of another sixty years the criticism of the Hammonds still calls for an answer. The experience of building new towns, and of the whole programme of 'urban renewal', does, however, make for recognition of a fact that is relevant to an interpretation of the nineteenth century; that it is one thing to build a town, quite another to construct a community. Rapid growth delays the emergence of a forceful 'community spirit' while, at the some time creating problems that demand communal action. Historians, meanwhile, have done much to explain the economics of urban growth in the nineteenth century, and to reveal the extremely wide range of issues with which it confronted contemporary society.

[23] LIVING IN TOWNS: HOUSING

No room to live? The pressure of population

The spontaneous redistribution of the population from the countryside into towns was accompanied by some unavoidable deterioration in living conditions. Village housing was often poor, the houses damp and badly ventilated, and the accommodation too small for the family. Sanitation scarcely existed. But these were inconveniences which were modified, to an extent, by the more spacious environment of the village house. Whatever its drawbacks the village house had clear advantages over the majority of town houses available to the working class in this period. Town houses were often better furnished and less subject to damp (a much higher proportion of town houses were newly built): but they were smaller, had fewer rooms, rarely any garden, and were easily overcrowded. These, at least, are the generalizations suggested by Edwin Chadwick's *Report on the Sanitary Condition of the Labouring Population of Great Britain* (1842): the conclusion of the agent of the Manchester Statistical Society (founded 1833 and responsible for the pioneer social surveys of the city), after comparing housing in three villages in Rutland, and in Manchester and Dukinfield (a small cotton town east of Manchester: its population trebled 1821–31) was that:

The rents of the houses in Rutlandshire would appear to be very low compared with those in large manufacturing towns. Not only is the average cost of the former less than half of the latter, but for that diminished cost the dimensions of the houses are double those in large towns, with comforts and conveniences which the latter never can possess. (*Report*, ed. M. W. Flinn, Edinburgh University Press, p. 221.)

The same survey found that, while 14 per cent of the families in two of the villages, and 19 per cent in the third, slept three or more to the bed, the comparable figures in Dukinfield and Bury were 33 per cent and 35 per cent.

Although the quality of urban housing varied very much from

town to town, its standards were determined by a few, well recognized, considerations. Urban land values were high and few working people could afford to live far from their workplace. Everything encouraged high density housing. Building land was, of course, cheaper on the outskirts of the town but, as yet, the low-cost transport necessary to suburban growth was not available. The middle classes, as might be expected, were the first to break the ancient practice of living 'at' work and move out to suburban homes. The Census Commissioners of 1851 already advocated suburban evacuation for the majority, little aware of the problems which, in its turn, the 'rush hour' would bring:

Facilities for the distribution over wider areas, and for the periodical concentration of the town's population, can be made by the agency of railways; and as the working people go and return to the shops at regular hours, they may evidently be conveyed at as little cost as any kind of merchandise; and thus we may hope that the worst of all Birth-places – the crowded room, or the house of many families – will never be the Birth-place of any considerable portion of the British population. (Census Reps., 1851, H. C. 1852–3, lxxxviii, p. cviii)

One family, one house was the English ideal, even in 1851 (the Census found, in Manchester, 45,000 families living in 37,000 houses, in Liverpool 47,000 in 35,000, and in Newcastle 19,000 in 11,000: Clapham, Vol. I, p. 547n). Most building in this period implied the same equation even if the reality was often very different.

The worst overcrowding did not necessarily occur in close association with industry. It was probably in the great cities, and some of the seaports (like Liverpool, which had to absorb so many immigrant Irish, and Hull), that squalor and congested living conditions were most pronounced. In his *Report* Chadwick noted that:

The most wretched of the stationary population of which I have been able to obtain any account, or that I have ever seen, was that which I saw in company with *Dr Arnott*, and others, in the wynds of Edinburgh and Glasgow. (op. cit., p. 97)

The Scottish cities differed from the English in that the tene-
ment was commoner than the separate house. Here, however, as
in London, and in most ancient towns that grew at all rapidly in
this period, once respectable property had the habit of becoming
transformed into working-class tenements: decayed central
areas of this type – comparable, perhaps, to the 'twilight zones'
of the modern city – provided grotesque examples of overcrowding and were the particular objects of attack by sanitary
reformers. Especially sordid were the notorious 'rookeries' of
London's West End, St Giles, or Seven Dials where, as Dickens
observed, 'every room has its separate tenant, and every tenant
is . . . generally the head of a numerous family'. He went on to
describe the teeming chaos of a typical house in the same district:

The man in the shop, perhaps, is in the baked 'jemmy' line, or
the firewood and hearthstone line, or any other line which requires
a floating capital of eighteenpence or thereabouts: he and his family
live in the shop, and the small back-parlour behind it. Then there is
an Irish labourer and *his* family in the back-kitchen, and a jobbing
man – carpet-beater and so forth – with *his* family in the front one.
In the front one-pair, there's another man with another wife and
family, and in the back one-pair, there's 'a young 'oman as takes in
tambour-work, and dresses quite genteel'. . . . The second-floor front
and the rest of the lodgers, are just a second edition of the people
below. (*Sketches by Boz*, Scenes, Ch. V)

Districts like these, with their tangled populations of artisans,
street-sellers, casual labourers and the rest, interspersed with an
underworld of beggars, prostitutes, and thieves, belonged to
society that was less touched by the Industrial Revolution than
we sometimes suppose. They were more the outgrowths of a
demographic, than of an industrial revolution. In London the
main features of such quarters were well established by the
mid-eighteenth century (see M. D. George, *London Life in
Eighteenth Century*, Ch. II). If their history was to be altered by
the Industrial Revolution, it was through providing better paid
employment for their inhabitants. Public action against city
'black spots' was at first haphazard: the building of the first

railways into city centres often required the demolition of house
property of this type, even if the short-term effect was to increase
overcrowding in nearby streets.

If some of the most glaring and well known problems of urban
expansion occurred in towns and cities whose population was
only indirectly linked to the Industrial Revolution, the growth
of the industrial towns was, nevertheless, spectacular. Where
towns were growing at between 30 and 40 per cent, and sometimes more, in a decade the pressure upon the housing supply
was often intolerable. It was this pressure which was, of course,
reflected in high urban rents. As the town population mounted
in the early nineteenth century so did expenditure upon rent:
in 1801 rent accounted for 5·3 per cent (£12·2 million) of an
estimated National Income of £232 million, in 1851 it had risen
to 8 per cent (£42·6 million) of a National Income of £523·3
million (*The Abstract of British Historical Statistics*, p. 366).
Despite his higher wages the industrial worker could rarely
afford a rent of more than 2–3/– a week and, when his house cost
approximately £60–100 to build, the return upon capital was
not high by contemporary standards. The model cottages, which
were convertable into flats, built for the Great Exhibition were
intended to yield 7 per cent on an outlay of £110–120 (plate **16**).
Even if building was, in the long term, certain to chase demand,
short-term business crisis usually hit the small speculative
builder very hard – his activities were among the first to feel the
effect of any tightening of credit. Certainly in the factory towns
a depression could be visibly measured by the number of empty
houses, either completed and awaiting a first occupier, or
abandoned as families which had moved to a new house in a
prosperous year now moved out again as they found they could
not afford the rent. In this context building was a risky enterprise. The best return was found meeting middle-class demand
for the suburban villa; as a correspondent to *The Builder* wrote
in 1848:

Whilst we are exhausting our ingenuity to supply villas with 'every
possible convenience' we are leaving our working classes to the
enjoyment of every possible inconvenience, in wretched shells to

which men of substance would not consign their beasts of burden.
(quoted in J. Parry Lewis, *Building Cycles and Britain's Growth*,
Macmillan, p. 87)

New working-class districts provided dismal evidence of the
stratagems of the 'jerry'-builder: the commonest examples were
the over-development of sites, sometimes by building the
cottages 'back-to-back', sometimes by increasing the capacity
of the house by including a cellar to house a second (or third)
family, by generally skimping on materials, digging inadequate
foundations, and rarely, until tighter local authority supervision
was applied, attending to the basic environmental services like
paving, and the provision of sufficient privies and sewers.

'Jerry' building was a feature especially of the postwar years
after 1815: the word derived from the seaman's term 'jury', i.e.
makeshift, and was first applied to the building trade in the
immigrant-swamped Liverpool of about 1830. What identified
the jerry-built was its flimsiness:

The walls are only half-brick thick, or what the bricklayers call
'brick noggin', and the whole of the materials are slight and unfit for
the purpose. I have been told of a man who had built a row of these
houses; and on visiting them one morning after a storm, found the
whole of them levelled with the ground (this was in Manchester). . . .
I recollect a bricklayer near London complaining loudly of having to
risk his credit by building a house with nine-inch walls, and declared
it would be like 'Jack Straw's House', neither 'wind nor water tight':
his astonishment would have been great had he been told that
thousands of houses occupied by the labouring classes are erected
with walls of $4\frac{1}{2}$-inch thickness. (Assistant Poor Law Commissioner
Mott in Chadwick, *Report*, op. cit., p. 344)

In Professor Ashton's view: 'It was emphatically not the machine, not the Industrial Revolution, not even the speculative
bricklayer or carpenter that was at fault. . . . The fundamental
problem was the shortage of houses' ('The Treatment of Capitalism by Historians' in *Capitalism and the Historians*, ed. F. A.
Hayek, Routledge, p. 51). This shortage went back, at least, to
the beginning of the nineteenth century. In 1801 the number of
families in England and Wales exceeded the number of houses

by 274,000: by 1851 the discrepancy had risen to 280,000. From the point of view of the number of people per inhabited house there was, however, some slight improvement. Building did not respond at all evenly to *need*:

England and Wales: increase of 'separate occupiers' and housing stock, 1801–51

	Families	Houses
1801–11	275,000	216,000
1811–21	321,000	309,000
1821–31	419,000	444,000
1831–41	—	516,000
1841–51	800,000 (1831–51)	314,000

(*Note*: the increase in the number of families is the best guide to housing needs, but the Census category 'separate occupier' included many who would have set up their own homes if they could. Sharing increased during periods of unemployment. *Figures* from J. Parry Lewis, op. cit., p. 167). The table shows that there appear to have been two periods when house building trailed behind need: in the first twenty years of the century, and again in the 1840s.

The economics of housing

The first of these two important slumps in building activity was the result of the Napoleonic War. Industrial and urban growth in the last quarter of the eighteenth century had been accompanied by an associated boom in the building trade. Houses were being put up exceptionally rapidly in the 1770s and again, in even greater numbers, from 1785 to 1793 (although there was a pause in 1788). Building was clearly beginning to respond to the insistent demands created by a growing and migrating population, although how far needs had been met, or standards improved, it is difficult to say (much of this building was for the middle class). Certainly at this stage industrial growth and building appear to have been complementary processes. Apart from two feeble rallies, the first associated with the Peace of Amiens, the second running from 1805 to 1810, the war years

were a period of acute depression in the building trade. The
decision to finance the war by heavy borrowing was a fateful one
in terms of the housing standards of the next generation. With
interest rates legally pegged at 5 per cent (under the Usury Act,
1714: the ancient body of usury legislation was not repealed
until 1854), and with the safe return on Consols held at 4·2+ per
cent (often 4·5 per cent, occasionally 5 per cent) from 1794 to
1816, credit was often quite unobtainable for a risky enterprise
like building. The brick duty, and the timber duties, were also
responsible for some inflation in building costs. Both continued
to affect prices after the war although not, perhaps, as much as
by adding £20 to the cost of what would have been a £40 cottage,
as Joseph Hume argued in 1850. The building boom of the early
1820s was a response to the accumulated demand of the previous
twenty years: there is a strong presumption that this demand
was primarily for working-class accommodation.

In the postwar decades the relationship between the Industrial
Revolution and housebuilding was not only closer but it was
freed from the distorting influence of government policies dictated by the needs of war. Funds for housebuilding now had to
compete with industrial and overseas investment. In general
house construction followed in the wake of, for example, factory
investment and was geared to fluctuations in the prosperity of
local industry. The industrialists themselves, apart from the
greatest employers, had little spare capital for speculation in this
field and in the industrial towns the cottages were usually run
up by small jobbing builders whose operations centred on cheap
credit. House building was thus highly vulnerable to a check in
business activity, or unduly keen competition for building
materials. Neither of these factors operated evenly across the
country. There was also some correlation between steady, or
falling exports and a high rate of housebuilding, perhaps because
export booms were so closely interlocked with British overseas
investment. The 1840s constitute a special case: investment in
this decade was distorted by the railway mania. Railway construction depended upon bricks as the main building material
for stations and other buildings as well as engineering works like

bridges and viaducts. Although brick production rose well above the level of the 1830s, 200,000 fewer houses had been added to the housing stock by the end of the 1840s than in the previous decade. The discrepancy was, no doubt, less than it seemed because the railway programme entailed the demolition of some houses and their replacement formed a new consideration; the situation was, nevertheless, serious and the result was an increase of overcrowding, especially among the very poor. Once again the present had to suffer for the benefit of the future. A good supply of bricks was essential to the building industry. The canals had assisted the growth of the brick industry in the late eighteenth century and the railways were soon to diffuse cheap building materials even more widely. There was little technical change on the brickfields until the introduction of a brick-cutting machine in the 1850s: the industry's capacity was probably stretched to its limits in the 1840s. There was certainly a conflict between *growth* and *comfort* in this decade.

Obviously, if houses had cost even less, and rent been lower, the demand for them would have been greater. This is only another way of pointing out that many labouring families found their incomes swallowed up by paying for food and clothing. Housebuilding could not become a priority until higher real incomes established a stronger demand for new homes. In addition housebuilding required better credit facilities than existed in this period: the permanent building society only made an appearance in the later 1840s. It should be remembered, too, that in this century the provision of new homes has only been partly met by the market mechanism: without the contribution of local authority housing British housing standards in the twentieth century might not make such favourable comparison with the nineteenth. Only the larger industrialists of the early Industrial Revolution had the freedom to pursue an enlightened housing policy, in which the first criterion was not immediate profit – although, as is well known, they did get a return in the shape of a more stable and reliable work force. Where an employer did adopt a progressive housing policy the living habits of his workpeople could be significantly altered:

Having had such opportunity of observing the great inconvenience
arising from small dwellings where the families were large, both as
regards bed-rooms and living-rooms, few cottages having more than
two bed-rooms; and where there were children or young persons of
both sexes, the indelicacy of this arrangement was apparent; we
therefore concluded to build larger cottages, and make them with
three bed-rooms in each. These houses were sought after with the
greatest avidity, and families allowed to move into them as an especial
favour; the increase of rent of 1/- to 1/6 a week was a small consideration in regard to the additional comfort afforded to the family
where the income was from 24/- to 50/- or 60/- a week, as is frequently the case with families employed in the manufactories. (from
evidence by Henry Ashworth of Turton, near Bolton, in Chadwick,
Report, op. cit., p. 304)

In a paternalistic context like this, as at Disraeli's Millbank, an
employer might expect to shape a community according to
received middle-class values. Elsewhere, while intolerable overcrowding was, no doubt, resented by almost all working-class
families, there did not yet exist anything like a modern insistence
upon privacy. Even in some of the best early industrial housing
the accommodation provided was restricted to one or two rooms:
initially housing standards were derived from the traditional
practice of the region. Traditionalism also goes some way to
explain why families expected to go on keeping a pig in the
yard, or back area, no matter how great the inconvenience both
to themselves and others. Observers who expected working-class
families to use higher earnings (when they were available) to
purchase better housing ignored not only the widespread pre-
cariousness of earnings, but the continued grip of pre-industrial
and pre-urban habits. And it should be remembered that, if the
working classes were disinclined to alter ancient family habits,
the nation as a whole was disinclined to enter an era of communal regulation, even in such crucial fields as the disposal of
sewage or the provision of water.

[24] LIVING IN TOWNS: THE COMMUNAL PROBLEMS

However the Industrial Revolution affected the supply of houses, it certainly created an environment which was often hostile to clean and comfortable living. It is difficult now to appreciate quite what it was like to live in a city in which the pollution of streams and rivers, and the air itself, went virtually unchecked. Visitors to the industrial centres persistently recorded their dismay at the pollution of the air by smoke. To approach Manchester was to enter a zone of darkness:

For several miles before they reached Milton [i.e. Manchester], they saw a deep lead-coloured cloud hanging over the horizon in the direction in which it lay. (Mrs Gaskell, *North and South*, Ch. 7)

To Taine 'the air and the soil appear charged with fog and soot', and the heroine of *North and South*, on first settling in Manchester, felt that the air in her bedroom was heavy with smoke. Although manufacturers could be prosecuted for allowing their furnaces to pollute the atmosphere, action was rarely taken. Like so many other evils that of smoke was preventable:

The appearance of the towns on the Sunday, when nearly all the furnaces are stopped, when there is little more than the smoke from the dwelling-houses, when everything is comparatively bright, and the distant hills and surrounding country that are never visible through the atmosphere of the town in week-days may be seen across it, presents nearly the appearance which such towns would assume on working days, if the laws were duly executed, and the excessive smoke of the furnaces prevented. (Chadwick, *Report*, op. cit., pp. 356–7)

Dirty clothes and dirty homes were the first evils of smoke; the health hazard was presumed, even if it could not be proved.

The health of towns had become a topic of continuous public debate by the 1840s. After the publication of Chadwick's *Report* in 1842, if not before, educated opinion could be in no doubt about the alarmingly high death rates among urban populations. This, again, was a general problem of urban growth and not the specific outcome of Industrial Revolution. In outline at least the solution to most of these problems was well known by the mid-nineteenth century; effective and disinterested public administration, the supervised installation of well engineered schemes of sewage disposal and water supply, and generally improved standards of medical knowledge and personal hygiene. Public health administration, however misunderstood and resented, had come into being by 1850. As its efficiency depended upon local backing the impact upon health standards was variable and there was no general and marked drop in the death rate until much later in the nineteenth century. It is not correct to regard the major impediment to progress in this field to have been the spirit of laissez-faire. Parochialism and ignorance were the main obstacles to change. Among the middle classes there was often predictable hostility to an increase in rate expenditure and, even more, to the intrusion of centralized initiative into local affairs. Yet the sanitary reformers, who emphasized the economic wastefulness of (especially) epidemic disease, were certainly no enemies – in the short term – to the dominant philosophy of individual enterprise. Of course there were powerful vested interests, like the water companies, or established commissions of sewers, who were naturally hostile to thoroughgoing sanitary reform. Medical opinion was seldom unanimous and its verdict was consequently muffled. Yet Chadwick was probably right to identify 'fatalism', the ancient habit of resignation and acquiescence in the face of disease, as the first barrier to break down. The sanitary reformers had all the naïvety of those who imagine that traditionalism is easily overthrown. As Charles Kingsley reminded them in his essay 'A Mad World, My Masters' (1858) it was absurd to expect the automatic assistance of the clergy (easily the most influential body of persuaders):

they [the sanitary reformers] actually expected that parish rectors, already overburdened with over-work and vestry quarrels – nay, even that preachers who got their bread by pew rents, and whose life-long struggle was, therefore, to keep those pews filled, and those renters in good humour – should astound the respectable house-owners who sat beneath them by the appalling words: 'You, and not the "Visitation of God", are the cause of epidemics; and of you, now that you are once fairly warned of your responsibility, will your brothers' blood be required'. (in *Sanitary and Social Essays*, 1889 ed., p. 275)

It was mistaken, in Kingsley's view, to suppose that the preacher believed 'the mortal lives of men to be inexpressibly precious'.

At least by 1850 the progress of engineering technique, and the much increased production of iron, meant that society possessed the resources for efficient sanitary engineering. The steam engine could be utilized to supply water under pressure and to pump away sewage. The advantages of the glazed earthenware, or iron, sewage pipe over their rival, the brick sewer, were beginning to be understood. What was emerging here was a technology of urban services. It was not only apathy which hindered its progress. Like the doctors, the engineers could not always agree among themselves. They resented the persuasive intrusion into their profession of Chadwick and the General Board of Health (established by the Public Health Act, 1848, for a six-year period which was not extended). Bazalgette, the engineer to the Metropolitan Commission of Sewers, was a known opponent of Chadwick's pipes and his consultant engineer, Robert Stephenson, had once declared 'As to pipes he would not touch one'. Despite such professional wrangles, and widespread suspicion of the General Board, 182 towns, with a population of over 2 million, had been brought under the Public Health Act by 1853: 'the general picture was one of steady and accelerating progress' (R. A. Lewis, *Edwin Chadwick and the Public Movement*, Longmans, p. 341). The cholera epidemic of 1853–4, while not so severe as in 1848–9, was a sobering reminder of how much progress had still to be made in the field of sanitation and water supply. Amost everywhere the well and cesspool, the shared privies and open sewers, and the intermittently flowing stand-cock (providing water for, perhaps, a whole terrace), indicated the survival of private and public habits from another age.

Even a nation of countrymen settled in towns could not permanently resist those pressures which were forcing them to organize their life more efficiently. It was what was begun in the 1840s, rather than what was achieved, which mattered for the future. There was another indication that towns had 'come of age': the recognition of the need for public parks. In the eighteenth, and early nineteenth century when most towns, including the largest, were still small by the standards of the mid-nineteenth century, this problem had scarcely arisen. Since the end of the eighteenth century some towns had lost valuable open space by the enclosure of commons (often no bad thing for housing densities) and garden land on the outskirts had often been used for building – this was the case at Birmingham:

Within the last half century the town was surrounded by land which was divided into gardens, which were rented by the mechanic at one guinea or half a guinea per annum. Here the mechanic was generally seen after his day's labour spending his evening in a healthy and simple occupation in which he took great delight. This ground is now for the most part built over, and the mechanics of the town are gradually losing this source of useful and healthy recreation. (Chadwick, *Report*, p. 335–6)

In Sheffield, which at the beginning of the century had been well provided with commons, 'scarce a foot of all these common wastes remain for the enjoyment of the industrial classes' (1843). To walk out into the country was no pleasure, as Dr Kay pointed out in 1833, when this meant trudging along turnpike roads which were 'alternately dusty or muddy'. Townsmen were being sealed off from the country by the growth of the town itself. In London this process was fancifully compared to the work of locusts:

Although, in fact, these little devastators do not trouble us; in effect, Londoners are the victims of equally efficient destroyers of their green places. Bricklayers are spreading the webs and meshes of houses with such fearful rapidity in every direction, that the people are gradually being confined within narrow prisons, only open at the top for the emission of what would be air if it were not smoke. . . . The lungs of London have undergone congestion. (in Dickens's family magazine, *Household Words*, Vol. I, 1850, p. 451)

There was an acute need for public action. In Manchester, described as 'singularly destitute of those resources which conduce at once to health and recreation':

The prospect of obtaining any wide area to be appropriated as a public walk or otherwise for the use of the labouring classes, becomes more remote each year, as the value of land within the neighbourhood of the town increases. (C. Mott, in Chadwick, *Report*, op. cit., p. 336)

Although the lack of playgrounds and open spaces was a problem, above all, of the great city, it could be found even in the village where, as Chadwick complained, the children often had nowhere to play but in dirty back-lanes. The result of breakneck urban growth in the early nineteenth century was that many cities were left, for the remainder of the century, with densely populated quarters where there were virtually no parks and open spaces. But, as with the provision of essential services, progress was being made by the 1840s: central and local initiative had together begun to equip the great cities with their first public parks. In London the royal parks, which served the West End, were improved in the early 1840s; Green Park was drained, and Regent's Park, which had been created by Nash and the Prince Regent after the land had reverted to the Crown in 1809, was made fully open to the public. The need was now to provide 'lungs' for the city's industrial population. In the east, Victoria Park, Hackney, was laid out 1842–5. Quick action was also wanted in South London. The old commons were neglected, and shrinking in size:

Kennington Common is but a name for a small grassless square, surrounded with houses, and poisoned by the stench of vitriol-works, and black, open, sluggish ditches. (Thomas Miller, *Sketches of London*, 1852, p. 228)

To the west 'Wandsworth had set out in good earnest to reach Lambeth' and it was to prevent the formation of a continuous suburban and industrial sprawl south of the Thames that the government decided to create a public park at Battersea. The suggestion to convert what, until recently, had been Battersea open fields into a public park was first made to the Royal Commission on Metropolitan Improvements in 1843: the Commission reported favourably on the scheme in 1846. An Act at once empowered the Commissioners of Woods and Forests to purchase 150 hectares (320 acres) in the fields and to lay out a park. By 1857 £187,000 had been spent on the purchase of land, and the once waterlogged and marshy site had been transformed by the construction of a costly embankment. The Park was a deserved success; 12,000 visitors were not unknown on summer days and, on Sundays, when Chelsea Bridge was toll free, the visitors sometimes numbered 50,000. Yet parks could be dull and dispiriting places. More people may have come out to Battersea Fields on a Sunday earlier in the century when they were the scene of 'the low amusements of the dangerous classes'. Parks iike this were not simply 'improvements' in the physical sense: for the respectable the park stood for the quiet, civilized, family recreations of which they approved, as against the disorderly and often riotous pleasures of the past.

Outside London other towns made a beginning with their parks in the same period. Birkenhead obtained the first local Act for the provision of a public park in 1837, Manchester had its first park by the mid-1840s, and Joseph Strutt gave Derby 4 hectares (11 acres), laid out as an arboretum, in 1840. Parks were not, of course, the only amenities appearing within the new towns by 1850. Schools, chapels, churches, reading rooms and Mechanics' Institutes, the ubiquitous public house, the pleasure garden and the concert rooms, were the products of faith, philanthropy, and a lusty, if primitive, entertainment industry. To these public and private enterprise was adding, perhaps, a bath and wash-house, a new cemetery (to replace old and overcrowded burial grounds), and the plant of service industries, like water-works. What had been constructed was not yet very impressive. Much that was basic, the proper paving of streets, the insistence on minimum building standards, and the elimination of open sewers lay in the future. Urban death rates were still high, often still rising. Despite all this the framework of an urban civilization was in being.

[25] THE TOWN DWELLER: A NEW MAN?

Traditional religion under stress

Within this new civilization attention has been concentrated on two events; the divorce between the majority and the practice of Christian worship, and the emergence of class consciousness and class hostility. Was the Industrial Revolution the cause of the declining support for Christianity which became evident in this period: or was it the result of other, perhaps less easily identifiable, forces? In fact the concept of 'decline' is one that should be applied only with strict caution. There was certainly a decline in attendance at religious worship, in 'the religious habit'. It is equally clear that, by the end of the eighteenth century and throughout the early nineteenth century, there was a body of atheist and 'freethinking' opinion (its most obvious expression was the popularity of Tom Paine's *The Age of Reason*). What significance can be attached to either of these developments? This depends, of course, partly upon their scale but, more importantly, upon the extent to which they represent a marked departure from past experience. The free-thinkers were undoubtedly more numerous than atheists had ever been before: but their numbers were too small to suppose that they exercised any substantial influence. It is, to go further, impossible to know how to evaluate the religious *belief* of the early modern, but pre-industrial, centuries. Conventionality has to be assumed, but it cannot be mapped with any precision. Church attendance was a recognized obligation for the majority: there is little to suggest that the obligation was not met.

That conventional religion did not satisfy thousands was evident from the success of Methodism. This discontent was more than the anticlericalism which had always been prevalent in massively conformist Christian communities. Like other revival movements Methodism was a search for 'real' religion, in the sense that its followers wanted to meet higher demands than those of 'established' religion: from the emotional, psychological upheaval of 'conversion', in which the experience was one of release, the Methodist went on, having 'joined a society', to find the initial freshness of first conviction preserved within a dramatic pattern of worship of which the main elements were hymn-singing and sermon. Without the parallel event of the Industrial Revolution Methodism might have been expected to do little more than supplement the existing body of Dissent. The impetus must surely have faltered. So of course it did, but not before Methodism had stamped its character on the first industrial communities (and much of the countryside as well). Methodist church *membership* (old connexion) rose from 90,000 in 1800, to 358,000 in 1850 – the most rapid growth had been achieved in the two opening decades of the century. By 1850 the Wesleyan Methodists were no more than the dominant group within the movement; the Religious Census of 1851 recorded that, while 654,000 Wesleyans attended chapel on the evening of 30 March 1851, 229,000 attended Primitive Methodist chapels, the largest of the Methodist sects. In many of the manufacturing towns, but especially in the West Riding, Methodists dominated the older Dissenters: as Dean Hook of Leeds admitted in 1837, 'the real fact is that the established religion of Leeds is Methodism'.

The Industrial Revolution was thus accompanied by a remarkable religious revival. Whatever the value of Methodism, however much the associate of 'uprooting' and 'transplanting' a population, to become a Methodist was an act of choice: it was not habit that took a man to chapel. That this was so was made plain by the 1851 Census. The Census assumed that the churches needed to provide seating for 58 per cent of the population (10,398,013 people) if they were to meet a minimum requirement of one attendance at church on Sunday. Of the 10 million which Horace Mann, who compiled the Religious Census, computed 'to be at liberty to worship at one period of the day', over 5 million were '*altogether absent* every Sunday': this was the result of their own 'free choice' and had nothing to do with a shortage of seats. Yet it was true that townspeople were particularly poorly served by the churches. In the large towns in 1851 the churches could seat only 44·7 per 100 of the population: in 1821 the position had been worse (37 per 100), but since then the Church of England had striven hard to build new churches. Outside the large towns the provision of seating was satisfactory, 70 per 100. In these towns nearly one in four of the seats provided was in a Methodist chapel; between 1801 and 1821, when the total number of seats provided was growing at a slower rate than the population itself, the Methodists had increased their accommodation by more than 80 per cent per decade. It was often in the towns where Methodism had taken little root that the provision of seats was most inadequate. In London the only boroughs to provide *more* than 30 seats per 100 were the City, Westminster, and Greenwich, and the worst figures for the large towns as whole were recorded in Lambeth (24·8) and Tower Hamlets (25·6). The average for the capital was 29·7. In Birmingham it was 28·7.

There could be no hesitation about the Report's conclusion: among the urban working class the habit of attending religious worship had been lost. Mann admitted that they were, for the most part, 'unconscious secularists' rather than atheists, but their absence from church was, nevertheless, 'attributable *mainly* to a genuine repugnance to religion itself'. Mann saw the labouring population as 'really as ignorant of Christianity as were the heathen Saxons at Augustine's landing' and he believed that there was no hope of their reconversion until serious missionary effort penetrated into 'the dingy territories of this alienated nation' (for extracts from the Report see *English Historical Documents*, Vol. XII (I), pp. 370–94). Methodism had, after all, provided some grounds for optimism. In a period of religious revival it might not seem fanciful to suppose that if the majority had lost contact with religion through negligence and the accidents of urban migration they might also, if properly approached, be persuaded to return to Christianity by missionary enterprise. As yet, there was no reason to think that industrial society as such was a hostile environment for religion. The industrial workers, especially the skilled, were not demonstrably more irreligious than the working class as a whole: the division was between townsmen and countrymen, between the middle classes and those below them (and often, until the Evangelical Movement had done its work, those above them). Furthest from religion were those town dwellers like the costermonger interviewed by Mayhew who had *heard* of Christ, but had never been in a church, and to whom the word 'Redeemer' prompted only the sad reflection, 'Well, I only wish I could redeem my Sunday togs from my uncle's'.

The decline in church-going could be, and often was, seen as a symptom of wider social dislocation. But the distress it caused owed something to the heightened religious sensitivity of the late eighteenth and early nineteenth centuries. When witnesses were examined before the Royal Commission on the labour of women and children in mines (1842) they were questioned about both their education and religion. The answers could be alarming:

[Janet Cumming, aged 11, coal-bearer, East of Scotland coalfield] I am learning to read at the night-school; am in the twopenny book; sometimes to the Sabbath-school. Jesus was God; David wrote the Bible; has a slight knowledge of the first six questions of the Shorter Catechism.

[Elizabeth Day, aged 17, working in a Barnsley Pit] I don't go to Sunday-school. The truth is, we are confined enough on weekdays and want to walk about on Sundays; but I go to chapel on Sunday night. I can't read at all. Jesus Christ was Adam's son, and they nailed him to a tree; but I don't rightly understand these things. (both extracts from E. Royston Pike, *Human Documents of the Industrial Revolution*, Allen and Unwin, pp. 171, 264)

The mining communities were, in some respects, unusual and the mining village was a very different environment from that of a large town: some remained almost untouched by religion, others were profoundly influenced by Methodism. Yet the central problem, that of communicating religious beliefs, was much the same here as in the greatest city. Church attendance in the villages of pre-industrial England was probably uneven, but it could be, and perhaps usually was, remarkably complete: in the Kent village of Goodnestone all but 16 of those villagers who had been confirmed (128 out of total population of 281) received

communion in Easter Week 1676, at Clayworth in Nottinghamshire the figures were 200 out of 401 (P. Laslett, *The World we
have lost*, University Paperbacks, pp. 71, 73). *Literal* Christians
(in Laslett's phrase) that these villagers were, one wonders how
they would have fared before a Royal Commission of the 1840s.
Some were obviously more devout than others, if very few could
write most may have known the catechism, and all were
encompassed by traditional belief and institutions.

The issue of class

When people moved into the towns and industrial districts
(where the parish system, and the surveillance of the squire,
were as impossible to maintain as in many towns), they
moved outside this ancient framework. If a majority were now
to retain their religion they would have to do so by *choice*,
as the Dissenters had been used to doing in the past. The
Industrial Revolution, by intensifying migration, did assist the
breakdown of the religious habit by undermining the position
of the Church of England. But it is difficult to see that the early
industrial 'way of life' was, in itself hostile to religious belief.
Within a town the paths that led to church and chapel were not
those of the village; it was not always instinct to follow your
betters but, sometimes, to go the other way – yet, as with the
Primitive Methodists or the Baptists, this was still the way of
religion. Industrialization was a complex influence. Some employers cared for the religious well-being of their workpeople
and themselves provided for the building of churches. While
many were deterred by middle-class support for religion, others
undoubtedly associated church attendance with respectability
and success. Throughout society it has to be remembered that
the language of religion was part of a common culture. Revival-
ism was always capable of stemming, and even reversing, the
drift to secularism. Further, as many historians have pointed
out, the significance of contemporary religion, especially of
Methodism, was enhanced by its ability to supply both an
experience in community life and a means of emotional release.

Religion had to compete with the public house, but not yet with a modern entertainment industry.

Estrangement from religion was known to follow class lines. Horace Mann admitted the deterrent affect of the common division between the rented pews and the free seats, which had made religion appear 'a purely middle-class propriety or luxury'. Perhaps even more important was,

... the influence of that broad line of demarcation which on weekdays separates the workman from his master [and] cannot be effaced on Sundays by the mere removal of a physical barrier. (*English Historical Documents*, Vol. XII (I), p. 390)

The Industrial Revolution has long been held accountable for a social, as well as economic, transformation. Modern class divisions and class consciousness, which had no counterpart in agrarian, pre-industrial society, were, it has been thought, the first artefacts of industrial revolution. By the mid-nineteenth century the facts appeared incontrovertible. In his essay of 1829, entitled *Signs of the Times*, Thomas Carlyle, after characterizing 'this age of ours' as 'the Age of Machinery', an age when

We war with rude nature; and, by our restless engines, come off always victorious, and loaded with spoils,

went on to reflect,

What changes, too, this addition of power is introducing into the social system; how wealth has more and more increased, and at the same time gathered itself more and more into masses, strangely altering the old relations, and increasing the distance between the rich and the poor. (*Critical and Miscellaneous Essays*, 1839, ed., pp. 147–8)

Although they were to draw very different conclusions from their analysis, Carlyle's diagnosis was impressively close to that of Marx and Engels:

In proportion as the bourgeoisie, i.e. capital, is developed, in the same proportion is the proletariat, the modern working class developed – a class of labourers, who live only so long as they find work, and who can find work only so long as their labour increases capital. . . . The modern labourer . . . instead of rising with the progress of industry, sinks deeper and deeper below the conditions of existence of his own class. (*Communist Manifesto*, Progress Publishers, Moscow, pp. 49, 58)

Modern industry, itself the creation of the resourceful bourgeoisie, demanded the formation of a proletariat. In this process the ancient distinction between labourers and craftsmen is destroyed and, with the massing of population in towns, combined with broadening vulnerability to the business cycle, the result is accelerating class conflict. In time this conflict will be enacted at a national level as 'the collisions between individual workmen and individual bourgeois take on more and more the character of collisions between two classes'.

The class theory of the Manifesto (1848) had been both outlined, and documented, in Engels's *The Condition of the Working Class in England*:

The middle classes have more in common with every other nation in the world than with the proletariat which lives on their own door-steps. The workers differ from the middle classes in speech, in thoughts and ideas, in customs, morals, politics, and religion. (Engels, op. cit., p. 139)

In remarkably similar language Disraeli warned his readers of the divide between the rich and the poor: 'Two nations; between whom there is no intercourse and no sympathy' (*Sybil*, Bk. I, Ch. 5). Of Manchester Mrs Gaskell's southerner, Margaret Hale could say:

I see two classes dependent on each other in every possible way, yet each evidently regarding the interests of the other as opposed to their own; I never lived in a place before where there were two sets of people always running each other down. (*North and South*, Ch. 15)

Middle-class opinion was, of course, unwilling to admit that there were real differences of economic interest between the classes: towards the starker facts of poverty its attitude was all too often just evasive. When, in *Our Mutual Friend*, Mr Podsnap was tactlessly reminded of some recent cases of death by starvation his first response was to say 'I don't believe it', and his second to exclaim 'Then it was their own fault' (this point has been made by W. E. Houghton, op. cit., p. 415). However hypocritical the Podsnaps may have been (they can hardly have remained quite unaware of social realities by the 1830s and 1840s) the geographical separation of the classes in the suburbs of the large cities does help to explain much contemporary ignorance among the middle classes. Engels was not inclined to excuse, but he admitted:

these plutocrats can travel from their houses to their places of business [in Manchester] ... by the shortest routes, which run entirely through working-class districts, without even realizing how close they are to the misery and filth which lie on both sides of the road. This is because the main streets which run from the Exchange ... are occupied almost uninterruptedly on both sides by shops, which are kept ... in a clean and respectable condition. (op. cit., p. 55)

Even a man with a keen social conscience, like George Godwin, editor of *The Builder,* could see serious obstacles to individual voyages of discovery into the poorest working-class districts:

it is necessary to brave risks of fever and other injuries to health, and the contact of men and women often as lawless as the Arab or the Kaffir; in addition ... there is among the very poor a strong feeling against intrusion: few persons venture into these haunts besides the regular inhabitants, the London missionaries, the parish surgeon, and the police, and thus the extent of this great evil [the slum] is imperfectly understood. (*A Glance at the 'Homes' of the Thousands,* London 1854, p. 1)

Friction and misunderstanding between the classes were, in part, the consequence of their increasing isolation within the great cities.

The existence of immense disparities of wealth was a fundamental feature both of pre-industrial society, and of the countryside throughout the whole period of the Industrial Revolution. Of the 20,686 men who died in Cambridgeshire 1848–57 only 1,630 (5 per cent) left property valued at £5 or more: out of the total deaths for the county, 40,483, 0·2 per cent left nearly 50 per cent of the total wealth. 400 people, about 1 per cent of the deaths, left £3·3 million out of the total for the county of £4·4 million (J. R. Vincent, *Pollbooks, How Victorians Voted*, Cambridge, p. 36). The urban migrants of this period were, for the most part, propertyless – only 53 labourers, and 45 servants, figured among the Cambridgeshire testators. They were accustomed to show 'deference' towards the landowner and the gentleman, and the very remoteness between them no doubt encouraged the labourer to acceptance of his 'lot' and 'station'. For large sections of the labouring population to discard their respect for property, to begin to see the interests of 'labour' in competition with the interests of their employers, required not only some generations of experience in an industrial environment, but also increasing contact with *ideas* of sufficient relevance and vitality to destroy traditional inhibitions. Eighteenth-century urban Radicalism, infused with the hostility of the French Revolution towards aristocratic privilege, and later stiffened by Nonconformist resentment of the Established Church, provided a structure within which a significant degree of working-class self-consciousness could be realized. In the late eighteenth century, and in the postwar decades, aristocratic and landed privilege drew the attacks of a Radicalism that was based equally upon the support of wealthy individualists, a large section of the business community (from small producers and shopkeepers, to bankers and greater manufacturers), and the artisans of the cities. The greatest victory of early Radicalism, the Reform Act of 1832, was also the cause of its later fragmentation. The redrawn franchise of 1832 was received by the working classes as an act of exclusion: their response was Chartism, 'an insurrection expressly directed against the middle classes' (Annual Register, 1839). A new era of class bitterness dates from the 1830s when the New Poor Law was introduced into the manufacturing districts: the Act was widely interpreted as an attack upon the 'productive classes' for which the middle class was primarily responsible. Engels believed that the whole middle class was behind the New Poor Law (op. cit., p. 331).

Perhaps most of the large manufacturers were, but the shop-
keepers often took a different approach – their anxiety as ratepayers submerged by the threat to business implied by the
withdrawal of outdoor relief.

Behind the achievement, in this period, of a sense of shared
objectives among the working class lay the differing contribu-
tions of ideas, circulated by an enterprising Radical press, and
experience. Robert Owen's repetitive emphasis on the importance of labour belongs not only to the spread of cooperative
(as distinct from competitive) venture as to the process through
which the working class acquired a heightened awareness of its
own existence. Overambitious and precocious as the Owenite
movements were, they clearly pointed to the opening of a new
phase in working-class history. As organizations the subsequent
working-class movements of the 1830s and 1840s were weakly.
Ideas were not quickly or easily translated into effective institutions. The most successful working-class action was industrial,
despite the bitter hostility of both employers and government
towards trade unions. Nevertheless the will to persist, and stick
together, in the face of adverse conditions and the threats of
employers, was quickly undermined. Machine breaking and
intimidation were often indispensable if the men were to force
employers to meet them with any concessions. The context for
such action was not necessarily the more modern and highly
mechanized industries: the grievances of the Leicester stockingers
against frame rents turned them, at different stages, into Lud-
dites and Chartists. Class hostility was not restricted to the
cotton towns and to factory industry, although it was here that
it attracted most attention – as Mr Thornton irritably remarked
'at a time like this [a strike was imminent] our doings are sure to
be canvassed by every scribbler who can hold a pen' (North and
South, Ch. 15).

Even after the 1840s it was apparent that the working class
was not unanimously committed to the practice of class conflict.
In the People's Paper the Chartist leader Ernest Jones expressed
his exasperation with the failure of many working people to
recognize the truth – as he saw it, that,

Amid the mass of factory tyranny which meets us on all sides, amid the mass of murmuring and indignant misery, there is nothing more sickening to my mind, than the language and sentiments of a certain portion of the working classes, who are perpetually talking of 'the mutual confidence of employers and employed' – 'the identity of their interests' – 'the kindness of their good masters', – 'the excellence of their intentions' – 'the duty to their employers', and other sickening and disgusting epithets, in which either ignorance or cowardice wait on human degradation ...

Now what say you to 'identity of interests'?

My friends I'll tell you plainly how the interests really lie: IT IS YOUR INTEREST TO RUIN THEM AND IT IS THEIR INTEREST TO RUIN YOU. (1852, quoted in Cole and Filson, op. cit. pp. 418–19)

What struck Jones as 'ignorance or cowardice' is likely to strike us as a survival of traditional attitudes. The further interest of his remarks is that they apply to men and women (a large proportion of factory workers were, in fact, children) who belonged to the Marxian proletariat. For those who dealt, not with large employers, but with small masters, whose fortunes closely followed their own, 'class' must have seemed an unconvincing explanation of their difficulties and problems.

The Radicalism of artisan craftsmen certainly included an insistence on 'the rights of labour', but its objectives were primarily political not social revolution. With some justification Henry Mayhew argued that the real threat to social *disorder* in London came not from the well-informed and politically conscious artisans, but from the unskilled labourers. They were

as unpolitical as footmen, and instead of entertaining violent democratic opinions, they appear to have no political opinions whatever; or, if they do possess any, they rather lead towards the maintenance of 'things as they are,' than towards the ascendancy of the working people.

In comparing the (unskilled) coalwhippers with the operative tailors Mayhew described the former

as extremely proud of their having turned out to a man on the 10 April 1848, and become special constables for the maintenance of law and order on the day of the great Chartist demonstration.

Yet theft, drunkenness, and brutality were markedly more common among the labourers than among artisans: they were

nine times as dishonest, five times as drunken, and nine times as savage as the rest of the community.

Like the coalheavers, the London dustmen had no politics, and only the slightest appreciation of what Chartism was about, but

they have a deep-rooted antipathy to the police, the magistrates, and all connected with the administration of justice.

The costers generally believed that 'working-men know best' and gave their support to Chartism, but their fiercest resentment was also against the police:

I am assured that in the case of a political riot every 'coster' would seize his policeman. (*Mayhew's London*, ed. P. Quennell, Spring Books, pp. 536–7, 347, and 53)

These were truly the dangerous classes. They were not, at the same time, sharply class-conscious despite the fact that their poverty and way of life divided them so irrevocably from the middle class: they were, as yet, too ignorant, their lives too crowded with the struggle for existence, for them to participate in radical, urban politics.

The industrial town fostered political awareness because it demanded that working people should develop their own institutions, unsupervised by a 'ruling class', and largely untouched by an established religion whose object (among others!) had always been to inculcate social obedience. By the end of this period clearly the formative institutions, trade unions, chapels, friendly societies, cooperatives, pubs, the early music halls, and the street, have already begun to alter the balance of power within society. Yet, this said, it was also apparent that the working class was not capable, even in the 1840s when the incentive from distress was compelling, of effective independent action. Economically the working class was not homogeneous. Its institutions belonged, for the most part, to a minority. The strongly shaded regional character of British industrial development added further variety to working-class objectives. The national framework of working-class agitation was more ambitious in the Chartist era than at the beginning of the century, but it was still flimsy. Above all the structure of contemporary politics, either before or after 1832, while it could accommodate a popular, Radical onslaught on the privileges of the old order, obviously discouraged a working-class attack upon property and wealth. Education and self-improvement promoted social harmony as much, or more, than they promoted social discord. In the Introduction to *Self-Help*, Samuel Smiles described how the idea of the book had come to him after a visit to a 'northern town' where he had been invited to speak to an audience of young working men who had rented a hall – once used as a temporary Cholera Hospital – as a school room and meeting place:

[he had] addressed them on more than one occasion, citing examples of what other men had done, as illustrations of what each might, in greater or less degree, do for himself; and pointing out that their happiness and well-being as individuals in after life must necessarily depend mainly upon themselves – upon their own self-culture, self-discipline, and self-control – and, above all, on that honest and upright performance of individual duty which is the glory of manly character. [Smiles's visits were in 1844]

Whatever the pressures driving men into classes, and particularly working men, it would certainly be unwise to discount the impact of the appeal to individual, and not class, solutions to the disturbing experiences of industrial and urban life.

Further Reading

A good first approach to this subject is to compare Clapham's two chapters on 'The Face of the Country', Vol. I, Chapter 1 and Vol. II, Chapter 12 (in *An Economic History of Modern Britain* [Cambridge University Press, 1930]). Asa Briggs's *Victorian Cities* (Odhams, 1963) is extremely useful but deals only with the nineteenth century. There are an increasing number of good local studies, and recent additions to the *Victoria County Histories* contain valuable urban histories. There is regrettably nothing on the nineteenth century to match M. D. George's *London Life in the Eighteenth Century* (London School of Economics, 3rd ed., 1951), but H. J. Dyos's *Victorian Suburb* (Leicester University Press, 1961) is a pioneer study. Geoffrey Martin's 'The Town', *Visual History of Modern Britain* (Vista Books, 1961) is useful but has disappointingly few illustrations of industrial towns. T. W. Freeman's *The Conurbations of Great Britain* (Manchester University Press, 1959) contains a great deal of invaluable information.

On housing, M. W. Barley's 'The House and Home', *Visual History of Modern Britain* (Vista Books, 1963) is an essential starting point. Both Engels (Further Reading, Part II) and Chadwick (Further Reading, Part III) provide much contemporary information. T. S. Ashton's *Economic Fluctuations in England 1700–1800*, Chapter 4 (Oxford University Press, 1958) and Parry Lewis's *Building Cycles and Britain's Growth* (Macmillan, 1965) set house building in its economic context. John Summerson's *Georgian London* (Pelican, revised ed., 1962) has a general bearing on this chapter even though it is concerned primarily with houses of architectural merit.

On religion, E. P. Thompson's *The Making of the English Working Class*, Chapter XI (Pelican, 1968) has some sharp comments on Methodism and also argues that working-class consciousness was fully developed by 1830 (Chapter XVI). G. Kitson Clark's *The Making of Victorian England*, Chapter VI (Methuen, 1962) is a survey which extends back to the beginning of the century. The early sections of the chapters on the major churches in K. S. Inglis's *Churches and the Working Classes in Victorian England* (Routledge, 1963) are vital. O. Chadwick's *The Victorian Church* (Black, 1966) has a chapter on the Church and the labourer (Chapter 5). Asa Briggs's 'Economy and Society in the 1780s', *The Age of Improvement*, Chapter 1 (Longmans, 1959) touches upon many of the issues raised in this chapter.

PART IV
Government in the Early Industrial State

[26] WHY GOVERNMENT MATTERS

No society in the modern world could hope to achieve an Industrial Revolution without the energetic support of its government. This is why the efficiency of government is a matter of high priority for the underdeveloped countries. A misgoverned society cannot industrialize. In the advanced nations government now takes the leading role in economic planning: it is also a major investor in, and customer of, industry. In any description of the modern economy government and its policy occupy a central position.

By contrast the British Industrial Revolution was not the brainchild of government planners and economists. But this does not mean that the activities of government were irrelevant to either the causes or progress of the industrial revolution in Britain. 'Government' is the expression of a political system and the social structure which supports it. That eighteenth-century government in Britain did not obstruct the Industrial Revolution (or those who led it) was largely because British society was based upon a firm recognition of the rights of property. Property in Britain was not at the mercy of absolute monarchy. Nor was it weighed down by obligations to peasant farmers of a type often imposed on the European nobility by military minded monarchs. The English labourer had few traditional rights by the end of the eighteenth century. The decline of paternalistic central government was hastened by the collapse of the Stuarts and the Revolution of 1688. The first industrial revolution occurred in a country in which the activities of government were contracting and where it was widely believed that they should contract still further.

Paradoxically the Industrial Revolution was not followed by the withering away of the state. Apart from national defence the main business of the state was certainly the protection of property: the protection of 'labour' was very much a secondary consideration. But the Industrial Revolution created problems which could only be solved by an extension of the powers of the state. To defend property it became necessary to regulate the terms on which banks might operate. The opening of railways posed certain inescapable problems of regulation and the need to define a public interest. British government did not handle these problems with great relish but it did not altogether avoid them. Too great an emphasis on laissez-faire obscures the extent to which government had gone, by 1850, to equip itself with new powers and to achieve, however imperfectly, a role of great significance for the future of industrial society.

Even to carry out its limited functions eighteenth-century government had to be financed. The century of Industrial Revolution also included periods of prolonged and expensive wars. Government expenditure made an impact upon the economy which it is necessary to follow and assess. Taxation had economic as well as social consequences. Tariffs on commerce were essential to the revenue throughout this period: they also constitute the most obvious form of economic policy. The great debate on free trade was a debate about what economic policy was most effective for an industrial economy.

[27] GOVERNMENT REASSESSED: THE RISE OF LAISSEZ-FAIRE

Eighteenth-century government inherited a wide initiative in economic affairs. It could regulate both industry and commerce. An elaborate system of external tariffs had evolved from the Crown's ancient right to levy customs duties. Since the seventeenth century the customs revenue had been supplemented by a variety of 'excise' dues (or purchase taxes) on articles or foodstuffs in common use. Both customs and excise led to the widespread intrusion of government officials into economic life and provoked resentment as well as evasion. The main purpose of these taxes was to raise revenue but the customs also supplied a means of protecting British industry from its competitors. Government had no qualms about protective tariffs: nor did it hesitate to place an outright prohibition on foreign imports where these could not be controlled by tariffs. Merchants accepted this policy and so did most producers. The most favoured were given immunity from foreign competition. By contrast some exports, including corn, were encouraged by the payment of export bounties. British merchant shipping was shielded by the Navigation Act (1660) which restricted trade with the colonies to British ships sailing with British crews. There was no secret about the motive of these frankly interventionist policies. Statesmen could never forget, as Sir Josiah Child had written in 1694, that 'Profit and Power ought jointly to be considered'. This belief was the essence of what has since been called *Mercantilism*. Even Adam Smith, who had little time for most existing commercial policy, admitted that

as defence, however, is of much more importance than opulence, the act of navigation is, perhaps, the wisest of all the commercial regulations of England. (*Wealth of Nations*, 1776, Bk. IV)

Merchant seamen were essential to seapower and the link between commercial success and naval superiority was obvious to everyone in the eighteenth century.

The state's power to intervene and regulate was not confined to commerce. Both workshop and market place were subject to legislative control. The Elizabethan Statute of Artificers (1563) had empowered the J.P.s to fix the terms of apprenticeship and even to assess wages. The Poor Law went beyond the ancient Christian duty to provide for the destitute; it punished (severely) those who refused 'to labour as a true subject ought to do'. To establish a claim for relief the pauper had to prove 'settlement' in a parish and, because this was so often open to dispute, the parish officers exercised a real degree of control over the mobility of labour. Traditional government was hostile, at least in theory, to what is now known as 'labour migration': the migrant was often dismissed as a vagabond and a criminal. Regulations of this kind created a crowd of petty tyrants to harass the poor man and the labourer, but they were not as harmful economically as might appear at first glance. They were not, and probably could not, be enforced rigorously. In the case of the Poor Law the issue of settlement was invoked by parish officers who wished (as most would) to disclaim responsibility for a man and his family; *successful* migration was of no interest to them. Similarly the ancient powers of the justices to fix the price of bread were scarcely ever exercised.

The fabric of state intervention was, then, already dilapidated by the eighteenth century. Interventionist policies were discredited after the Stuarts had misused them in an attempt to buttress the position of the Crown. A new emphasis upon the role and claims of the individual came to compete with the older view which made government responsible for social harmony and national well-being. The whole apparatus of regulation, including the working of the taxation system, was then brought under the enlightened enquiry of Adam Smith. Laissez-faire became articulate. Government regulation, it was argued, hampered and distorted enterprise. The smuggler, for example, acquired the character of a child of (economic) nature whose sins were really attributable to a perverse environment: he was

a person who, though no doubt highly blameable for violating the laws of his country, is frequently incapable of violating those of natural justice, and would have been, in every respect, an excellent citizen, had not the laws of his country made that a crime which nature never meant to be so. (*Wealth of Nations*, Bk. V, Ch. 3)

It was absurb to think that government knows best. In his enthusiasm for individual action Smith was often close to absurdity himself. By seeking his own gain, he argued, the individual

promotes the interest of society more effectually than when he really intends to promote it.

This warning was particularly applicable to government:

The statesman, who should attempt to direct private people in what manner they ought to employ their capitals, would not only load himself with unnecessary attention, but assume an authority which could safely be trusted, not only to no single person, but to no council whatever, and which would be nowhere so dangerous as in the hands of a man who had the folly and presumption enough to fancy himself fit to exercise it. (Bk. IV, Ch. 2)

It was just this authority which government claimed when it favoured the domestic manufacturer:

To give the monopoly of the home market to the produce of domestic industry, in any particular art or manufacture, is in some measure to direct private people in what manner they ought to employ their capitals, and must, in almost all cases, be either a useless or a hurtful regulation.

In place of a government inclined to protect and regulate Adam Smith looked to one which would allow free trade and permit buyers and sellers, consumers and producers, to meet in a free market.

There is an attractively close link between the ideas of the *Wealth of Nations* and the needs of an early industrial society. His attack upon the apprenticeship regulations of the Statute of Artificers was also an assertion of his belief in a free market for labour:

The patrimony of a poor man lies in the strength and dexterity of his hands; and to hinder him from employing his strength and dexterity in what manner he thinks proper without injury to his neighbour, is a plain violation of this most sacred property. . . . To judge whether he is fit to be employed, may surely be trusted to the discretion of the employers whose interest it so much concerns. The affected anxiety of the lawgiver, lest they should employ an improper person, is evidently as impertinent as it is oppressive. (Bk. I, Ch. 10, Part III)

The 'proper' person was the qualified apprentice: craftsmen themselves clearly had no quarrel with legislation which protected their position. But in the new industries the apprenticeship regulations did not apply. The apprenticeship clauses of the 1563 statute were repealed in 1813 and 1814. The benefit to 'poor men' was far from clear. Together with the apprenticeship regulations had gone the attempt to determine wages by public action. When the Nottingham stockingers appealed to Parliament in 1812 for some alleviation of their hardship they did not imagine that it would consider a minimum wage for their trade:

It is true that Government has interfered in the regulation of wages in times long since gone by; but the writings of Dr Adam Smith have altered the opinion, of the polished part of society, on this subject. Therefore to attempt to advance wages by parliamentary influence, would be as absurd as an attempt to regulate the winds. (quoted in E. P. Thompson, *The Making of the English Working Class*, p. 536)

The alteration in opinion was not all the work of Adam Smith. It went back at least into the early eighteenth century.

In this new society men had to look to themselves, to their own enterprise and thriftiness, and to their own hard work to see them through. This outlook was central to the message of the great Victorian publicist, Samuel Smiles:

Whatever is done *for* men or classes, to a certain extent takes away the stimulus and necessity of doing for themselves; and where men are subjected to over-guidance and over-government, the inevitable tendency is to render them comparatively helpless. . . . Laws, wisely administered, will secure men in the enjoyment of the fruits of their labour, whether of mind or body, at comparatively small personal sacrifice; but no laws, however stringent, can make the idle industrious, the thriftless provident, or the drunken sober. (*Self-Help*)

If this was the prevailing view by the 1850s then the history of government during the Industrial Revolution might well be described as one of progressive withdrawal, of the triumph, in fact, of laissez-faire.

There is some truth in this. Statesmen certainly spoke the language of laissez-faire. In the same year that the Nottingham stockingers made their appeal to Parliament, Lord Liverpool, the Prime Minister, noted that 'it was undoubtedly true that the less commerce and manufactures were meddled with the more they were likely to prosper'. His Home Secretary, Lord Sidmouth, had even written an ode to Adam Smith; not surprisingly Sidmouth's attitude to the distress of 1812 was that 'man cannot create abundance where Providence has inflicted scarcity'. Another source of this complacency and pessimism was Thomas Malthus's famous *Essay on Population* in which he predicted that population would outrun the resources of agriculture. Adam Smith advised governments to do nothing because this would encourage expansion, Malthus because nothing they could do would prevent the equation between population and food supply from moving to its own, inexorable, solution. Yet in many ways laissez-faire was a counsel of perfection. Governments could not pursue it without criticism and nor could it always be reconciled with conscience. The traditional view of government's responsibilities, especially towards the weak and helpless, was never totally submerged.

Even more important was the fact that some features of the new society demanded that government undertake some new tasks. British governments in the nineteenth century had none of the resources which would have been required for anything like a modern attempt at economic planning. The drift of intellectual opinion was against interventionist policies and, in consequence, it was difficult for government to approach its problems with a coherent strategy. If corruption gradually weakened its hold over administration this did not mean that what took its place was a clear philosophy of government. As Sir John Clapham has written:

'Things were in the saddle and rode mankind', and the state let them ride. Sometimes it seemed to be acting on a reasoned policy of abstention; more often, perhaps, it was not acting because it had no clear idea of what to do for the best. (*Economic History of Modern Britain*, Vol. I, p. 378)

The virtues of government were, then, largely negative. It succeeded in preserving order during the period of the Industrial Revolution and, in the nineteenth century, there were clear signs that it was doing so with increased efficiency. It succeeded, although only just, in providing an expanding economy with a stable and adequate coinage. A serious shortage of small coin had arisen by the late eighteenth century. Some manufacturers were forced to pay their workpeople in tokens of their own minting. The supply of copper coins did not improve until the first recoinage of copper was contracted out to Matthew Boulton in 1797–9 but not until 1821 was the Mint, now completely reequipped by Boulton, able to meet all the demands made on it for copper coins, and the issue of private tokens was made illegal. In 1817 Boulton's machinery had brought the first of a new series of silver coins, thus halting the less widespread, but more disturbing, issue of private silver tokens. Prolonged failure to reform the Mint could well have had serious economic and social repercussions. Quite as important as the provision of these basic services was the comparative cheapness of eighteenth-century government. Between the end of the seventeenth century and about 1770 the proportion of the national income devoted to government and defence may have fallen from 7 per cent to 4 per cent (Deane and Cole, *British Economic Growth 1688–1959*, p. 156). The dangers of 'public prodigality and misconduct' did not escape Adam Smith but he was confident that

The uniform, constant, and uninterrupted effort of every man to better his condition . . . is frequently powerful enough to maintain the natural progress of things towards improvement, in spite of the extravagance of government, and of the greatest errors of administration. (*Wealth of Nations*, Bk. II, Ch. 3)

Taxpayers had to accustom themselves to a much higher level of government expenditure during the Napoleonic War. In the nineteenth century the demand for cheap government became insistent. It was then closely linked to middle-class hostility towards what was believed to be aristocratic mismanagement. The Administrative Reform Association campaigned during the Crimean War for the remodelling of public administration on the lines of successful private business. Unfortunately the war eventually provided as much evidence of the dishonesty of businessmen as the incompetence of aristocrats. In any case quiet reform in government departments had been begun under the Younger Pitt.

[28] COMMERCIAL POLICY AND TRADE

Trade regulation and its effects

The commercial policies of the eighteenth century were insufficiently restrictive to prevent a notable expansion in international trade. It is true that the most remarkable growth was in the trade with colonial, non-European regions, and with the Mediterranean area, rather than with Britain's nearer neighbours in North-Western Europe. It was, significantly, French luxuries which figured prominently in the smugglers' cargoes. The colonial trade, which fed into Britain either raw materials or popular consumer goods unobtainable in Europe, was organized in Britain's interest (or, as some would have had it, in the interests of the merchants engaged in the trade). It was the basis of the highly profitable entrepôt trade. Under the Navigation Acts of 1651 and 1660 (which were modified, but not abandoned in 1822 and 1825) colonial trade was restricted to British ships: other colonial powers pursued similar policies into the nineteenth century. The Navigation Acts were naturally favoured by the shipping interests: perhaps colonial trade might have been

brisker had Britain allowed other trading nations to compete in
the freighting of colonial cargoes. In fact the presence of American merchants in the West Indies was recognized by Pitt in
1795: they were not permitted to ship West Indian goods to
England, but it is difficult to believe that imports of West
Indian goods were much curtailed by the Navigation Laws. This
may have been the effect of the taxation of sugar, and certainly
the preference given to West Indian sugar after the Emancipa-
tion of 1833 did deprive the British consumer of the cheaper
'foreign' sugars (which were still slave grown). In colonial
markets, as elsewhere, there was a fundamental mechanism con-
necting imports and exports: rising national income in Britain
enabled imports to rise and stepped up the purchasing power of
Britain's customers. In the West Indian trade, where Britain
had become accustomed to an adverse balance of trade, exports
grew more rapidly than either imports or the total volume of
trade in the second half of the eighteenth century:

Official Values

	Imports	Exports	Total Volume
1750–1 (England)	£1,484,000	£449,000	£1,933,000
1797–8 (U.K.)	£5,982,000	£4,612,000	£10,594,000

(*The Abstract of British Historical Statistics*, p. 312)

The expansion of the West Indian trade took place within the
framework of imperial regulation: the same cannot be said for
trade with mainland America, or at least with the U.S.A. after
Independence. The economies of the sugar islands and the
mainland were similar in one important respect: the need to
import manufactured goods from Europe. The Navigation Acts
required the West Indians to sell their sugar, and the Southern
planters their tobacco, in England. This was no imposition because English manufactures were cheap and of good quality.
The North felt differently because its own mercantile development was hampered and because its farmers had, as yet, little
to sell to Europe. After Independence the rapid shift to cotton
growing in the South linked the economies of Britain and the
U.S.A. in an Atlantic trade which was of the utmost importance

to the Industrial Revolution. By 1850 25 per cent of British imports came from the U.S.A.: from 54 per cent in 1815 the U.S. share of the supply of raw cotton to Britain had risen to 81 per cent by 1846–50. By the 1830s Britain was the major market for American wheat and wheat flour: even in the first quarter of the nineteenth century the U.S. was exporting an average of 1,029,000 kilos (81,000 quarters) of grain (mostly wheat) to Britain. In the export trade a significant feature of the Atlantic trade was the important role of manufactured goods *other than* cotton fabrics or yarn: from 1816 to 1850 British woollens almost invariably commanded a larger market than cottons, and the Americans were Britain's best customers for bar iron, unwrought steel, hardwares and cutlery (for details see J. Potter, 'The Atlantic Economy 1815–1860', in *Studies in the Industrial Revolution*, ed. L. S. Pressnell, 1960). Britain thus secured crucial advantages from the enterprise of American pioneers: the Atlantic trade provided valuable encouragement to the diversification of industrial growth in Britain.

The Americans financed their adverse balance of visible trade with Britain (although this was ending by 1825) through their own international commerce, by the sale of their farm produce to the West Indies and the other areas of European settlement in the Americas, and British investment. The Americans were as much reliant upon the British economy after 1783 as they had been earlier in the century. Despite the quick growth of the American cotton industry from the 1820s it was scarcely less true in the second quarter of the nineteenth century than it had been in 1766 that

The American is apparalled from head to foot in our manufactures . . . he scarcely drinks, sits, moves, labours or recreates himself, without contributing to the emolument of the mother country. (*London Magazine*; quoted in E. Wright, *The Fabric of Freedom*, 1965)

Yet while the Americans won some concessions from British governments after Independence it was not until the nineteenth century that Britain made any serious modification in the policy of trade regulation. The economic facts did not call for panic

measures to 'liberalize' trade. Quite the contrary: they argued
for a tougher policy or, at least, for one of 'no change'. In the
long term government might have been well advised to encourage Anglo-American trade by allowing the Americans free
access to the West Indies. But 'courting' the Americans was
rejected because, as one of its opponents insisted

Every day's experience shows that this country, from the nature and
quality of its manufactures, and from the ascendancy it has acquired
in commerce, will command three-fourths of the American trade. The
American merchants solicit a correspondence and beg for credit,
because they feel their own want of capital, they know our traders
are more liberal, and our goods cheaper and better, than any in
Europe. (Lord Sheffield, 1783; quoted in W. Brock, *The Effect of the
Loss of the American Colonies upon British Policy*, Historical Association, 1957, p. 7)

The Navigation Acts continued to ensure that the commercial
advantages of the Atlantic trade remained with Britain. The
vitally important (for the Americans) West Indian trade was
restricted to British ships until 1830 (the Jay Treaty of 1794
allowed only small U.S. coasters into West Indian ports).
Restrictionist as this policy was, and despite its unfortunate
side effects like diplomatic tension between Britain and the U.S.,
the war of 1812–15, and the postwar tariffs imposed by the
Americans on imported manufactures, it did not seriously
hinder the growth of the Atlantic trade.

However trade regulation operated in the Atlantic after 1783
it did not curtail American demand for British goods. But by
the time of the Younger Pitt it was apparent that Britain's
trading relations with Europe were in some need of overhaul
and reassessment. A policy of high tariffs was ill suited to an
industrial and trading nation which had already won an important lead over its rivals. Of course the secret of English success
in foreign markets was the cheapness and the superiority of
English products combined, as in the well known case of Josiah
Wedgwood, with professional salesmanship. If the economies of
scale and technical innovation were to be held it was vital to
enlarge markets and contact new sources of demand (there are

similar considerations behind Britain's present anxiety to enter
the Common Market). It was not just his success at home which
made Wedgwood keen to sell abroad. In March 1771 he reasoned
that his stock was too large 'and nothing but a *foreign* market
... will ever keep it within any tolerable bound'. Neither high
tariffs nor the traditional supremacy and prestige of French
porcelain deterred him from planning anything less than the
'conquest' of France in Burslem. His entry into the European
market was planned with the greatest care. Wedgwood fully
understood the position of the aristocracy as the arbiters of
taste and his first effort was to place his products in their salons
and dining rooms. He set up foreign warehouses to ensure quick
delivery, he offered credit and tempted first customers with
discounts, he prepared catalogues in the European languages:
in a memo of November 1773 he noted that 'we shall want some
hundreds of small dishes to send abroad as patterns the next
spring' (his was a classic consumer trade, dependent upon new
designs, their secrets jealously guarded). Wedgwood's success
was remarkable and it was achieved without any widespread
demolition of European tariffs. But his interests in new markets
and his confidence in the superiority of British manufactures
made Wedgwood argue for commercial conciliation if not for any
wider strategy of free trade. His was one voice which urged upon
Pitt the desirability of a commercial treaty with France: this
was actually concluded in 1786 (the Eden Treaty).

Adam Smith had already drawn attention to the importance
of the French market for English manufactures: 'national
animosity' and 'mercantile jealousy' had prevented the development of Anglo-French commerce. Both parties should think
again:

The wealth of a neighbouring nation, though dangerous in war and
politics, is certainly advantageous in trade. In a state of hostility it
may enable our enemies to maintain fleets and armies superior to our
own; but in a state of peace and commerce it must likewise enable
them to exchange with us to a greater value, and to afford a better
market, either for the immediate produce of our own industry, or for
whatever is purchased with that produce. ... If those two countries,

however, were to consider their real interest ... the commerce of France might be more advantageous to Great Britain than that of any other country. (*Wealth of Nations*, Bk. IV, Ch. 3, Part II)

Smith went on to emphasize the scope offered by an easily accessible market of 24 million as compared with the smaller and distant market afforded by the North American colonists. When Pitt presented his case for the commercial treaty with France to the Commons in 1787 he, too, stressed the size of the French market. He saw the British and French economies as largely complementary and had few fears for the British manufacturer. He asked the House

Would not more of our earthenware, and other articles, which, under all the disadvantages that they formerly suffered, still, from their intrinsic superiority, force their way regularly into France, now be sent thither; and would not the aggregate of our manufactures be greatly and eminently benefited in going to this market loaded only with duties from twelve to ten, and in one instance with only five per cent? ... A market of so many millions of people – a market so near and so prompt – a market of expeditious and certain return – of necessary and extensive consumption, thus added to the manufactures and commerce of Britain, was an object which we ought to look up to with eager and satisfied ambition. To procure this, we certainly ought not to scruple to give liberal conditions. (*English Historical Documents*, Vol. XI, p. 557)

Objections against the treaty with France were, of course, political. Pitt was eloquent in persuading the Commons to forget old hatreds: 'to suppose that any nation could be unalterably the enemy of another was weak and childish'. But the manufacturers were not all on the side of the future. In 1785 they had opposed Pitt's scheme to place England and Ireland on a common tariff and, in 1787, they were divided over the French treaty. Wedgwood and the Birmingham men were, however, enthusiastic in 1787: economically they feared the Irish more than the French. James Watt wrote to Wedgwood to cheer him with news of Birmingham support for the treaty:

I was present ... at a public meeting with about 100 of the principal inhabitants, merchants and manufacturers, where success to the treaty and a perpetual peace with France were drunk and followed by three unanimous cheers. (Mantoux, *The Industrial Revolution in the Eighteenth Century*, p. 391)

The treaty did lead to an increase in trade with France. Wedgwood had cause for satisfaction. In 1785 exports of earthenware to France were valued at £641: by 1789 they had risen to £7,920. Yet there was to be no sudden switch from an era of high tariffs and mercantilist regulation. The French Wars put an end to Pitt's experiments in freer trade: revenue now took precedence over other considerations and the government's main contribution to demand came from its own increased expenditures on war materials.

The coming of free trade: the motives and implications

The relaxation of tariff policy and trade regulation did not immediately follow the close of the great war in 1815. Perhaps the explanation of this immobility in policy which makes most sense was the heightened importance of the customs to the total revenue of government after the Commons insisted on the repeal of the Income Tax in 1816, showing what Castlereagh correctly, but tactlessly, described as 'ignorant opposition to taxation'. While the customs had rarely provided more than 25 per cent of government income in the last quarter of the eighteenth century, from the 1820s the customs frequently contributed 40 per cent or more and its share did not begin to fall until after 1850. Further, the Corn Law of 1815, which prohibited the entry of foreign grain into Britain until the domestic price had reached 80/- a quarter, was an act of protection which discouraged any experiment in freer trade by Britain's neighbours. Farmers and landowners hoped that protection would ensure them the high prices and rents to which they had become accustomed during the war. Although manufacturers were by no means prepared to move into an era of free trade in 1815, the Corn Laws were quickly seized upon by Radical opinion as an example of the misuse of political power by the landed interest. The 1815 tariff was modified in 1822, and replaced by a sliding scale of duties in

1828: this scale was itself revised in 1842. After the formation of the Anti-Corn Law League in 1838 the corn tariff was the central issue in a dramatic and colourful confrontation between the landed interest and the industrial middle class. The League argued that the tariff cut away the purchasing power of both Britain's overseas customers and her own working population. This emphasis on the importance of stimulating demand is interesting and clearly had some relevance during the world depression of the late 1830s and early 1840s. The League was cogent evidence of a new aggressiveness among manufacturers, a self-confident assurance that their products were what the world wanted. The financial journalist and commercial diplomat, John Bowring, who later negotiated Britain's commercial 'entry' into China and the Far East, told a Manchester audience in 1839 of

What a satisfaction it is to every man going from the West to the East, when he finds one of the ancient Druses clothed in garments with which one of our industrious countrymen provided him. What a delight it is in going to the Holy City to stop within the caravan at Nazareth – to see four thousand individuals and scarcely be able to fix upon one to whom your country has not presented some comfort or decoration. (quoted in W. L. Burn, *The Age of Equipoise*, p. 64)

Yet this market was unlikely to be affected by the Corn Laws. This was more likely to be the case with Britain's European customers. There was also reason to believe that the Corn Laws, even under the sliding scales, favoured fluctuation in bread prices – and that tariffs and the excise bore most heavily upon the working-class budget and sapped home demand for industrial goods.

Various gestures towards inflating home demand by lifting tariffs or excise duties were made by the Whigs in the 1830s, but the first important approach to free trade was that made by Sir Robert Peel between 1841 and 1846. Peel was well aware of the need to inflate demand in the early 1840s, and the depression had also aroused concern about Britain's access to international markets, but the most direct incentive to his reforms came from the growing weight of official opinion behind the case for the simplification of the tariff system. The failings of an over-elaborate tariff, the administrative advantages of a simpler book of rates, had been seen by both Pitt and Huskisson and, of course, by the customs officers themselves. Tariff cuts were known to encourage trade and reduce smuggling. In 1784, when the absurdly high duty of 119 per cent on tea was cut to $12\frac{1}{2}$ per cent, the result was startling: while only 2,250,000 kilos (4,962,000 lb) went through the customs in 1784, the figure for 1785 was 7,396,000 kilos (16,307,000 lb). If it was primarily revenue that the customs were meant to provide then this might as well be served by tariff reductions as by a Chinese Wall of high tariffs which either provoked smugglers' evasion or, worse, prevented trade altogether. A thoroughgoing reform of the customs demanded straight thinking about the basic *purpose* which they were intended to serve. By the end of the 1830s this could not be delayed much longer. As the challenging report of the Select Committee on Import Dues (1840) put it:

The Tariff of the United Kingdom presents neither congruity nor unity of purpose; no general principles seem to have been applied ... [it] often aims at incompatible ends; the duties are sometimes meant to be both productive of revenue and for protective objects, which are frequently inconsistent with each other; hence they sometimes operate to the complete exclusion of foreign produce, and in so far no revenue can of course be received. ... They do not make the receipt of revenue the main consideration, but allow that primary object of fiscal regulations to be thwarted by an attempt to protect a great variety of particular interests, at the expense of the revenue, and of the commercial intercourse with other countries. (*English Historical Documents*, Vol. XII (I), p. 419)

The Committee's plea for the 'simplification' of the tariff found a response in Peel's fiscal programme after 1841: in cutting the duties on imported raw materials, like timber, and on foodstuffs, Peel showed that he was able to distinguish between the revenue and protective functions of the tariff. Because he inherited from the Whigs a history of deficit budgets it was considerations of revenue to which he attached most weight. Trusting to the continuance of the commercial expansion of the twenty-five years since 1815, Peel risked a policy of serious tariff reduction. He thus related government income more closely than before to commercial growth and accepted the implication that, should it falter, further tariff cuts might be a necessary instrument in encouraging the revival of business and trade.

Had it not been for the tragedy of the Irish famine Peel might have delayed indefinitely an answer to the charge that he had sacrificed protection to free trade. If protection seemed important to the Tory squires it had long since ceased to dominate the thinking of government and its advisers. The alliance between government and the world market did not begin in 1846. The Corn Laws were largely an irrelevance to the problem of Britain's food supply during the decades of industrial revolution: repeal helped to stabilize prices in periods of scarcity (which usually affected all Europe) but did not enable overseas farmers to undercut British prices until much later in the nineteenth century. The Corn Laws were parliamentary, not government, policy. Administrative reform of the customs had begun under Pitt. He had consolidated the customs and excise duties in 1787 and his work of reorganization was taken up again after the war and was especially rapid during Huskisson's period at the Board of Trade (1823–7), during which a wide range of import duties were lowered. In 1803, as a complement to the policy of dock extension at the major ports, the entrepôt trade was relieved of cumbersome negotiations with the customs by an act which allowed reexports to be stored in 'bonded' warehouses. The attainment of a more rational, or less irrational customs system owed much to the administrative enterprise of nineteenth century customs officials. Their contribution was important because rationalization was almost invariably linked to the reduction of duties. A major landmark in this field was the publication in 1825 of J. Deacon Hume's *Consolidated Laws of the Customs*. When the 'Custom House Bible', as it was known, was revised in 1833 another official noted that the changes consisted 'almost wholly of Reductions of Duties and Easements of Restrictions'. Perhaps it is equally significant that one of the best accounts of industrial and commercial growth in the early nineteenth century should have been provided by an official of the Board of Trade, G. R. Porter, who had set up the Board's statistical department in 1834 and published his *Progress of the Nation* in 1836.

In embracing free trade Britain gave formal recognition to the importance of overseas trade to the British economy. It became equally doubtful whether the old system of regulating trade was either useful or necessary. There was no hurried relaxation of the Navigation Acts after 1815. The argument that it was necessary to protect British shipping because the merchant marine amounted to a reserve Navy continued to carry weight and, indeed, did so until the time when it could be forecast that the Navy would rely on ironclads in future wars – and not on the 'wooden walls'. Again, although there was little left after 1815 of the eighteenth-century world of competing commercial empires, European nations and the U.S.A. were all prepared to exploit trade regulations and discriminatory tariffs as the basis of their commercial diplomacy. British policy was naturally a matter of wide concern to other states. Concessions had to be made to the Americans and the continental powers lost no opportunity to press for equal treatment. But there was no hurried retreat from past policies, merely a recognition that Britain had more to lose than to gain from commercial warfare. As Huskisson explained in 1826:

His Majesty's Government have thought it more prudent and more dignified to enter into amicable arrangements with other powers, founded on the basis of mutual interest, and entire reciprocity of advantages, rather than embark in a contest of commercial hostility and reciprocal exclusion. (*English Historical Documents*, Vol. XI, p. 568)

Nevertheless Huskisson's Navigation Act of 1825 was entitled 'an Act for the encouragement of British shipping and navigation': it persisted in the enumeration of goods which could only enter the country in British ships, or in ships of either the producing nation or of that from which the goods were imported. Non-European products could not be imported from Europe. Even where trade was opened to foreign shipping it did not necessarily compete on equal terms in British ports and it was in this field that the 'reciprocity' arrangements of Huskisson operated. Further changes in British policy became unavoidable by the 1840s. The Free Traders included the Navigation Laws in their criticism of traditional policy. European powers were still irritated by the regulations. From an administrative viewpoint the reciprocity treaties had made for complexity rather than the opposite. In 1847 the Navigation Laws were suspended, and in 1849 they were repealed.

Britain's fumbling progress towards free trade was a response to market conditions after 1815. Until the mid-1820s Britain faced an adverse movement in the *terms* of trade in the international market – i.e. export prices fell faster than import prices: in the first decade after the war export prices dropped quite sharply and, although this was matched by some fall in import prices, during the 1830s import prices threatened to return to the levels of the early 1820s. Under these conditions there existed a powerful incentive to increase exports and, of course, the cheapness and quality of British manufactured goods enabled this to be done. At the same time northern European markets, while remaining the greatest single outlet for British products actually contracted in the 1820s (wartime purchases had been boosted by British subsidies to the allies) and only began to grow again in the late 1830s (for the figures see Part V, Overseas Trade, Table D, p. 224). This was a disappointing result but it was not to be explained by tariff or trade policies. Continental purchases of British goods did not begin to forge ahead at all dramatically until industrialization began its progress in Western Europe after 1850. Even then Britain was usually in deficit on her *visible* trade with Europe. What was worrying about the postwar period was that Britain's overall surplus on transactions with other nations remained rather small. It was income from shipping, insurance, and other services, together with rising earnings from overseas investments, which made it possible for Britain to support a deficit on visible trade. The deficit also helped other nations in their purchases of British goods. In this difficult postwar period the

self-confidence of British manufacturers was, however, sufficient
to challenge the wisdom of traditional trade policies:

> Look yonder where the engines toil:
> These England's arms of conquest are,
> The trophies of her bloodless war:
>   Brave weapons these.
> Victorious over wave and soil,
> With these she sails, she weaves, she tills,
> Pierces the everlasting hills,
>   And spans the seas.
> (W. M. Thackeray, 'May Day Ode', 1851, quoted in Clapham,
>   Vol. 2, p. 1)

By 1852 industry stood exposed to whatever winds might blow:
apart from silk, which carried a duty of 15 per cent, no duty
higher than 10 per cent faced any manufactured commodity
entering a British port.

Free trade was an outcome of the Industrial Revolution not
its cause. But its significance was immense. By committing the
British economy to international trade, by attaching the
British Industrial Revolution to a mechanism of world demand,
the governments of the mid-nineteenth century willed the
emergence of a world market and ensured that the Industrial
Revolution should not remain an isolated event. With typically
thorough insight Marx could already read the signs of the
twentieth-century world in 1848:

In place of the old wants, satisfied by the productions of the country,
we find new wants, requiring for their satisfaction the produce of
distant lands and climes. In place of the old local and national seclu-
sion and self-sufficiency, we have intercourse in every direction,
universal inter-dependence of nations. (*Communist Manifesto*, Progress ed., p. 45)

The wider context within which the Industrial Revolution
occurred is often forgotten. In 1750 world population was
between 650 and 850 million: by 1850 it had reached 1,100–
1,300 million. In Europe population had risen from 110–130
million to 210 million (265 million if Russia is included). The

American population had gone from 10–20 million to 50–70 million and the population of Asia was almost as large in 1850 as the world total a century earlier. In all history the opportunities for enterprise had never been so great as they were in this remarkable century.

[29] FISCAL POLICY AND THE ROLE OF GOVERNMENT SPENDING

The needs of the state were simply defined in the eighteenth and nineteenth centuries. A revenue was required to defend Britain from her enemies and to protect the rights of property at home. Fiscal skills were employed to curtail expenditure and to keep taxation at a minimum. Except during the emergency decades of the Napoleonic War government did not control a sufficiently large share of national resources to exercise a profound influence upon economic development. In 1792 total government expenditure (including local government) was £22 million or 11 per cent of the Gross National Product. By 1814 expenditure had climbed to £123 million or 29 per cent of the GNP: this proportion fell to 19 per cent in 1822, 16 per cent in 1831, 11 per cent in 1841, and 12 per cent in 1850. Nevertheless in absolute terms expenditure rose between the late eighteenth century and the mid-nineteenth century; government spent £66 million in 1850, or £20 per head as compared with £14·4 in 1792 (figures from Alan T. Peacock and Jack Wiseman, *The Growth of Public Expenditure in the United Kingdom*, Princeton, 1961). As price levels had fallen between 1792 and 1850 the increase in expenditure was, in effect, rather more than the figures suggest. Throughout the period government expenditure was concentrated upon three services; the support of the army and navy, the relief of the poor, and debt charges (which usually accounted for approximately 50 per cent of expenditure). Government income was primarily derived from the customs and excise, but also from stamp duties and post office charges; the only important direct tax on wealth or income in the eighteenth century was the Land Tax. Until the 1780s the excise yielded an income comparable to the customs, but from then onwards was progressively dwarfed by it. Until the later 1820s the excise retained its eighteenth-century primacy as the preeminent source of revenue. But from the 1830s it was rapidly supplanted in first place by the customs. Despite the overwhelming preference for indirect taxation throughout this period, necessity twice dictated the introduction of an income tax; it was first imposed in 1799, was quickly dropped in 1802 only to be brought back in the following year and to last out the war until it was abolished in 1816. Robert Peel restored the income tax in 1842. The result was to upgrade the importance of direct taxation but, even in 1850, the Land and Income Taxes between them produced only £10·1 million in revenue while the customs and excise together yielded £37·3 million.

What were the implications of these fiscal policies? Government was clearly not attempting to use taxation to redistribute income. Indirect taxation bore heavily upon the working class. Government expenditure created employment, in its own offices, in shipyards and armaments works as well as in the army and navy, and a high proportion of the payments which it made took the form of transfers to individuals, either government stock holders or paupers. Under the exceptional conditions of war, with swollen armed forces and continuous contracts for their needs of food, clothing, and weapons, some sections of the working class might benefit from government activity. After the war this ceased to apply. The Poor Law of 1834 led to a quite drastic cut in expenditure upon poor relief and there was little significant increase in the provision of services which benefited the working class: local government provided only the most basic amenities. In the eighteenth century trunk roads were committed to the care of turnpike trusts. The paving, lighting, and cleansing of streets, together with the laying of sewers, frequently became entrusted to independent commissions, owing to the state only their right to corporate existence and the power to levy a rate. Water supply was the province of private companies. Although there were indications of change by the 1830s it remained true that local 'government' was largely confined to the relief of paupers and the harrying of vagrants. Where 'improvement' was wanted, and when the capital could be raised, it was first instinct to allow these services to be run as business ventures.

Between 1756 and 1815 there were thirty-six years of war. Since the national debt had first been floated at the end of the seventeenth century, war was financed primarily by long-term loans secured through the issue of Bank of England stock. As the new system of public finance proved itself, and the national debt became a source of confidence rather than alarm (it was £78 million in 1750, £241 million in 1792, £840 million in 1820), interest rates fell. In the first quarter of the eighteenth century interest rates, understood as the yield on bank stock, fell from around 8 per cent to around 5 per cent: thereafter 3–4 per cent was the normal rate, although higher yields were experienced in both the American and French wars after 1778. Because the usury laws kept other interest rates to 5 per cent (the government was always entitled to exceed this) the creation of a differential of 1–2 per cent exercised an important influence over eighteenth-century investment. Insofar as industry was financed from its own savings the interest rate was of limited impact. But it is generally agreed that low interest rates did encourage eighteenth-century investment in 'public utilities' like canals, turnpikes, docks and harbours, or urban improvements. These were the projects which suffered most when interest rates rose, as they did if the government was forced into heavy short-term borrowing. But confidence in the nation's public finance was a precondition for investment on the eighteenth-century scale and it was reflected in low interest rates. After the upheaval of the Napoleonic War the yield on consols settled down at about $3\frac{1}{2}$ per cent. Consols were an essential instrument in the financial system: they were the most 'liquid' (easily disposable) investment as well as the most secure and the banks customarily kept a proportion of their assets in government stock.

[30] BANKING AND CREDIT: A GOVERNMENT RESPONSIBILITY?

The wartime banking boom

Waging war is a wasteful activity and it is a mistake to suppose that the Napoleonic War was any exception. During the war government certainly commanded a large share of the nation's resources: some industries, like the iron industry, received a sudden stimulus. The large subsidies paid to allies were partly returned in orders for British industry. But in general the war was a difficult time for industry as wages and costs were pushed up by the inflationary impact of high government expenditure. Large incomes were more heavily taxed. Yet there was nothing like a modern attempt to restrict profits or direct labour. Although capital was diverted from private to public use during the war its control remained as markedly concentrated as before. Where the war was influential was in prompting the rapid development of the banking system. One estimate indicates that the number of banks rose from 280 in 1793 to 626 in 1815. Despite a rash of failures after 1815 an informed observer could write in 1821 'there are bankers, or bankers' agents within ten miles of every place, almost'. The reasons behind this boom in banking are complex. High agricultural earnings in wartime were certainly one cause of rising deposits: government itself gave business to the banks by using them in the collection and forwarding of taxation. The banks were already relieving the shortage of currency by issuing their own notes (cheques were only in common use in the London area, where the Bank of England had a monopoly of note issue). But the major cause of the wartime increase in note issue was the Bank of England's decision to suspend cash payments – the convertibility of its notes into gold – in 1797. The suspension was the Bank's, and the government's answer to exceptional conditions. To finance continental allies Britain had to export gold. The unusually high price which gold was making in international markets created a further problem by widening the existing discrepancy between the Mint (face) value of the British gold coinage and its metallic value. From 1797 to 1821 gold coins virtually disappeared from circulation: instead the country relied upon bank notes, about half of which were Bank of England notes while the remainder were issued by the country banks.

Bank notes were one way of extending credit. Of course there was a risk that banks would overissue in relation to their deposits. The war years produced its crop of bank failures, but most bankers seem to have acted responsibily enough under novel and tempting conditions. The war also caused greater use of other credit instruments. The most important of these was the bill of exchange. A bill was an undertaking to settle an account at a fixed date, say three months, which had been 'accepted' by a bank: it could then be sold at a discount (i.e. less a charge for interest and risk) and the bill then circulated as paper, collecting any number of subsequent endorsements until it matured. Like notes, bills were thought to contribute to wartime inflation. The Bank of England, which customarily acted as the discounter of last resort, refused to discount bills which matured after sixty-five days or those which were not secured by a real exchange of goods. In fact the volume of discounting undertaken by the Bank did mount in the war. The bill was an indispensable instrument of trade and the Bank's policy clearly took this into account. But there were countless bills which the Bank would not handle and, further, the whole mechanism of discounting was threatened by the high return on money which the war brought about. Although the Usury Laws were still in force they could not prevent speculative dealings on the Stock Exchange where it was possible to make 'capital gains' which represented a return on money far in excess of the legal 5 per cent. As the country banks found that their London agents were increasingly unwilling to discount they were forced to make use of specialized bill brokers. The war initiated a process which was to take discounting largely out of the hands of the London banks. But the London banks did not simply retreat from this field. By the second quarter of the nineteenth century they had developed the practice of buying a 'bundle of bills' from a discounter or broker as a highly convenient way of holding assets in a state of high liquidity (as the bills matured, perhaps within days of purchase, they provided the bank with the cash to meet demands made upon it by its own customers).

Throughout the Industrial Revolution the growth and development of banking was interlocked with the expansion of the economy itself. From the middle of the eighteenth century a network of country banks arose to supplement the existing London banks. The country banks met two main needs of those businessmen and landowners (including the professional classes) whose affairs rarely took them to London: they provided a safe deposit for money and facilities for receiving and making payments. The country banks measured out credit to their customers by the twin instruments of discounting and note issue. From some points of view the country banker could be thought of as primarily a lender: a work of 1827 contrasted the London banker who 'takes care of his customers' money' and the country banker who 'has chiefly to advance money to his customers'. Against his accumulated securities (his own capital and customers' deposits, represented by gold or Bank of England notes, deposits with his London agent, government and other stock, mortgages and loans) the country banker issued notes and it was in these that he discounted bills brought to him by local traders. Discounting was short-term lending and the cautious banker was advised (by Thomas Joplin who was, however, a keen advocate of joint-stock banking) to confine his loans 'to the discounting of such short dated bills . . . as through its London agents can be turned at any time into cash'.

The suspension of cash payments by the Bank of England was an encouragement to note issue by the country banks – which explains the rapid increase in their number – and it was by this means that the credit was supplied for the war effort. Paper money also solved some of the difficulties caused by the current scarcity of coin. At a comparatively early stage in the history of the country banks Parliament had prohibited the issue of notes under the value of £1 (in 1775) and, then, under £5 (in 1777).

These restrictions were withdrawn in 1797, although the prohibition on notes under £1 was reimposed in 1808 when bank notes also became subject to an issuing licence. Banks and bank notes were thus a very familiar feature of life by 1815. Few men of any substance made do without bank accounts by the 1820s. Of course a local crisis, and still more a national one, could quickly result in a 'run' on the banks, but it was perhaps now rather unusual to keep large sums of money at home rather than deposited in a bank. Of course banks served a small public: many had no more than 200 accounts and a bank which handled 500 was certainly a large one. Very few labourers had bank accounts and, indeed, many banks refused deposits under £10 or £20. Nevertheless many working people were paid in bank notes and their savings clubs and friendly societies sometimes kept an account with a country bank.

Banking after 1815

A readiness to use banks and accept paper money was as much a distinguishing feature of Britain by 1815 as the advanced nature of her industrial economy. The nation's primary education in banking was completed. But, not surprisingly, after an era of frequent failures as well as rapid expansion, the stability of the banking system was a subject of nervous concern. The war sponsored a feverish, intricate, and pioneering debate on the principles of sound banking. In many minds the banking boom was almost inseparable from wartime inflation and a return to cash payments seemed to promise both sounder banking and lower prices. The farmers were not entirely happy about resumption of cash payments: they had come to rely heavily upon credit from the banks and no doubt sensed more difficult times ahead. A resumption of cash payments was, in fact, delayed until 1821 (although this was two years ahead of the final schedule laid down in Peel's Act of 1820). The country banks had already begun to contract their note issue: they were bound to be particularly cautious immediately after resumption. To make matters worse – for the farmer – 1820–1 were good harvest years and agricultural prices were consequently low. The impact of the depression in agriculture was felt throughout the economy: farmers were certainly to take a more jaundiced view of banks in future. To an extent this crisis was the result of government policy: resumption could be expected to have deflationary consequences but its introduction in 1821, at a time of low farm prices and sluggish international trade, was particularly unfortunate. The medicine was nasty and it didn't, and couldn't, cure. The resumption of cash payments was intended to ensure secure banking by compelling bankers to be more circumspect in their note issue. Yet within four years the nation was caught up in an acute financial crisis during which over sixty banks were forced to close their doors.

It was too much to hope that a return to a gold standard was sufficient by itself to regulate the credit given by the banks through their note issue. Bankers issued notes as much to attract business as to make a profit. As one Midlands banker put it in 1832:

I think it [note issue] gives a sort of éclat to the establishment; it answers the purpose of the address card of a tradesman; it makes the Bank notorious, and makes it a subject of conversation, and brings deposits and customers. (quoted in L. S. Pressnell, *Country Banking in the Industrial Revolution*, Oxford, 1956, p. 157)

It was indeed a matter of opinion whether there was a profit to be made on the issue of small notes at all. Because every bank was an individual and local concern there was no such thing as a commonly accepted ratio between a bank's deposits and its note issue. This was a matter for the banker's judgment. The public clearly looked for integrity in a banker and a bank's reputation in this respect was naturally vital to its success. The prominent group of Quakers in banking, to take a notable example, needed few lessons in how to deserve the confidence and loyalty of their customers. If bankers came to grief it was usually because they had made the same mistakes as those around them and because the economy, unduly sensitive as it still was to fluctuations in the harvest yield or of popular overseas markets, was extremely unpredictable. The crisis of 1825 impressed upon both bankers and public the extent to which banking was dependent upon factors largely outside the control of bankers themselves.

In the first place the banking system was sufficiently integrated by the 1820s for disaster to leap rapidly from London to the provinces or vice versa. Difficulties came suddenly: a bank might find itself fighting off a 'run' by its customers and noteholders – who, of course, wanted their deposits in cash – where days, or even hours, before its dealings had been perfectly normal. Assets had to be mobilized at very short notice. This may best be illustrated from the history of one particularly well documented bank. In 1822 the Banbury New Bank, then owned by R. and C. Tawney, was purchased by two other Quakers, Joseph Gillett and his brother-in-law, Joseph Gibbins. Gillett had already worked for the other Banbury bank, Cobb's, and had used his wife's capital in 1821 to enter another Oxfordshire bank as a partner; Gibbins was already in partnership in banks in Birmingham and Swansea. The purchase provided that Richard Tawney's son, Henry, should enter the partnership when he came of age. The bank lost business when Gillett took over from the Tawneys and its note issue had fallen to under £4,000 by the end of 1823.

Not surprisingly the financial crisis of 1825 put the firm in danger. On 11 December 1825 Gibbins arrived in Banbury, informed Gillett that he was going to London to raise cash for his Birmingham bank, and advised him (he managed the Banbury bank) to do the same. Gillett at once wrote to his own brother and asked him to obtain at least £10,000 in gold from their London agent: Gibbins himself was asked to cover some part of the £27,000 which he owed the Banbury partnership. These precautions were taken only just in time. On Monday, 12 December, a large London bank, Pole & Co., with forty-three country 'correspondents', failed: fortunately Joseph's brother, William Gillett, successfully obtained £11,000 from their own London agent, Curtis's, including a 'a Box of £6,000 intended for some other Bank'. William arrived in Banbury on Tuesday at the same time as the news of Pole's failure. Almost at once customers and noteholders began a run on Gillett's. On Wednesday another important London bank failed. That morning Gillett received a parcel of bills from his partner, Gibbins: of course bills were now of very little help and Gillett decided to go at once to Birmingham to demand cash from his partner. William Gillett returned to London in the hope of finding someone there prepared to discount the bank's bills. Neither were successful: at Birmingham Gillett was told bluntly that there was no cash to be had. On Thursday afternoon Gillett's were forced to stop payment on their notes but there was no panic, presumably because the bank had paid steadily so far. By Friday morning Gillett was desperate. At last he decided to take all the bank's bills to London. As the London Mail had already left Banbury the flustered young banker had to hire a chaise which overtook the mail coach at Aynho. In London Gillett learnt that his father had already raised £5,000 to relieve the Banbury New Bank. It was not easy to raise money in London that Friday. Gillett was accompanied to the Bank of England by a representative of Curtis's: the Bank refused to discount any of his bills themselves but was sympathetic enough to refer Gillett to a discount house where the Bank's support could be expected to help him. On Saturday morning he obtained £6,200 (he had come to London with £20,000 of bills) from a discounter and immediately returned to Banbury by chaise. All this was not enough to reopen on the following Wednesday, as Gillett had hoped: the Bank remained closed until mid-January or later (for details see Audrey M. Taylor, *Gilletts: Bankers at Banbury and Oxford*, Oxford, 1964, pp. 5–13).

Banking legislation 1826–44

What had gone wrong at Banbury? Clearly very little. If Gillett was inexperienced he nevertheless acted with commendable sense and alacrity. There was no hint of dishonesty. Perhaps Gillett needed more time to bring the bank's business back to the level it had enjoyed under the Tawneys: the crisis caught him at a weak moment. For the bank's customers there was consider-

able inconvenience but remarkably little loss of confidence – it
was customers' support which enabled the bank to reopen when
it did. What the nation as a whole read into the 1825 crisis was
another lesson in the dangers of note, and especially, small note
issue. The banking legislation of 1826 indicates the lines along
which people were thinking. All small note issue under £5 was
to cease from 1829. The Bank of England was to set up provincial branches for the supply of coins and notes. Most important of all for the development of English banking (joint stock
banks had always been legal in Scotland) the Bank of England's
monopoly of joint stock banking was ended: joint stock banks
could now be established *outside* the London area (105-kilometre
[65-mile] radius). It took time for joint stock banks to come
into being and attract custom: not until the late 1830s, and in
the 1840s, did they begin to outstrip the older country banks in
importance. The rapid growth of joint stock banking was foreshadowed in legislation of 1833 which permitted their creation
within the London area, although these banks were not to be
allowed to issue notes. By the same Act Bank of England notes
became legal tender. A final settlement of private note issue was
reached in the famous Bank Charter Act of 1844: in future a
bank's note issue could not exceed the average of its note issue
for the twelve weeks preceeding 27 April 1844. This fixed the
private issue at just over £8·5 million (maximum). Private bank
notes did not lose importance at once and their contraction took
place very slowly. There was still a circulation of £84,000 in
1914. If a bank were to fail at any time it lost its right of note
issue forever under the 1844 act and, naturally, no new banks
were to acquire the right of issue.

Banking legislation was not solely concerned with the regulation of private banks. Perhaps its most important objective
was to define the role of the Bank of England. Although the Bank
had long been the agent of government there could be no
question of bringing the Bank under direct government control
at this date. But the Bank's note issue was thought to be a
suitable field for legislative control. The 1833 act, which made
the Bank's notes legal tender and empowered it to set up pro-

vincial branches, also imposed upon the Bank the duty of making regular returns to the Chancellor of the Exchequer of its bullion reserves and note issue. After the resumption of cash payments the private banker had been in the unenviable position of having to pay his customers gold on demand even if, as Gillett's experience in 1825 showed, gold was virtually unobtainable: from 1833 a Bank of England note was the equivalent of gold. Thereafter the problem of credit supply seemed to many to centre on the note issue of the Bank itself quite as much as on the private note issue. Thus the Bank Charter Act of 1844 restricted the Bank's right to issue notes quite severely. It could, of course, issue any amount of notes to the value of its bullion (gold and silver) reserves but, beyond this, it was limited to an issue of £14 million in notes against any securities it might hold. This was known as the fiduciary issue and the Bank required an authorization from the government to exceed it. The Act thus subjected the note issuing department of the Bank to legislative supervision while leaving it free to conduct its banking how it pleased. There was an admirable neatness about this solution. If domestic prices were rising to such heights that imports swept upwards (because Britain had become an especially attractive market) and exports remained either static or moved downwards (as British goods became more expensive abroad) then the limitation that was placed upon credit by the fiduciary issue was expected to right the situation by an automatic process. But in the financial crisis of 1847 the government found itself forced to give the Bank permission to exceed the fiduciary issue – although, in the event, the Bank didn't need to do so – in order to restore basic confidence in the financial system.

The Bank Charter Act did not, and could not, provide a code of practice for a 'central' bank. It did resolve the currency issue. But it overlooked the vital significance of the Bank's own banking activities, and especially its discount policy. Because the Bank was the holder of the nation's bullion reserve, and because it was the lender of last resort (neither of these functions had been laid down by statute), its policies had repercussions throughout the whole banking system. If the Bank encouraged easy credit it was virtually impossible for other banks not to follow suit, and if it pursued credit stringency, again, it was impossible for other banks to offer easy credit. What mattered here, granted the inevitable fluctuations in business activity in this period, was the timing of the Bank's policies: that it should not make credit easier than it ought to be, so that unsound projects could find backers, and that it did not impose stringency when what was needed was the opportunity for expansion *or* when it was too late to prevent a crisis. As yet the Bank had not fully grasped its responsibility in this direction. The crises of 1825 and 1847 were both preceded by speculative booms which went partly unregulated because the Bank wished to exploit its own opportunities to lend. That there should be similarity between these crises confirmed the arguments of those (the 'Banking School', as opposed to the 'Currency School') who thought it impossible to control credit satisfactorily by rationing money. Certainly the Bank was too slow in raising bank rate in 1846–7: from 1844 until October 1847 bank rate was consistently below the market rate of discount.

The banking crisis of 1847

The crisis of 1847 began with the harvest difficulties of 1846 which coincided with a poor cotton crop in the U.S.A. Wheat prices were exceptionally high into the spring of 1847 but this had the curious consequence of ferreting out fresh supplies abroad while, at home, the prospects for the next harvest seemed excellent. The result was a crop of failures among corn dealers and commercial houses in both Lancashire and Scotland. To this situation railway investment made an uncertain contribution. Because construction work had to continue on those schemes that went forward after 1846 interest rates were pushed to very high levels. From the beginning of October the Bank was actually rationing its discounts. As in 1825 these circumstances put pressure on banks which had inadequate capital reserves. This time the Banbury New Bank survived the crisis without shutting its doors. Its capital position was worrying. Gillett had a great deal of capital tied up in various family businesses (a common practice among country bankers which went back to the origins of the country banks) and at the end of 1846 the Bank had only some £8,000 of reserves to meet losses on £128,000 advanced to customers. One of the features of 1847 was the failure of a number of joint stock banks. Shareholders in the new banks were not yet protected by limited liability; in 1844 Peel gave joint stock banks whose capital was £100,000 or over the right to register as companies, which meant that they could take action at law through their officers, but banks were not covered by the privilege of limited liability until 1858. Until then a shareholder in a bank was at least technically liable should the bank fail and even if this was not strictly observed the failure of a joint stock bank naturally caused more hardship than had been the case with the older country banks. In Mrs Gaskell's *Cranford* elderly and innocent Miss Matty was almost wholly dependent upon the income from her stock in the Town and Country Bank of Drumble. When the bank failed Miss Matty felt personally responsible. News of the failure reached Miss Matty while she was shopping in Cranford's drapery stores; a farmer, buying a shawl for his wife, had his note from the bank rejected by the shopkeeper. She insisted upon giving him gold for his note:

'... I don't pretend to understand business: I only know that if it is going to fail, and if honest people are to lose their money because they have taken our notes – I can't explain myself', said she, suddenly becoming aware that she had got into a long sentence with four people for audience; 'only I would rather exchange my gold for the note, if you please', turning to the farmer, 'and then you can take your wife the shawl. It is only going without my gown a few days longer', she continued, speaking to me. 'Then, I have no doubt, everything will be cleared up.'
'But if it is cleared up the wrong way?' said I.

Miss Matty was old fashioned. She felt towards the bank's customers much as the earlier, private, family country banker must have done. But at the same time she represented the new era in banking. She was a stockholder and the type of banking practised by her bank (however unsuccessfully) differed sharply from that of earlier country banking. Not only was capital greater, but branch banking was rapidly developed by the joint stock banks. Despite the incident in the draper's shop the private note issue was dwindling. The cheque was circulating much more widely. And the bankers of the 1850s had the important advantage of being able to make advances to their customers against new and conveniently realized securities like railway stock.

[31] PARLIAMENT AND THE PUBLIC COMPANY

Joint-stock conceded?

The state made much use of the banks. After the opening of provincial branches of the Bank of England it was possible to look for a new system of tax collection which dispensed with the outdated and unprofessional 'receivers'. These were replaced by inspectors of taxes in 1831 and a new Board of Inland Revenue was set up in 1849. For all this the existence of a developed banking system was essential. At the same time, however tentative banking legislation may have been, the state had at last given encouragement to the more advanced joint stock banks and this just as a new phase of large-scale enterprise and international investment stepped up the demand for capital. But the state had interfered very little in the detail of bankers' affairs. Despite some recognition of a legitimate public interest in banking procedure the state had done no more than give a nudge, in 1844, to the movement towards increasing the capital of banks. Beyond this it offered no guidelines to the banker and scant protection to his customer or shareholder. Men must look after their own affairs: as Peel put it, 'What security can I give you to a Bank that has £600,000 of paid up capital and lends £500,000 to one house?' The answer, of course, was 'none', but this should not be allowed to conceal the fact that the great debate on banking in the early nineteenth century implied that a solution to its problems naturally included a degree of public intervention.

Banking legislation was scarcely an energetic exercise in interventionism: it carried with it no administrative control of banking by the state and its most far-reaching provision, the withdrawal of the Bank of England's monopoly of joint stock banking, was long overdue. Company legislation was equally an attempt to frame law to suit altered circumstances. Until the repeal of the Bubble Act (1720) in 1825 'unincorporated' joint stock companies had an uncertain title to legal existence (incorporation was normally granted through an Act of Parliament: shareholders' liability was limited to their investment in the company and not, as in a simple partnership, to the full amount of their possessions). The Registration Act of 1844 established a procedure for the setting up of a company which was controlled by a Registrar of Joint Stock Companies: prospectuses had to be submitted to the Registrar (until 1847), directors were to accept appointments in writing and to refrain from dealing in the company's shares, proper accounts had to be kept and inspection permitted. Such a company then possessed the right to sue, or be sued, in its own name but it did not possess limited liability. This privilege was first offered to companies by an act of 1855 which was almost immediately replaced by the Joint Stock Companies Act of 1856. This act simplified the procedure for forming a company: most of the detailed supervision of the Registrar – which had, however, been easily sidestepped – was jettisoned in favour of the acceptance of a model set of rules. But these did allow shareholders to ask for an inspection of the company by the Board of Trade and required that a balance sheet should be presented at an annual meeting of shareholders. The achievement of a new legal code for companies was a protracted process and it was not complete even in 1856. Lawyers reacted to the change with tenacious conservatism and their attitude was shared by many others who felt that limited liability was an incentive to fraud. The ancient procedure for incorporation had ceased to be workable, but Parliament could not simply leave the definition and status of companies to be decided in the courts.

The railway companies: a test case?

In practice neither the banking nor company legislation were a serious challenge to the principles of laissez-faire. What interventionism there was here was muted. But, for a moment, Parliament's handling of the early railway companies promised a different outcome. Perhaps this was because the formation of a public utility company, through the familiar mechanism of a private Act, always meant some public discussion of the specific issues – as well as much lobbying behind the scenes. Thus both canals and turnpikes had already created a precedent for some regulation of railways: it was usual, for instance, to fix tolls charged by canal companies in their enabling Act. Something could have been learnt too of the need to insist upon uniform operating practices when licensing a new type of transport undertaking: the canals had been built without system, their locks and tunnels of different widths and heights. In any case changes in the transport services were clearly a matter of public interest. They might affect the strategy of national defence and they had implications for the maintenance of public order which, throughout this period, depended as much upon troops as on local officers. Like the canal companies, the railways were invested with powers of compulsory purchase and in a Parliament of landowners this was certain to make for interest in their affairs. The opportunity for the state to direct the growth of the railway system in Britain was, however, allowed to slip away during the late 1830s and early 1840s.

The machinery of a private Act was defective. The first condition which promoters had to satisfy was that there was a *local* need for a railway. An adequate capital had to be raised to support the venture and, to control the flood of new projects in 1845–6, Parliament did insist that 5 per cent of the capital should be deposited with the Accountant-General as a test of good faith (over £11 million was involved). The Liverpool and

Manchester Railway had been required by its Act to lower freight charges should it pay a dividend over 10 per cent but, although much discussed, dividend control was not applied to other companies. The Acts also included maximum tolls for freight or passengers but as the companies were easily able to operate below the statutory rates these clauses were of little importance. Some anxiety about railway management was beginning to be expressed in the later 1830s. Wellington thought that the Whigs had been 'very improvident' in not placing tighter reins on the companies. The monopolist aspect of the situation led even a self-made draper, James Morrison, M.P. for Ipswich, to argue either for effective dividend control or parliamentary revision of rates at the end of twenty years. Edward Baines, the Leeds newspaper proprietor, considered this proposal 'a very extraordinary interference with property' (Clapham, I, p. 415).

When Parliament at last (in view of the speed of development) took action in 1840 it set up a Railway Department of the Board of Trade: the department's three officials were to watch the progress of railways under construction and to collect statistics of traffic and accidents. In 1840 the first concern of Parliament was with public safety but when Gladstone reopened the discussion on railway legislation in 1844 it was clear that a more radical measure was imminent. Responsible opinion was by now much more favourable to stricter control of the companies. In the event Gladstone's Act of 1844 was a mild measure. The original proposals authorized the Board of Trade to survey the position of railway companies fifteen years after they had been set up: it was to be empowered either to purchase the company or, if its dividend had reached 10 per cent in the preceding three years, to revise its charges and then to retain a degree of direct control over its management. The provisions were not retrospective and so could never apply to the main trunk routes which had already been built, but this did not prevent the railway interest from referring to the 'railway plunder Bill'. The railways were never plundered: the state's right of purchase under the bill was never exercised. Much more important was the protection which it gave to third-class passengers and the obligation imposed on the companies of running at least one third-class train a day.

The railway debate raised some interesting issues. The state did not establish even an ultimate control over the railway system (not until 1871 did it acquire powers to take over the railways in the event of war). Perhaps the most important event in railway history in 1844 was not Gladstone's Act but George Hudson's first successful amalgamation of small companies into a railway colossus, the Midland Railway. The London & North Western, the Manchester, Sheffield & Lincolnshire, and the Lancashire & Yorkshire followed in 1846–7. Hudson realized that the future lay with the large company but he rejected any form of state initiative to prompt or direct amalgamations. Yet the large company was a potential, if not actual, monopolist. Hudson himself didn't believe that competition among railway companies was either really possible or even desirable. Gladstone, too, knew how strong were the arguments against uncontrolled competition among railway companies and because what Parliament was sanctioning was often close to monopoly he wanted some measure of state control. Failing this the state had to employ its existing, indirect, authority: as he put it, 'the power of encouraging or if need be creating competition . . . is an engine of great capabilities in the hands of the State'. One form of competition which Parliament would have liked to exclude was that between a narrow and a broad gauge, the absurd inconvenience of which seems only to have been realized when the gauges met for the first time at Gloucester in 1844. The Gauge Act of 1846 did at least aim at uniformity: companies were expected to lay a narrow gauge unless they obtained an exemption. Everywhere, of course, the junction of two lines caused confusion and in this area the arbitration of the Railway Department might be welcome. The usefulness of the Department's work indicates that its lack of formal powers was not quite such a handicap as at first appeared. While its efforts to assess the practicality of railway projects during the 'Mania' in 1845 aroused only suspicion (although the parliamentary committee was ill adapted to this work), its reports on safety, and other matters of public interest, helped shape an opinion which the companies could always afford to ignore.

How well the state might have supervised the railways had it been allowed the freedom to do so is, of course, a matter of guesswork. As it was the inspectors of the Railway Department didn't escape abuse. They were recruited from the Royal Engineers: granted the novelty of their work they performed it with considerable skill. A civil service of this type had to be composed of experts, or of men whose training would enable them to-become experts quite quickly. The growth of a 'scientific' civil service was a feature of the period 1830–50 and, in retrospect, it seems a clear indication that the Industrial Revolution was compelling government to undertake new tasks. The work of these new officials was surrounded by controversy. Not only did they have to contend with resentment against any kind of central agency or intrusion into private interests, but they themselves had only a dawning appreciation of how to carry out their functions (the legislation which created their departments was as amateur and imprecise on detail as again only inexperience can explain). Because their coercive powers were usually very limited the officials were often tempted into open controversy with their opponents with the result that they were freely accused of personal animosity. That public officials were trying to be impartial was something which contemporaries could scarcely understand. The age of impartiality and patronage necessarily overlapped.

[32] SOCIAL REFORM: MERELY AN ADMINISTRATIVE FAILURE?

Professor Ashton has argued that the failure of the state to keep pace with the changes in society as a whole largely explains the disappointingly slow advance in living standards achieved in this period:

If the Industrial Revolution was not able to bring its rewards in full measure to the ordinary man and woman it is to the defects of administration, and not of economic processes, that the failure must be ascribed. (*Industrial Revolution, 1760–1830*, p. 141)

The meagreness of reform in Britain until the second quarter of the nineteenth century was partly a consequence of the war: thereafter a feeling that government and its institutions were out of joint with the times did make itself apparent. But a failure to administer may imply an unwillingness to administer or to accept that evils could be eradicated or lessened by it. Government in Britain during the Industrial Revolution meant government by magistrates and parish officers: central government did very little which directly affected the mass of the people. Such a society was able, perhaps better able, to produce an Industrial Revolution than its continental counterparts but it was not necessarily better equipped to revolutionize its government in the administrative sense. In Britain to 'centralize' was to be 'continental' and alien. Thus it is true that the early Factory Acts suffered from an administrative 'defect' in that they were to be applied by magistrates and not by a central inspectorate, equally true that the early inspectorate was only modestly successful because its powers were so slender and ill defined. Not until 1844 did the inspectors possess undisputed right of entry to factory buildings or did penalties exist for obstructing them in carrying out their duties. What was being remedied here was a failure by Parliament to supply the means of enforcing its legislation. The early factory Acts were in effective because they were disregarded by the manufacturers and factory regulation remained ineffective until the inspectors were properly empowered to hunt out abuses. There were certainly many practical problems to be solved here, and a new type of civil servant to be trained, but there was also substantial and determined resistance to the imposition of an industrial code by the state or to limiting the employers' freedom of action in any way.

Nevertheless the social legislation of the Industrial Revolution clearly belonged to its times. It was concerned with different problems from those which had bothered governments in the sixteenth and seventeenth centuries. The Elizabethan Poor Law was a police measure. It envisaged, if it did not realise, a stable society: entitlement to relief was based not so much on need as on settlement. In the rural society the labourer was expected to know poverty at various times in his life: what mattered was to establish the responsibility of a particular parish for his relief. The Poor Law of 1834 had a much narrower economic purpose. Destitution was defined by an administrative test. The destitute were those who came to the workhouse and entered it as paupers. The object was to cut the cost of relief, especially in rural areas, and to make labouring families hunt for work. The secondary purposes of the Act, to provide more efficient relief services or to improve the education of pauper children, were much less effectively realized. The Act's diagnosis of poverty was faulty: it did not take into account the type of periodic and inescapable unemployment which so often affected the industrial areas. It assumed that those needing relief could always be accommodated in the workhouse. In practice the Act was more loosely applied. The new boards of guardians, whose creation broke up the old pattern of local government, proved to be more responsive to local pressures than central directives: the assistant poor law commissioners quickly grasped that their work, in the field, was to advise and persuade the guardians to respect a central policy. But perhaps what was significant about the Act (apart from the bitter working-class hostility which it aroused) was that it did bring local representatives and officials into frequent contact with Westminster.

Industrial legislation had limited objects. It aimed at protecting children and young persons who worked in factories. The Act of 1844 defined a factory as premises within which mechanical power was used in preparing, manufacturing, or finishing cotton, wool, hair, silk, flax, hemp, jute or tow: buildings within the factory perimeter where children were at work were also covered by the Act even although they might not contain machinery. The Mines Act of 1842 extended its protection to women. In this case protection consisted in prohibiting the employment of women and children underground. Children who did not work in factories or mines went unprotected. The reason for this was no doubt partly administrative. Difficult as it proved to regulate factories it was as nothing with the difficulty in controlling other places in which children might be found at work. The lamentable plight of the child chimney sweeps even after the Act of 1840, which prohibited anyone under twenty-one from climbing a chimney, and which should have abolished the sweeping of domestic chimneys by climbing altogether, illustrates both practical problems of regulating work *outside* the factories and the callous indifference of the public which humanitarianism had to overcome. In the factories all workers were affected by the limitation of children's working hours, as everyone concerned with the factories had realized that they would be. The safety regulations introduced under the 1844 Act were intended to protect children who were agreed to be particularly at risk while attending power-driven machinery, but some of the more basic regulations in the Act applied to adults as well. Despite what was probably a commonly held view that it took the operative 'not a little perverted ingenuity to get into danger' (W. Cooke Taylor, 1842), the notion of employers' liability had begun to make progress. One of the factory inspectors could argue in 1846 that

. . . sound limbs are a main part of the working man's capital, and it should be exposed as little as possible to the risk of irrecoverable diminution. (Leonard Horner)

Of course if the worker were to be protected his employer had to be coerced. In general the courts were unwilling to apply this coercion. The early factory legislation was most suspiciously scrutinized in the courts and, wherever Parliament's intention had not been made quite clear, judgment invariably favoured the manufacturer. The Ten Hours Act of 1847 was defeated in the courts and had to be modified by the so-called 'compromise' Act of 1850. But the reverse process could also take place. In 1840 Lord Ashley supported a young millgirl in an action against her employer for damages resulting from injuries sustained when she had been caught up by a revolving shaft. The mill-owner was found liable and had to pay damages and very heavy costs. The case made a legislative definition of liability much more desirable. In drawing up their recommendations which formed the basis of the 1844 Act the inspectors drew extensively upon their experience of the way in which the better manufacturers already fenced their machinery. For the majority of manufacturers factory legislation was certainly something imposed from without. But what was imposed on them was often already the practice in the more progressive and enlightened mills.

[33] PUBLIC POLICY IN THE INDUSTRIAL REVOLUTION: THE ISSUES AND THE PROBLEM

It was a general feature of the problems of the new society that they called for accurate definition. No doubt the rapid upsurge in population also helps to explain the growing interest in statistics in the late eighteenth and early nineteenth centuries. Even so it was a long time before government could rely upon adequate statistics. The first census was taken in 1801 but it took half a century to develop the census into a systematic description of national life. From the 1830s the government began to be much better equipped: in 1832 the Board of Trade set up a statistical department and, from 1837, the civil registration of births, marriages, and deaths was required by law.

In 1833 the British Association formed its own statistical section and this was followed by the formation of local statistical societies. From the 1830s politicians had to live with figures. Canning, it was said, once admitted to Brougham that there was nothing he feared more than facts and figures: in Chadwick's opinion what he should have dreaded was 'the wretchedly imperfect figures' then available. The mere possession of statistics was not enough to compel government action. But they could be used to judge the moment when action had become appropriate and intervention justified. Almost all public health legislation was permissive; it made powers available to a local authority which was ready to act because local opinion agreed that action was necessary. In this context the role of statistics was persuasive. The Public Health Act of 1848 allowed local boards of health to be set up, in the first instance, after a petition had secured the signatures of one-fifteenth of the ratepayers. But the Act permitted this procedure to be ignored if the local death rate had reached the figure of twenty-three per thousand. Where statistics did not persuade they also constituted an argument for intervention.

The motives of nineteenth-century social and industrial legislation have often been discussed. The most straightforward explanation of it is to see here a process of readjustment to the needs and pressures of an expanding industrial society. One historian has, for example, argued that

The new enterprisers wanted new freedoms, but also new services, and extracted both from the state. The old enterprisers and the new workers were stripped of old protections and used their political weight to create new protections. (J. B. Brebner)

The British political system was admittedly based upon a balance of interests in this period, but not all parties in the new industrial society had equal access to it. As men of substance, some important manufacturers, especially if they bought land, could expect to share in the status and influence which was traditionally accorded to property. Lesser men, who had little contact with the gentry (if one remained) and none with the capital and its society, had to be content with very much less. The labouring poor, however hard sections of it might press for redress and relief, could only hope that others would take up their cause. Who, then, to take an obvious example, 'extracted' factory legislation from the state? Certainly not the manufacturers, although some of them gave the Factory Movement their support and were willing to observe the factory Acts in spirit as well as letter. The operatives of course wanted legislation and it was the object of the Factory Movement to urge Parliament and government to act. But the Movement would have been helpless without the leadership of Tories and Evangelicals and, above all, without Ashley's ability to convince a broad spread of opinion in the Commons that

the State had an interest and right to watch over and provide for the moral and physical well-being of her people. (1844)

Even so the legislation fell as far short of achieving all that the operatives wanted as it went beyond what many masters regarded as legitimate.

By the 1840s the factory inspectors were making a significant contribution to the demand for further control of hours and conditions. The principle of inspection was a vital one in enabling the state to undertake new roles. If inspection was not solely the brainchild of the social philosopher Jeremy Bentham (1748–1832) and his disciples it was a central feature of Benthamite thinking. Bentham attacked the traditional notion that the first duty of government was to respect vested interests. While Benthamism accepted the current emphasis in thought and behaviour on individualism, it also put the state at the service of the majority – its actions should aim at securing 'the greatest happiness of the greatest number'. Law should be both unambiguous and enforceable: to be properly enforceable it had to be backed by centralized agencies. Thus the Report of the Royal Commission of 1833 recommended the setting up of a factory inspectorate because its proposals 'were not conducive to the immediate interests either of the master manufacturers, or of the operatives, or of any powerful class, and are not therefore likely to receive continuous voluntary support'. To a Benthamite enthusiast, like Edwin Chadwick, the 'voluntary' principle in legislation was, in practice, more a concession to vested interests than a valid defence of the individual from unwarranted state intervention. Perversely the majority were hostile to Benthamite legislation. To them it looked like oppression. Chadwick was the author of the disappointing Factory Act of 1833, the Poor Law of 1834 and its twin, the Rural Police Act of 1839. To the working classes he was a sinister influence. There was, of course, something in this: the Poor Law was ill-conceived, and the diagnosis of poverty on which it rested was faulty. The Poor Law 'Bastilles' were the dour expression of a belief that much, perhaps most, poverty was caused by improvidence and could be treated as a crime. But the responsibility here was not all Chadwick's. The measure put to Parliament by the Royal Commission contained proposals for much improved care of the aged and orphans: as, enacted it was shorn of some of its progressive features. The gentry were obsessed by their eagerness to reduce the poor rates. As administered by the Boards of Guardians the Act was sometimes more tolerant of outdoor relief than Chadwick would have allowed, but neither was it free from scandalous examples of local, petty, meanness. Through his interest in poverty Chadwick was brought to discover and publicize the needless waste of life imposed upon the whole community by the uncontrolled spread of epidemic disease. Here positive amelioration for the working class seemed at least a possibility: but the public health campaign was never well supported and the working class largely ignored it.

Centralized action had no entirely reliable allies and no completely predictable enemies. What the state could perform was after all, a largely unknown quantity. Middle-class suspicion of government action was based much less upon an estimate of its usefulness than upon resentment against the methods of patronage and preferment which seemed to typify the *ancien régime* of the eighteenth century. Sections of the working class began, in the nineteenth century, to look to the state for protection. But, in general, the working class did not expect improvement to come from an increase in government action. Perhaps the Chartists did see beyond an extension of the franchise to the achievement of a 'welfare' state. Yet the grievances which were given most weight in the Chartist Petition of 1842 were those that could have commanded middle-class support. In an attack upon the civil list the Chartists contrasted themselves as 'the producing millions' not against capitalist employers but against the traditional rulers, members of the royal family, and the Archbishop of Canterbury. Their programme for the distress of the early 1840s was scarcely revolutionary:

That notwithstanding the wretched and unparalleled condition of the people, your honourable House has manifested no disposition to curtail the expenses of the state, to diminish taxation, or promote general prosperity.

Nevertheless Macaulay, in a speech opposing the Petition, sketched a future in which property would be at the mercy of democracy, with disastrous consequences for the nation. He claimed to detect

a constant and systematic attempt for years to represent the Government as being able to do, and as bound to attempt that which no Government ever attempted . . . it has been treated as if the Government possessed some mine of wealth – some extraordinary means of supplying the wants of the people; as if they could give them bread from the clouds – water from the rocks . . .

Were government to engage the 'spoliation' of one class to assist another the great historian could see only political chaos ahead out of which would arise that bogey of all Whigs and Englishmen, 'a military despot'.

The Macaulays of the early nineteenth century advocated a very lightweight state indeed. They were equally unwilling to allow the workingman a right to collective self-defence: wages were fixed by market forces and based upon individual contract. 'Combinations' of workmen, trade unions, were, however, a fact which neither a hostile law, suspicious governments, nor frightened employers could ever quite submerge. In dealing with trade unions government preferred to believe that it was handling a problem of public order rather than championing a laissez-faire economy. The restrictive Combination Acts of 1799 and 1800 were intended to prevent the outbreak of organized conflict in industry and provided for the arbitration of wage disputes before magistrates. Such arbitration was impossible when the J.P.s were interested parties. But government saw itself as the enemy of combination, not of wage demands. The distinction was perhaps academic. After the repeal of the Combination Acts in 1824 trade unionism could still find itself oppressed, as under the Whigs in the 1830s, by a law which barely tolerated the essentials of strike action and by employers, encouraged by the government, applying victimization against trade unionists. The belief that trade unions were mere ill-tempered conspiracies died hard. That collective bargaining had a future in the industrial state was something which few saw; to the traditionalist the idea was too novel, and to the employer it offered only a threat. It took sound observation to notice, as Henry Mayhew did, that the trade unions (among artisans) were a real expression of working-class self-help and deserved consideration and respect, not ill-informed condemnation. Ironically, in developing trade unions the skilled working class had begun to fashion institutions which, in time, would be able to make much more precise demands upon the state for protective legislation than could be envisaged in this early period. Yet however uncertain the ultimate direction of state intervention in an industrial society, by the end of the 1840s it could at least be seen that government had acquired new techniques and a jumbled, but not insignificant array of new powers.

Further Reading

The books mentioned in the further reading for Part I also cover the questions raised in this chapter. E. Victor Morgan's *A History of Money* (Pelican, 1965) is a convenient historical introduction to government finance and banking. L. S. Pressnell's *Country Banking in the Industrial Revolution* (Oxford University Press, 1956) is an exhaustive study and the same author's 'The Rate of Interest in the

Eighteenth Century', *Studies in the Industrial Revolution*, London University Press, 1960) examines both the pattern and importance of interest rates in the eighteenth century. T. S. Ashton's *An Economic History of England: The Eighteenth Century*, Chapter VI (Methuen, 1955) is an excellent account of eighteenth-century financial history; for the nineteenth century it is still probably best to turn to Clapham, Vol. I, Chapters VII and XIII. Perhaps the best way of approaching the history of banking is through the history of a single firm; Audrey M. Taylor's *Gilletts: Bankers at Banbury and Oxford* (Oxford University Press, 1964) is a fascinating detailed study.

The nineteenth-century attitude to government is discussed in J. Brebner's 'Laissez-Faire and State Intervention in Nineteenth-Century Britain' (1948) (reprinted in *Essays in Economic History*, Vol. III, ed. C. Carus-Wilson, Arnold, 1962). Brebner regards government action in the nineteenth century as a largely unplanned response to industrialization; a rather similar approach is evident in G. Kitson Clark's *The Making of Victorian England* (Methuen, 1962) and in W. L. Burn's *The Age of Equipoise* (Allen and Unwin, 1964) which is a study of the years 1852–67, but contains much on the earlier nineteenth century that is relevant to this subject, especially in Chapter 4. Jennifer Hart's 'Nineteenth-Century Social Reform: A Tory Interpretation of History', *Past and Present*, No. 31 (1965), vigorously defends the more traditional view that social reform was directed by Benthamite thinking, a view unpopular among recent historians and much criticized by O. MacDonagh's *A Pattern of Government Growth, 1800–60: The Passenger Acts and their Enforcement* (McGibbon and Kee), especially in the concluding chapter (16). The problems facing the sanitary reformers are fully discussed in R. A. Lewis's *Edwin Chadwick and the Public Health Movement* (Longmans, 1952) and in the introduction to M. W. Flinn's new edition of Edwin Chadwick's *Report on the Sanitary Condition of the Labouring Population of Great Britain, 1842* (Edinburgh University Press, 1965).

PART V
Statistics of the Industrial Revolution 1750–1850

This Part provides a short summary of some of the basic statistics of economic change from 1750–1850. The statistics are presented, for the most part, in a highly simplified form. Annual statistics have been abbreviated, wherever possible, to an *average* return for a five-year period (i.e. a 'total' for 1785 will consist of an average for 1783–7). Any average can be misleading. The five-year average is capable of ironing out short turn fluctuations in trade or output. Because it is essentially an arbitrary division it cuts across fluctuations, sometimes making them seem more important than they were and sometimes having the opposite result. Readers who wish to refer to annual series will find them in B. R. Mitchell and Phyllis Deane, *The Abstract of British Historical Statistics* (Cambridge University Press 1962). This book is indispensable for any statistical approach to this period and without it this chapter would have been almost impossible to assemble. Where it is necessary this Part contains a description of the quality of eighteenth or nineteenth-century statistics. Each group of statistics is followed by some comment and interpretation: this is intended to supplement the text of Parts I–IV.

I hope this chapter will not be used simply as an appendix. Statistics are not an optional extra in economic history but an integral part of the subject. Without them accurate explanation is impossible. But this is not to say that the statistics are the only satisfactory evidence to be used by the economic historian. The statistics are often faulty. Above all they have to be understood as generalizations which summarize the individual decisions and actions of which social and economic life is composed. The function of statistics in economic history has been well put by Professor Court:

A figure, a table, or a graph can be critical in economic history, for it may bring to the final test our view of how or why things happened. At the same time it must be allowed that much statistical work is in the nature of description rather than explanation. Emphasis and degree are however important matters in history. Quantities may assist to define the limits of a problem, even if they do not serve to solve it. (*Approaches to History*, ed. H. P. R. Finberg, p. 29, 1962)

The statistics in this chapter are partly a description of the Industrial Revolution, and what was meant, in the nineteenth century, by 'the progress of the nation': they also provide material for an understanding of both the phasing of industrial acceleration and what it was in the general economic situation which shaped the history of particular industries.

[34] POPULATION

The sources

The population statistics of the Industrial Revolution are based on three major contemporary sources; the parish registers, the decennial censuses begun in 1801 and, from 1838, the *Annual Reports* of the Registrar General. The first census was, of course, a landmark. It arose out of the anxious debate on population growth in late eighteenth-century England: pessimistic views on the nation's ability to support a rising population had gained ground with the publication of Malthus's *First Essay on Population* in 1798. The 1801 census recognized a need to pursue the history of population growth back into the eighteenth century. Parishes had to supply details of baptisms, burials, and marriages for 1780–1800, and in 1836 John Rickman, the administrator of the early censuses, attempted to push the precensus history of population back to the late sixteenth century by asking the parishes to submit further details from their registers.

Much of this evidence is difficult to interpret. This has not prevented general agreement about the scale of population growth over the eighteenth century, but both the causes and the phasing of this demographic revolution have occasioned keen discussion. The limitations of the sources have determined the character of much of this debate. A successful analysis of population trends relies much more upon agreed birth, death, and marriage rates than upon an acceptable aggregate increase across half a century or more. Even after 1838 registration was not complete. But for the important years 1780–1810 the parish registers were very fallible; the Methodists did not bother with Anglican baptism or burial and the growing popularity of private cemeteries opened up another possibility for error in the calculation of births and deaths. These deficiencies may be partly remedied as local studies of the registers, and the records of Dissenters' and other burial grounds, become more intense.

1 Estimates of British population in the eighteenth century (in thousands)

England and Wales			Scotland		Ireland (C)	
1700	5,475 (R)	5,826 (B)	1755	1,265	1712	2,791
1750	6,467	6,140			1754	3,191
1780	7,953	7,531			1791	4,753
1790	8,675	8,247				
1800	9,168	9,156				

2 British population, 1801–51 (in thousands)

	England and Wales	% increase	Scotland	% increase	Ireland	% increase
1801	8,893	—	1,608	—	—	—
1811	10,164	14·00	1,806	12·3	—	—
1821	12,000	18·06	2,092	15·8	6,802	—
1831	13,897	15·80	2,364	18·0	7,767	14·19
1841	15,914	14·27	2,620	10·8	8,185	5·25
1851	17,928	12·65	2,889	10·2	6,552	−19·85
1911	36,070		4,761		4,390	

(R) Rickman, 1802   (B) J. Brownlee, 1916   (C) K. H. Connell, 1950

3 Baptisms, burials, and marriages: annual averages per decade 1780–1839 (in thousands)

England and Wales	Baptisms	Burials	Marriages
1780s	240	192	67
1790s	263	187	75
1800s	272	201	75
1810s	317	206	90
1820s	368	236	103
1830s	379	278	112

4 Estimated birth and death rates 1751–1840 (Brownlee), England and Wales (per thousand)

	Births	Deaths
1751–60	36·9	30·3
1771–80	37·5	31·1
1791–1800	37·3	26·9
1811–20	26·6	21·1
1831–40	36·6	23·4

5 Birth, death, and marriage rates, 1841–50. England and Wales (per thousand)

	Births	Deaths	Marriages
1841	32·2	21·6	15·4
1842	32·1	21·7	14·7
1843	32·3	21·2	15·2
1844	32·7	21·6	16·0
1845	32·5	20·9	17·2
1846	33·8	23·0	17·2
1847	31·5	24·7	15·9
1848	32·5	23·0	15·9
1849	32·9	25·1	16·2
1850	33·4 Av. 32·6	20·8 Av. 22·4	17·2 Av. 16·1
1913	25·5	14·6	15·7

6 Average death rates in different age groups 1841–50, England and Wales (per thousand)

0–4	5–9	10–14	15–19	20–24	25–34	35–44	45–54	55–64	65–74
71·3	9·2	5·1	7·1	9·5	9·9	12·8	18·2	31·8	67·5

7 Composition of the population of England and Wales by age groups, 1821–51 (by thousands and as a percentage of the total)

	1821	%		1841	%		1851	%
70+	311·3	2·95	70+	446·9	2·81	70+	503·3	2·81
60–9	480·7	4·56	60–9	699·4	4·40	60–9	808·8	4·51
50–9	694·4	6·59	50–9	1,026·2	6·45	50–9	1,253·1	6·88
40–9	983·3	9·30	40–9	1,526·6	9·64	40–9	1,767·6	9·90
30–9	1,243·2	11·9	30–9	2,051·5	12·9	30–9	2,364·7	13·2
20–9	1,657·3	15·7	20–9	2,833·4	17·8	20–9	3,137·1	17·5
10–19	2,218·2	21·1	10–19	3,318·9	20·8	10–19	3,670·6	20·5
0–9	2,942·7	27·9	0–9	4,011·2	25·2	0–9	4,440·4	24·7

(The returns of ages in 1821 were incomplete; 10,531 answered out of 12,000. The percentages in this table are therefore of total *replies*.)

Comment

The most remarkable phase of population growth during the Industrial Revolution took place in the early nineteenth century. Although the 1780s was a decade of rapid growth, the overall increase in population between 1750 and 1800 was much less spectacular than the increase marked up between 1800 and 1850. Again, it is at least *possible* that the long accepted contrast in population growth between 1700–50 and 1750–1800 has been exaggerated. If the estimates for 1700 are too high, as many now believe, the rate of growth for 1700–50 compares more favourably with the succeeding fifty years. It has recently been pointed out that by reducing Brownlee's estimate for 1700 by 10 per cent (not an extreme step) and by raising it by the same amount for 1750 (5–10 per cent margin of error can be assumed for all estimates) the rates of growth for the two periods narrow to 30 per cent and 35 per cent (G. S. L. Tucker, in *Economic History Review*, Vol. XX, 1967, p. 135). The validity of this calculation may be no greater than earlier estimates but it certainly serves to emphasize the danger of linking the early Industrial Revolution with an equally revolutionary upsurge in the rates of population growth. This was a nineteenth-century phenomenon.

As well as attempting to establish the size of the population in the eighteenth century historians have been equally anxious to describe the mechanics of its growth. The baptism and burial returns seem to show that the birth rate was approximately 36 per thousand for most of the century after 1750 while the death rate began to fall in the 1780s. An examination of the deficiencies of the registers in this period has, however, led J. T. Krause to question this familiar interpretation. He attributes the stability of the burial returns from the 1780s to the 1810s to under-registration and has argued that the death rate remained at about 27 per thousand until the end of the 1810s. The birth rate was, by contrast, much higher than had previously been thought, i.e. 40–42 per thousand over the same period. By the 1840s the birth rate had dropped significantly and the death rate had also fallen. Both approaches have difficulties. A sharp fall in the death rate in the late eighteenth and early nineteenth century is a little hard to accept even if the growing use of vaccination and the absence of severe epidemics (which subsided from the *mid*-century) are taken into account. Equally, a soaring birth rate depends upon a fall in the age of marriage and a relaxation of family limitation: there is, as yet, insufficient evidence for either.

How is population growth to be related to the Industrial Revolution? The exceptionally rapid growth of the early nineteenth century is most simply explained as a response to greater economic opportunity: by this date the Industrial Revolution was 'creating its own labour force'. This mechanism operated primarily through the birth rate. That it was the birth rate which responded most immediately to economic circumstances can be seen from the first decade of registration statistics (Table 5). Recovery from the slump of 1839–42 was reflected in a rising number of marriages during 1843–6: the return of bad times in 1847–8 again reduced the marriage rate. The birth rate, as might be expected, peaks in 1846 and again at the close of the decade. The death rate may have been marginally affected by hardship (1842?) but its fluctuations were mainly caused by the uncertain incidence of epidemic disease. 1846–7 were years of typhus and influenza epidemics and 1849 saw a return of cholera. In the 1840s births were a measure of optimism and while it would be a mistake to read this experience too far back into the eighteenth century something like it had been established by, or during, the 1780s.

To stress the importance of the birth rate is not, however, to relegate either the death rate itself or the contribution of population growth to the Industrial Revolution to a position of insignificance. As M. W. Flinn has argued *only* a falling death rate from the 1780s would entitle historians to regard population growth as a major factor in this crucial period: the birth rate 'theory' would make the growth of population either, as we have seen, an outcome of economic change or a quite separate and independent process (see Flinn, *The Origins of the Industrial Revolution*, 1966, pp. 29–36). But this need not preclude an important role for a fall in the death rate at other phases of the Industrial Revolution. When the death rate falls an increased number of children survive infancy and begin a working life. Similarly the expectation of life for adults rises. Both of these changes make an important economic impact. The proportion of young and mature adults in the population increases at the expense of the very young and the old (because, by modern standards, the expectation of life will not be great). It is this section of the population which is, by definition, most productive and the source of the greatest demand. An expansion of domestic demand was perhaps the most notable feature of the third quarter of the eighteenth century: industrial wages rose and so did the population of the more industrial regions. While in the later eighteenth century, and in the nineteenth century, the demand for industrial goods was kept buoyant by the *number* of consumers and rising exports it looks as though a rise in *per capita* incomes was more important in this earlier period. Of course the number of consumers was increasing too and the rise in the population continued to push up incomes of those dependent upon the land – it was this which lay at the base of the whole process.

The age structure of the population in the nineteenth century (Tables 6 and 7) demonstrates the importance of the death rate to early industrial Britain. Despite the high infant mortality children and adolescents dominated the population; the under 20s were 49 per cent of the total population in 1821, 46 per cent in 1841, and 45 per cent in 1851. Fully a quarter of the population were children under the age of ten. This must be taken into account in any attempt to assess the contentious issue of the use of child labour during the Industrial Revolution. Across the whole period there was a slight upward shift in the proportion of working adults in the population (Table 7); the 30–39 age group had expanded its share of the total by 1·3 per cent between 1821 and 1851 (but it *was* the survivor of a large generation), and the 20–29 age group by 1·8 per cent over the same period.

The expectation of life also seemed to be rising. For every male born in the decades 1761–70, 1771–80, and 1781–90 who survived to 1821, a corresponding 1·274, 1·363, and 1·479 of those born 1781–90, 1791–1800, and 1801–10 survived to 1841. Of course this may mean little more than that each generation was larger than the one before. There was certainly no dramatic fall in the death rate. Nineteenth-century sanitary reformers rightly believed that their first object should be to reduce the death rate among adults, especially among married men with families. Perhaps it was the cost of relieving widows and orphans (most of which was carried by their relatives) which made this aspect of the public health question seem so urgent. Chadwick was able to point out other consequences for the community in this persistent drain on the numbers of mature men and women. Their deaths left behind a population 'that is young, inexperienced, ignorant, credulous, irritable, passionate, and dangerous, having a perpetual tendency to moral as well as physical deterioration'.

[35] EXAMPLES OF URBAN GROWTH

8 Contrasts in urban growth 1801–51 (in thousands)

	1801	1811	1821	1831	1841	1851	1911
Nottingham	29	34	40	50	52	57	260
Manchester	75	89	126	182	235	303	714
Salford	14	19	26	41	53	64	231
Oldham	12	17	22	32	43	53	147
Leeds	53	63	84	123	152	172	446
Bradford	13	16	26	44	67	104	288
Halifax	12	13	17	22	28	34	102
Huddersfield	7	10	13	19	25	31	108

9 Contrasts in the rate of urban growth 1801–51 (% increase)

Nottingham	17·2	17·6	25·0	4·0	9·6
Manchester	18·6	41·6	51·0	29·1	28·9
Salford	35·1	36·8	57·7	29·3	21·0
Oldham	41·6	29·4	45·4	34·4	23·3
Leeds	18·9	33·3	46·4	25·2	13·2
Bradford	23·1	62·5	84·6	52·3	55·2
Halifax	8·3	30·7	29·4	27·3	21·4
Huddersfield	42·3	30·0	46·1	31·6	24·0

Mid-eighteenth-century estimates suggest that Nottingham's population at that date was approximately 12,000 and Manchester's 17,000 (1758).

10 Growth of population 1801–51 in the West Riding of Yorkshire, in the area of the (1951) West Yorkshire Conurbation, and in the five major towns of Leeds, Bradford, Halifax, Huddersfield, and Wakefield (in thousands)

West Riding		West Yorkshire Conurbation		Big 5	
1801	591	292		96	
1851	1,366	792		363	
	+775	+131·1%	+500	+171·2%	267	+ 272·4%

11 The Potteries 1801–51 (in thousands)

	Stoke*		Tunstall
1811	28		1,677
1821	35		
1831	35		4,673
1841	54		
1851	66 = +135·7%		9,566 = +470·4%
1911	235		

* Includes the townships of Burslem, Hanley, and Longton; 1911 figure includes Fenton and Tunstall as well.

12 Growth of population in Birmingham, in the West Midlands Conurbation, and in the combined population of the four towns of Birmingham, Dudley, Walsall, and Wolverhampton 1750–1851

	Birmingham	West Midlands	4 towns	4 towns as % of region
1750	24*			
1801	71	192	104	54·2
1851	233	650	347	53·4
		+458 238·5%	+243 233·6%	

* This figure is an estimate, the later figures are based upon the borough as created in 1838.

13 Glasgow 1755–1851 (in thousands)

		% increase	Clydeside Conurbation	
1801	77		(1755	63)
1811	101	31·2		
1821	147	45·5	1801	160
1831	202	37·4	1851	569
1841	275	36·1		
1851	345	25·4		
	+268	348·0%	+409 255·6%	
1911	784			

14 Greater London 1801–51 (in thousands)

		% increase	as % of England and Wales
1801	1,117		12·6
1811	1,327	18·8	
1821	1,600	24·6	
1831	1,907	19·2	
1841	2,239	17·3	
1851	2,685	16·6	14·9
1911	4,541 (L.C.C. area)		

Commentary

There is no single explanation for urban growth during the Industrial Revolution nor does it follow a single pattern. Under eighteenth-century conditions a rise in population did not lead to an immediate urban revolution. Clearly there was a drift to the towns and especially to those which could offer industrial work, either because they were established centres of a domestic industry or because they became growth points for consumer trades. But further industrialization in the eighteenth century primarily took the form of an expansion of the domestic industries and did not cause the emergence of the industrial *town*. The coal and iron industries did not centre on towns. For both industries the 'centres' were industrial villages, many of which were entirely new settlements. The larger unit here was the industrial region or area (the coalfield).

During the eighteenth century much of the increased population was retained on the land. In Ireland, where the population growth was quite as remarkable as elsewhere in Britain, it seems as though almost all the increase was held on the land. The nineteenth century did not totally supplant the settlement patterns of eighteenth-century industrialization. Industrial villages did not suddenly become out of date; the factory itself had appeared within a rural environment and continued to flourish there. Certainly the large industrial town now became a distinguishing feature of British society. Transport improvements and the use of steam power in industry created fresh possibilities for concentrating an industrial population in towns. By the 1840s urban migration was very pronounced and had clearly increased rapidly since the beginning of the century (Table 9).

Net gain (+) or loss (−) by migration in England 1841–61 (in thousands)

	London	Other towns	Colliery districts	Rural areas
1841–51	+274	+386	+82	−443
1851–61	+244	+272	+103	−122

(P. Deane and W. A. Cole, *British Economic Growth 1688–1959*, p. 10; based on calculations in A. K. Cairncross, *Home and Foreign Investment 1870–1913*)

What has to be understood by an industrial town in the nineteenth century is not always as straightforward as the statistics suggest. The registration of the urban population was itself an incredibly complicated task because the towns were growing so rapidly and because, in so many cases, there was no framework of local government to act as a guide. 'Towns' may be no more than statistical concepts. Even where the identity of a town and its inhabitants can be established without difficulty they may both have to be seen within the context of an industrial region. The early history of the modern industrial conurbations indicate how wrong it is to force together the Industrial Revolution and the industrial town in a simple partnership. In the West Riding (Tables 8, 9, 10), despite the exceptionally rapid growth of the major towns, their inhabitants were not in a majority even in the 'satellite' area comprised by the modern conurbation. Put this way the smaller towns and industrial villages appear as accretions to the leading towns: historically it was these towns themselves which were the accretion representing, as Bradford did, a secondary stage in the history of the woollen industry, the beginnings of power mechanization and the opening of town mills (Bradford had 1 mill in 1801, 67 in 1841).

The Potteries are a further example of an industrial region which developed only a loosely knit urban pattern. The transition from a local industry, using local raw materials, and with a limited market, into modern industry, dependent upon imported raw materials, with a national and international market distributing products from luxury articles and ornaments to common domestic earthenware, followed quickly upon the opening of the Trent and Mersey Canal in 1777. Although most potteries were modest concerns in 1851 the factory system was more advanced in the Potteries than in the woollen industry: some of the works, like the Wedgwood's Etruria (Hanley), the Fountain Place Works at Burslem (1,100 employed in the 1830s), and the Spode Works at Stoke (800 employed in 1840) were large by any standard. Steam power had not revolutionized the industry by 1850, but it was used in some places for mixing the materials. The larger works had attempted to employ steam power at an early date; Etruria had its first Boulton and Watt engine in 1782–4, another in 1792, and its third in 1802, while the Spode Works installed two engines 1802–6. But if the industrial organization of the Potteries was comparatively advanced its population was distributed in a disorderly clustering of small towns and industrial villages. The largest town in the Potteries was Burslem which had a population of some 13,000 in the 1840s (16,000 if *its* subordinate villages of Sneyd and Cobridge are included). Some of the most quickly growing communities in the nineteenth century were of very recent origin: pot-making had only just been established in Tunstall by 1800, yet there were 17 potteries there by 1838. The history of the Potteries in the nineteenth century is evidence of the tenacity with which people held to the immediate community, however small, for their deepest sense of identity and belonging.

As the early industrial towns continued to grow in the nineteenth century new industries arose to complement the pioneer industry on which the town's fortune had been built. In the textile towns perhaps the commonest new departure was into the manufacture of textile machinery. This became important in Nottingham after the effective mechanization of lace-making had brought this ancillary textile industry into the town to join the traditional hosiery trade. Nottingham's outward expansion was hindered in the early nineteenth century by the shortage of building land. The refusal of the burgesses (the 'cowocracy') to permit the enclosure of the town fields was the cause of appalling overcrowding:

I believe that nowhere else shall we find so large a mass of inhabitants crowded into courts, alleys, and lanes, as in Nottingham, and those, too, of the worst possible construction. (Royal Commission on the Health of Towns, 1845)

When the fields were enclosed in 1845 they were quickly covered with workers' houses and new factories but the slums had become a permanent feature of Nottingham life.

The growth of Glasgow (Table 13) was based upon a much wider range of commercial and industrial activities. Glasgow had prospered in the eighteenth century with the development of the Atlantic trade. From the 1780s the new techniques of cotton manufacture were quickly established in an area where there was already a successful linen industry. In the 1840s Glasgow was primarily a textile town: 25 per cent of its labour force was employed in textiles in 1851. The textile industry helped to sponsor the engineering trades in Glasgow, especially the manufacture of steam engines and, from the 1840s, of locomotives. Parallel, at this stage, to growth in the engineering industry was the spectacular rise of the Scottish iron industry from the 1830s. Cheaper Scottish iron thus became available at the opening of the railway era but, more influential for Glasgow itself, was the quickly established preeminence of the Clyde in iron shipbuilding during the 1840s.

[36] THE LABOUR FORCE

15 Estimated industrial distribution of British labour force, 1801–51 (in millions, and as percentage of the whole)

	Agriculture, forestry, fishing	%	Manufacture, mining, industry	%	Trade, transport	%	Domestic, personal service	%	Public, professional service	%
1801	1·7	35·9	1·4	27·9	0·5	11·2	0·6	11·5	0·3*	11·8*
1811	1·8	33·0	1·7	30·2	0·6	11·6	0·7	11·8	0·4	13·3
1821	1·8	28·4	2·4	38·4	0·8	12·1	0·8	12·7	0·3	8·5
1831	1·8	24·6	3·0	40·8	0·9	12·4	0·9	12·6	0·3	9·5
1841	1·9	22·2	3·3	40·5	1·2	14·2	1·2	14·5	0·3	8·5
1851	2·1	21·7	4·1	42·9	1·5	15·8	1·3	13·0	0·5	6·7
1911	1·6	8·3	8·6	46·4	4·0	21·5	2·6	13·9	1·5	9·9

(P. Deane and W. A. Cole *British Economic Growth*, pp. 142–3)

* These two columns do not correspond, because the percentage column also includes other miscellaneous groups (e.g. the unemployed).

16 Occupations: major groups. 1841 Census. England and Wales (in thousands)

	Men Under 20	Over 20	Women Under 20	Over 20	Total
Commerce, trade, manufacture	318	1,750	159	391	2,619
Agriculture	162	1,042	9	48	1,261
Domestic service	84	150	289	476	999
Living on means	5	119	14	308	446
Total occupied	724	4,062	505	1,416	6,707
Total unoccupied	2,936	239	3,157	3,059	9,391

Under 20s = 18·3 per cent of total occupied, 18·2 per cent of those employed in commerce, trade, and manufacture, 37·3 per cent of those employed in domestic service.

N.B. Tables 15 and 16: occupation details were not fully recorded until 1841. These estimates (i.e. Table 15) for the distribution of the labour force in modern industrial categories are only approximate and for 1801–21 Deane and Cole admit 'little more than guesses'.

17 Occupations: numbers employed in the major trades, 1851. Trades of 30,000 or more included (in thousands)

Agricultural labourer, farm servant, shepherd	1,461
Domestic servant	1,039
Cotton calico manufacture, printing, dyeing	502
Labourer (undefined)	377
Farmer, grazier	307
Boot and shoe maker	274
Milliner, dressmaker	268
Coal-miner	219
Carpenter, joiner	183
Army, Navy	179
Tailor	153
Washerwoman, mangler	146
Woollen cloth manufacture	138
Silk manufacture	115
Blacksmith	113
Worsted manufacture	104
Mason, pavior	101
Messenger, porter, errand boy	101
Linen manufacture	99
Seaman (at home)	89
Grocer	86
Gardener	81
Iron manufacture	80
Innkeeper, licensed victualler, beershop keeper	76
Seamstress, shirtmaker	73
Bricklayer	68
Butcher, meat salesman	68
Hose manufacture	65
School master/mistress	65
Lace manufacture	64
Plumber, painter, glazier	63
Baker	62
Carman, carrier, carter	57
Charwoman	55
Draper	49
Engine/machine maker	48
Commercial clerk	44
Cabinet maker	41
Teacher (various), governess	41
Fisherman/woman	38
Boat/barge, man/woman	38
Miller	37
Earthenware manufacture	37
Sawyer	35
Railway labourer	34
Straw-plait manufacture	32
Brick maker/dealer	31
Government Civil Service	31
Hawker, pedlar	31
Wheelwright	30

18 The labour force of the textile industry 1835–50: includes the cotton, woollen, linen (flax), and silk industries. Those employed in the cotton industry appear after the total in brackets (in thousands)

	Under 13		13–18		All ages		Total
	Male	Female	Male	Female	Male	Female	
1835	28 (15)	29 (14)	46 (28)	64 (38)	152 (100)	186 (119)	338
1850	20 (9)	21 (6)	68 (37)	— —	248 (142)	349 (189)	597

The under-13s were 16·8 per cent of the labour force in 1835, the 13–18s were 32·5 per cent, and women 55 per cent: in 1850 the under 13s were 6·9 per cent and women 58·5 per cent. The figures are based on returns by the Factory Inspectors.

Commentary

Table 15 summarizes the redistribution of the labour force in Britain accomplished by the Industrial Revolution. A complete census of occupations was not taken until 1841, although the occupations of men over 20 were covered by the previous census. The censuses of 1811, 1821, and 1831 aimed, in this field, at a simple classification into agricultural and non-agricultural occupations. The earlier figures in Table 15 have, as a result, to be regarded as approximate. Even so it is clear that there was a sharp fall in the proportion of the labour force engaged in agriculture, especially in the first thirty years of the nineteenth century, and a slightly larger proportionate rise of those engaged in industry over the same period. From the 1830s the fastest growth was in the services sector, although industry continued to grow and agriculture to contract. The origins of this crucial process of redistribution lay in the century, or century and a half, before 1800. It is unlikely that redistribution was proceeding at the nineteenth-century pace between 1750 and 1800; if it had then the proportion in agriculture must have been about 50 per cent in 1750. Calculations based on Gregory King's classification of the population in 1688 suggest that the agricultural sector then contained 40–60 per cent of the labour force. The lower of these estimates implies a substantial diversification of employment occurring in the sixteenth and seventeenth centuries which was continued through the eighteenth century. The higher estimate seems to make the eighteenth century itself the key period of redistribution.

The Britain which was transformed by the Industrial Revolution was already accustomed to specialized employment or, as Adam Smith called it, 'the division of labour'. For Adam Smith the labourer's coat set off a train of speculation:

s coarse and rough as it may appear, [it] is the produce of the joint abour of a great multitude of workmen. The shepherd, the sorter of the wool, the wool-comber or carder, the dyer, the scribbler, the spinner, the weaver, the fuller, the dresser, with many others, must all join their different arts in order to complete even this homely production. How many merchants and carriers besides must have been employed in transporting the materials from some of those workmen to others who often live in a very distant part of the country! how much commerce and navigation in particular, how many ship-builders, sailors, sail-makers, rope-makers, must have been employed to bring together the different drugs made use of by the dyer. . . . What a variety of labour too is necessary to produce the tools of the meanest of those workmen! . . . Were we to examine, in the same manner, all the different parts of his dress and household furniture . . . and consider what a variety of labour is employed about each of them, we shall be sensible that without the assistance and co-operations of many thousands, the very meanest person in a civilized country could not be provided, even according to what we very falsely imagine, the easy and simple manner in which he is commonly accommodated. Compared, indeed, with the more extravagant luxury of the great, his accommodation must no doubt appear extremely simple and easy; and yet it may be true, perhaps, that the accommodation of a European prince does not always so much exceed that of an industrious and frugal peasant, as the accommodation of the latter exceeds that of many an African king, the absolute master of the lives and liberties of ten thousand naked savages. (*Wealth of Nations*, Book I, Chapter I)

However closely historians search for an industrial 'take-off' in the late eighteenth century, it will remain necessary to admit the wider importance of the general economic maturity of eighteenth-century Britain.

The list of major occupations in 1851 (Table 17) shows the impact made by the Industrial Revolution upon employment. It must not be exaggerated. Agriculture and the traditional crafts (carpenter, tailor, blacksmith, bricklayer, cabinet-maker, sawyer, and brick maker) comprise one very large element of the labour force, while the distributive and retail trades comprise another. Among the industries the textile industry, in its various forms, was easily the largest employer of labour. Those working in the iron industry, as coal miners, as machine makers or on the railways as labourers, were equally representative of

the Industrial Revolution. So were those working in earthenware manufacture. But by 1851 the economy was sufficiently
integrated for concentration on 'representative' industries to be
a misleading guide to assessing the impact of the Industrial
Revolution. The straw-plait industry, organized on an outwork
basis, and centred on the counties of Buckinghamshire, Bed-
fordshire, Hertfordshire and Suffolk, was just as much a creature
of consumer demand as the textile industries and its rise as a
rural craft in the early nineteenth century helped to offset the
effects of a decline in the old lace and silk ribbon industries
which had previously given employment to the cottagers in
these counties. The importance to industry of the building
trades, of the carmen and bargees, or of the wheelwrights hardly
needs to be emphasized. What was important about the composition of the labour force in 1851 was not the proportion of
workers in it engaged in the 'revolutionized' industries, but
simply the range and extent of industrial employment.

It is not easy to put the role of child labour in the economy in
proper perspective. There certainly do not seem to have been a
disproportionate number of children and young people engaged
in 'commerce, trade, and manufacture' in 1841 (Table 16). The
under 20s formed only 13·6 per cent of the agricultural labour
force which suggests that there was not much that they could
usefully do on the land, particularly if they were girls. Young
people and women were clearly important to the textile industries: outside the textile districts domestic service swallowed up
the majority of working girls and women. Boys could find work
in most trades as apprentices or errand boys. Child labour under
the age of 10–13 was probably the exception rather than the
rule. The Factory Acts had helped to reduce both the number and
importance of children in the textile industries by 1850. Here
children's work was subject to some sort of control by the
inspectors. Elsewhere this was not the case. Domestic outwork,
either urban or rural, usually imposed some burden on the
children; if they were not themselves set to work (as in straw
plaiting) they were given domestic chores which would otherwise have fallen to adults. On the land children's work was

seasonal but it was none the less arduous for that. If the contribution of children to the labour force was only modest in numerical terms this does not mean that it was economically unimportant. In 1841 a population of nearly 16 million had to be supported by the work of under 4½ million adults; not surprisingly children were put to work whenever the opportunity presented itself.

[37] INDUSTRIAL PRODUCTION

Coal

19 Estimated output of the coal industry 1770–1850 (U.K. – in million tons)

1770	6·2	1830	22·4
1800	11·0	1835	27·7
1816	15·9	1840	33·7
1820	17·4	1845	45·9
1825	21·9	1850	49·4
		1913	287·4

(see P. Deane and W. A. Cole, *British Economic Growth*, p. 216, and Clapham, Vol. 1, pp. 430–1.)

Iron

20 Estimates of pig iron output in Britain 1720–1852 (in thousand tons)

1720	25	1806	244	1840	1,396
1788	68	1823	455	1847	1,999
1796	125	1830	677	1852	2,701
				1913	10,260

At the opening of the nineteenth century Staffordshire and Shropshire were the most important iron-producing counties. By 1852 South Staffordshire, South Wales, and the Scottish Lowlands were the leading centres of production.

Textiles

21 *Raw cotton imports 1750–1850* (in million lb). Five-year averages: 1750 = average for 1748–52

1750	2·9	1815–17	100
1760	2·3	1820	164
1770	3·7	1825	187
1780	6·9	1830	237
1785	16·0	1835	358
1790	28·9	1840	477
1795		1845	536
1800	47·2	1850	664
1805	60·6		
1810	81·1		

22 *Average annual prices of best quality mule yarn 1800–50*

Count	100	140	200
1800	8/–	13/6	
1807			25/–
1810	5/6	7/4	
1815	6/2	9/2	
1817–20			20/7
1820	5/1	7/1	
1825	4/4	6/10	
1830	3/3	5/8	
1830–34			16/8
1840	3/7	5/4	10/11
1850	3/2	4/8	9/3

Each year, except where indicated otherwise, is a five-year average.

(Based on Table II in T. S. Ashton, 'Some Statistics of the Industrial Revolution', in E. M. Carus-Wilson, *Essays in Economic History*, Vol. 3, p. 248. Ashton's average annual prices were those at which the firm of M'Connel and Kennedy sold their yarn over this period.)

23 Woollen cloth milled in the West Riding of Yorkshire 1770–1815
Five-year averages: 1770 = average of 1768–72 (in million yds)

	Broad cloth	Narrow cloth
1770	2·82	2·21
1775	3·04	2·39
1780	3·52	2·65
1785	4·65	3·53
1790	5·34	4·71
1795	6·99	5·07
1800	8·50	5·48
1805	9·40	5·80
1810	9·21	5·65
1815	10·77	5·84

24 Raw wool imports, estimated domestic wool clip, and *total consumption 1775–1849* (in million lb)

	Imports	Estimated domestic wool clip	Total consumption
1775		80	
1776–99	2·9	90	
1800–19	10·2	100	
1820–4	17·5	110	140·0
1825–9	28·1	115	153·3
1830–4	35·3	120	171·1
1835–9	52·9	120	177·9
1840–4	53·2	125	188·0
1845–9	70·4	130	209·5

(*Imports* for 1776–99 and 1800–19 are averages based on Elizabeth B. Schumpeter's *English Overseas Trade Statistics* and returns in the Parliamentary Papers, presented in *The Abstract of British Historical Statistics*, p. 191. The figures for estimated total consumption are those of P. Deane and W. A. Cole in *British Economic Growth 1688–1959*, p. 196.)

25 A group of consumer industries: candles, soap, paper, and beer production *1750–1850* (England and Wales)

a *Tallow Candles charged with duty 1750–1830.* Five-year averages: 1750 = average of 1748–52 (in million lb)

1750	36·0	1790	52·7
1760	39·8	1800	62·9
1770	42·3	1810	70·6
1780	49·2	1820	83·5
		1830	109·9 (1828–30)

b *Soap charged with duty 1750–1850.* Five-year averages (in million lb)

1750	28·6	1810	64·7
1760	28·8	1820	79·4
1770	30·8	1830	105·8
1780	36·5	1840	152·4
1790	40·2	1850	173·0
1800	49·3		

c *Paper charged with duty 1750–1850.* Five-year averages (in tons)

1750	4,075	1810	16,844
1760	5,265	1820	20,027
1770	6,446	1830	25,347
1780	6,502	1840	33,352
1790	10,866	1850	44,742
1800	12,290		

d *Beer charged with duty 1750–1830.* In thousand barrels (the barrel contained 32·6 gallons), strong and small beer included

1750	5,758	1800	7,168	
1760	5,855	1810	7,275	
1770	5,485	1820	6,970	
1780	6,134	1830	7,782	(1828–30)
1790	6,501			

Building

26 *Brick production 1790–1845,* England and Wales. Five-year averages: 1790 = average of 1788–92 (in millions)

1790	705·5	1820	984·3
1795	681·3	1825	1,442·0
1800	570·9	1830	1,075·4
1805	859·6	1835	1,319·5
1810	877·1	1840	1,504·8
1815	764·6	1845	1,726·8

Glass charged with duty 1750–1845, England and Wales. Five-year averages: 1750 = average of 1748–52 (in thousand tons)

1750	2·9	1815	6·7
1760	4·6	1820	7·4
1770	6·6	1825	9·4 (1826 for 6 months)
1780	6·0	1830	9·7
1790	8·1	1835	11·6
1795	7·9	1840	13·0
1800	8·0	1845	11·4
1805	8·9		
1810	8·9		

27 An index of industrial production 1800–50 (W. G. Hoffman)

This index has been estimated to include 77 per cent of total industrial production, including building, for the years 1801–30 and 1831–60. The Hoffman index is an annual index but has been averaged here at five-year intervals.

1913 = 100

1805	7·44	1830	14·6 (single year)
1810	8·22	1835	17·1
1815	9·03	1840	20·4
1820	10·5	1845	23·7
1825	12·5	1850	27·9

Commentary

The quality of production statistics available for the period of the Industrial Revolution is, quite naturally, extremely variable. Economic historians and statisticians have worked at the statistics, particularly those of the eighteenth century, with great ingenuity but their estimates have to be regarded as approximate. The popularity of the excise with the governments of this period has, at least, made it possible to follow the careers of some industries quite closely but, even here, much depends upon trust in the efficiency and honesty of the excise officers. For some industries the nature of the product, as with glass, made evasion difficult. For others the level of duty was decisive: the excise on bricks was so low that evasion was pointless. The excisemen were generally more effective in the London area and this means that their returns for an industry like soap-making, which was largely London based, are especially valuable. Some important

industries virtually escaped the taxman   ɔal shipped
from the North-East, or entering Lond   .easured from
contemporary statistics the rise of r   and industrial
areas, relying upon the canals for '   .e these returns
an inadequate guide to total   the nineteenth
century. Official annual estima   ᴜduction, as of iron,
did not begin until 1854. Fo   ᴜndustries it is possible
to supplement informatior   ᴜm the excise (on woollen
cloth or printed goods) a'   ᴜze of the finished product by
estimates of the *input*   ᴜterials. In the case of the cotton
industry progress is '   ᴜest measured by the quantity of
raw cotton import   ᴜpply it.

The question to ᴠ   production statistics ought to supply
an answer is: When did the Industrial Revolution occur? Is it
possible to isolate a comparatively short period of rapid growth?
The cotton industry clearly did experience, in the 1780s, a
decade of revolutionary advance when imports of raw cotton
rose by nearly 350 per cent. This was followed by a 110 per cent
rise in imports for the 1790s. No other industry really repeated
this experience. Even the cotton industry's exceptional history
does not compress all incident into one phase of 20–30 years. The
1770s have a special interest because it was in this decade (as
the foundation of some famous firms indicate) which created a
launching pad for its successor. Equally the growth of the
industry's output in the 1830s, as power weaving gave it a new
capacity for expansion, can scarcely be placed *outside* the period
of its industrial revolution. Just as the improved technology of
spinning brought down the prices of cotton yarn in the earlier
period, so the price of cotton cloth fell in the 1830s and 1840s.
In this later phase the industry finally shed its domestic outworkers and moved over to an almost wholly factory-based
structure. It could be argued that there were two industrial
revolutions in the cotton industry before 1850. In the woollen
industry it is doubtful if the term 'industrial revolution' really
applies to its history before the 1830s. Apart from the greater
technological problems encountered by the woollen industry, it
was also less easy to expand supplies of the raw material.

'Revolutionary' growth in this industry was delayed until the middle decades of the nineteenth century. The output of soap (Table 25b), of which the woollen industry was the greatest industrial user, rose very rapidly in the 1830s and again underlines the importance of this decade.

The history of the coal and iron industries also suggests that it is incorrect to try to apply too limited a chronology to the Industrial Revolution. In the eighteenth century the main use for coal was still as a domestic fuel: the opening of canals and the spread of steam power increased the industrial demand for coal quite considerably from the 1770s. But it was the revolutionary progress of the iron industry which had the greatest impact upon the coal industry. For both industries the era of the Napoleonic Wars was one of rapidly rising production and capacity (Tables 19 and 20). The second surge forward came with the opening of the railway age in the 1830s and 1840s. Both periods centred upon a step forward in the technology of iron manufacture: Cort's puddling process of 1784 and Neilson's hot-blast of 1829 (see Table 20, especially the astonishing growth of the Scottish iron industry after 1830). The expanding output of both these industries was essential to the long-term future of the Industrial Revolution. The abundance of coal, first made possible by the canals and then extended by the railways, released the economy from its dependence upon limited and uncertain sources of energy like timber and, valuable though they remained, wind and water power. Now available upon an unprecedented scale iron became, in effect, a new material as its use in building shows. Together coal and iron fathered the gas industry. The first large-scale experiments with gas lighting were made by William Murdock at Boulton and Watt's Soho Foundry at the end of the eighteenth century. By the late 1840s even small towns were generally gas-lit, investment in the industry amounted to over £11 million, and about a million tons of coal was consumed annually by the industry. By 1850 London had 3,200 kilometres (2,000 miles) of gas mains, and gas lighting, first used for streets and public buildings, was being rapidly installed in better-off homes.

The gas industry created a new technology: from its by-products were to come the first synthetic dyes. But its immediate success came from home demand based on an instant appreciation of what gaslighting meant as an amenity of family life. Candle and soap making were also industries which supplied the home. As both these industries used animal fat as the major raw material their fortunes were closely linked to those of agriculture and of the tanning and leather trades. Clearly a rising population called for a rising output from both industries and this could only be achieved – like the expansion of the woollen industry – by more intensive animal husbandry. Fluctuations in the statistics reflect the varying fortunes of both producers and consumers. Good harvests, high investment, and rising incomes made the 1790s a decade of growth for the consumer industries, although the declaration of war in 1793 created a setback in the middle of the decade.

Brewing was the first of the modern food industries. The success of the London brewers in the eighteenth century arose from the popularity of porter, a beer with good keeping qualities (it was first brewed in 1722) which enabled them to create a national market. Although the statistics may not tell the whole story beer production appears to have risen slowly, if at all, in the early nineteenth century. No doubt the excise itself was partly responsible: it was raised by $\frac{1}{2}$d a quart in 1799. Of course most beer continued to be locally brewed and this continued to be the case after the repeal of the beer duty in 1830. Production statistics for the industry as a whole cease to be available after this date. The next twenty years were eventful in the history of brewing. The famous pale ales of Burton-upon-Trent had been developed in the early nineteenth century to supply the Englishman in India with a lighter, cooler drink but, after Burton was put on the railway in 1839, pale ales became immensely popular at home. The output of Bass's brewery rose from 10,000 barrels in 1831 to 60,000 in 1847, and 130,000 in 1853 (see E. M. Sigsworth, 'Science and the Brewing Industry, 1850–1900', *Economic History Review*, Vol. XVII, 1965, p. 544).

The duty on bricks was low and evasion almost impossible:

the returns are, therefore, an accurate guide to total production. As population rose more houses had to be provided and the statistics confirm a long term upward trend in brick production (Table 26). But this did not mean that more houses were built every year. The ventures of the speculative builder were influenced more by the current rate of interest than by housing need. Interest rates were high in wartime and there was a marked recession in brick production during the Revolutionary War and again at the close of the Napoleonic War. After 1815 the need for houses was very great. By the 1820s a building boom had developed which lasted until 1826: house building did not revive again until after 1832. Whether builders responded to housing need depended upon the prevailing economic circumstances. The pressure of new families upon existing housing stock was not itself enough to draw funds into building. Housebuilding was in competition with other forms of investment. The statistics of brick production measure investment in all types of industrial buildings, as well as in public utilities like the canals, the railways, or docks. The new heights in brick output reached in the 1840s were certainly the outcome of railway construction (where bricks were used for most engineering works) and not another boom in housebuilding on the lines of the 1820s.

The Hoffman Index (Table 27) suggests that the Industrial Revolution entered a new phase from the 1820s. This is scarcely surprising. Within the century 1750–1850 not only was the range of industrial activity greatly extended but the output of all major industries was radically increased. Technical change and industrial reorganization have usually been regarded as the central process of the Industrial Revolution. Either could cause a fall in the prices of manufactured goods and so promote a new cycle of demand. But neither innovation nor reorganization could bring about as remarkable a growth in the potential market as the parallel revolution in transport. Transport economies were probably of much greater interest to the heavy industries, and to agriculture, than they were to millowners and the textile trades. But the impact of the transport revolution was progressive. It was also a lengthy revolution despite the fact

that its history seems so dominated by the decades of 'mania';
the canal age had scarcely begun in 1750 and it was only the
main outlines of a railway system which were complete by 1850.
An understanding of the Industrial Revolution requires a long
rather than a short view. The adoption of new technologies and
the reorganization of an industry cannot be accomplished over-
night. Both depend upon a period of experiment and there is
often a considerable (if diminishing) period of time lag between
the first successes and the elimination of old methods and
organization.

[38] OVERSEAS TRADE

28 *Official values of overseas trade 1750–1805,* in five-year averages: England and Wales 1750–85 and Great Britain 1790–1805
(in £ thousand)

	Imports	Domestic exports	Re-exports
1750	7,931	8,574	3,552
1755	8,741	8,436	3,395
1760	8,913	10,005	3,971
1765	11,231	10,112	4,578
1770	12,426	9,980	5,240
1775	12,350	9,354	5,129
1780	10,643	7,709	4,245
1785	14,515	10,681	4,246
1790	18,861	15,314	5,599
1795	21,696	16,629	10,147
1800	29,900	24,150	14,680
1805	27,300	23,200	8,600

29 Declared values of overseas trade 1810–50 (five-year averages in £ million)

	Imports	Domestic exports	Re-exports
1810	64·0	41·5	9·8
1815	68·8	45·4	15·3
1820	56·2	38·3	10·0
1825	57·2	36·3	7·4
1830	56·4	36·9	6·9
1835	69·2	44·8	8·6
1840	84·5	50·7	9·1
1845	87·4	57·5	9·2
1850	102·4	68·1	11·6

Note: Official Values 1810

	30·1	29·0	8·8

Official values are purely notional and are a guide to changes in the volume of trade and *not* its value. For this reason Table 28 should not be read on into Table 29; there was not the sudden increase in trade between 1805 and 1810 which these figures apparently suggest (see Commentary).

30 Values at current prices of British exports 1830–50 (five-year averages in £ million)

	Coal	Iron	Hardwares/ cutlery	Machinery	Non-ferrous metals	Cottons	Wool-lens
1830	0·16	1·2	1·4	0·2	1·3	18·1	5·0
1835	0·26	1·7	1·7	0·3	1·6	21·3	6·5
1840	0·6	2·8	1·6	0·6	2·0	23·7	6·2
1845	0·9	4·2	2·4	1·0	2·0	25·2	8·1
1850	1·2	6·3	2·7	1·0	2·1	25·6	9·0

31 Exports to major regions 1820–45 at current prices (five-year averages in £ million)

	1820	1825	1830	1835	1840	1845
Europe	8·7	7·4	6·7	9·0	11·1	12·9
Asia	3·7	4·1	4·4	5·4	7·9	10·2
U.S.A.	6·3	6·0	6·2	8·4	6·5	7·6
British N. America and W. Indies	6·1	5·3	4·8	5·3	5·8	5·8
Central S. America	3·1	4·7	4·7	5·0	5·4	5·5
India		3·7*		3·4		5·8

   * = 1827 only

Commentary

Statistics of English trade were kept by the Inspectors-General of Imports and Exports from 1696. Unfortunately the statistics took the form of *official* valuations which, in most cases, ceased to be adjusted to current prices during the early eighteenth century. The official £1 of the Customs was an entirely artificial unit and some historians have protested against deriving even an index of the volume of trade from these statistics (see T. S. Ashton, *An Economic History of England: the Eighteenth Century*, pp. 152–4). The figures certainly provide no guide to the *value* of trade and for this reason the reader should be careful to treat Tables 28 and 29 quite separately. Quite apart from the discrepancy between official values and current prices the statistics suffer still further where imports are concerned because of the evasion of the customs by smuggling.

Despite the limitations of trade returns based upon official values it is possible to derive from them an approximate idea of the increase in the volume of trade over the eighteenth century. By using the price series collected by Thomas Irving in 1796–8 Phyllis Deane and W. A. Cole have recently constructed an index for eighteenth-century trade which, for exports at least, shows reasonable correlation with an index based upon official values;

	Official values	1796–8 prices
1702–3	100	
1772–3	278	291
1797–8	498	521

(*British Economic Growth*, p. 44)

The history of British overseas trading from 1750 to 1850 is one of periodic stagnation as well as successful expansion. Total overseas trade grew rapidly from the mid-1740s until about 1760. The 1770s were a decade of recession made all the sharper by the difficulties of the American War of Independence. From the 1780s both imports and exports began an extraordinary upward spiral which is one of the best known features of the Industrial Revolution. The era of high trading lasted until the opening of the new century and returned again in the boom conditions which accompanied the closing stages of the Napoleonic War (Tables 28 and 29). The value of overseas trade fell after 1815 and it was twenty years before it equalled the level reached at the end of the war. But because prices also fell the quantity of goods passing through the ports did not fall as much as the declining value of trade suggests. Nevertheless the importance of trade to the economy lessened; Deane and Cole estimate, for example, that while exports had accounted for 13 per cent of the national income of England and Wales at the end of the eighteenth century, U.K. exports in the first half of the nineteenth century reached only some 10 per cent of national income (op. cit., pp. 309–10).

The official values are a poor guide to the *comparative* importance of individual export commodities. There is no doubt that the export trade was dominated by textiles throughout the Industrial Revolution, by woollens in the eighteenth century and by cottons in the nineteenth. Exports of woollens pushed ahead in the 1750s and 1760s but did less well in the 1770s and early 1780s, largely as a result of the repercussions of the American War of Independence. The woollen trade recovered vigorously in the late eighteenth century although from early in the nineteenth century its performance was increasingly overshadowed by the cotton industry – at least until the 1840s (Table 30). Cottons were both cheaper than woollens and suitable to a wider range of markets which included Asia and the Americas as well as Europe. Exports of coal, iron and steel, and other metals and metal goods also accelerated from the 1780s. By the end of the period British exports were much more diversified than had been the case in the eighteenth century. Britain's most rapidly growing export in the 1840s was iron and steel.

Apart from odd years (1816, 1821, 1822) Britain usually bought more abroad than she sold. The deficit which arose from Britain's exchange of goods with the rest of the world was offset by earnings from shipping and other services and, to an increasing extent in the early nineteenth century, by income on overseas investments.

The balance of payments, 1820–49. Totals in £ million per decade

	Merchandise trade	Overseas investment earnings	Other invisible trade
1820–9	−99·9	+42·9	+134·4
1830–9	−167·6	+63·6	+148·8
1840–9	−229·5	+82·6	+192·7

British imports were primarily of foodstuffs and raw materials. More or less continuous imports of grain began in the 1770s. There remained years, when the domestic harvest was particularly good, when imports were low, and the Corn Laws were certainly based on the belief that English bread should be made from English wheat – imports providing a supplementary inflow during a period of shortage. Rising corn imports from the late 1830s onwards indicate that the domestic harvest, however good, was now inadequate. Sugar, tea, and coffee ranked next to corn as the main consumer imports by 1850 but meat, butter, vegetable oils and tobacco were imported in significant quantities. The remaining imports were either raw materials for industry, like raw cotton (easily the largest of all imports), raw wool, dyes, etc, or, like timber, basic natural products of which Britain had an insufficient supply. Britain imported few manufactured goods and the most important of these from an industrial viewpoint, bar iron, dwindled in the nineteenth century to negligible quantities.

British imports were the means by which the rest of the world paid for the products of the Industrial Revolution. But historians have disagreed about the contribution of overseas trade to Britain's industrial success. While it is true that the most precocious industry, cotton, involved an essential transaction in international trade, and its affairs dominated British trade from the beginning of the nineteenth century, this does not mean that export demand can account for the Industrial Revolution. Britain's industrial growth did not depend upon overseas markets: it did not, for example, flag in periods of static, or even contracting exports. The 1770s were a notoriously difficult decade in international trade but they were an important, perhaps crucial, period of industrial experiment and change. A comparison of the Hoffman index (Table 27) for 1820–35 and export performance over the same years (Table 29) also shows that the Industrial Revolution did not always move most rapidly during an export boom. But, of course, the 1780s and 1790s were just such a period of boom in international trade and exports perhaps made their maximum contribution to the Industrial Revolution during these twenty years. It must also be remembered that the Industrial Revolution was a world event and was as much effect as cause of the emergence of the world economy. How far this process had already gone by the end of this period is apparent from the estimates of Britain's income from overseas investment and the provision of services to the rest of the world. The Industrial Revolution meant an economy of national surpluses and leaping output: this could not have been long sustained in a world of merely regional or even continental markets.

Because the British economy was heavily dependent upon overseas trade (taking the import and export trade together) it was especially liable to fluctuation. There was, inevitably, a higher degree of risk in supplying overseas markets, particularly when both news and goods travelled slowly. Overseas trade was almost certain to be interrupted by warfare. In the nineteenth century merchants and businessmen were only too familiar with what seemed an inevitable pattern of 'trade cycle' in which boom led into depression, depression into recovery, recovery into boom, and boom, once again, into depression.

In the nineteenth century there was also an apparent tendency for the economy to be subject to both long, and short-term, cycles. The repercussions of the trade cycle were clearly unwelcome: the onset of depression was marked by bankruptcies, unemployment, and falling production. The statistics of trade in this section, because they are based on five-year averages, do not reveal short-term fluctuations and sometimes distort the long-term cycle by dividing it into arbitrary periods. The trade cycle can only be studied properly in annual statistics and for these reference must be made to *The Abstract of British Historical*

Statistics itself. Yet the term *trade cycle* is slightly misleading if by it is understood the suggestion that all fluctuation in the economy can be attributed to fluctuations in overseas trade. In the eighteenth century a poor harvest inevitably brought some setback and harvest conditions were still an important factor determining economic fortunes in the first half of the nineteenth century. Weaknesses in the banking system and the supply of credit could both make a crisis more severe (and widespread) and added a permanent element of instability to all economic life. Even technical progress and a run of heavy investment might so expand an industry's capacity as to make it – in the short term anyway – extremely sensitive to any falling off in demand. This was certainly a consequence of the Industrial Revolution in the textile industries and as they were so important to the export trade it is not difficult to see why the trade cycle seems to dominate the forty years after 1815.

[39] BANKING AND INTEREST RATES

32 Number of country banks, England and Wales, *1784–1842*

1784	119	1825	544
1798	312	1830	439
1809*	799	1835	411
1815	699	1840	332
		1842	311

  * First year of official statistics.

There were 62 London *private* banks in 1832: in 1833 it became possible to form joint stock banks within the London area.

(Numbers of country banks from L. S. Pressnell, *Country Banking in the Industrial Revolution*.)

33 The yield on consols 1760–1850 (five-year averages)

1760	3·8%	1805	5·0%
1765	3·4	1810	4·7
1770	3·4	1815	4·7
1775	3·5	1820	4·1
1780	5·0	1825	3·6
1785	4·6	1830	3·5
1790	3·7	1835	3·3
1795	4·7	1840	3·3
1800	6·1	1845	3·2
		1850	3·1

34 Changes in the bank rate 1797–1850

1797	5%	1840	5%
1822	4	1842	4
1825	5	1844	2½
1827	4	1845	3, 3½
1836	4½, 5	1846	3
1838	4	1847	3½ rising to 8, down to 5
1839	5, 5½, 6	1848	4½, 3½, 3
		1849	2½
		1850	3

Commentary

The country banks linked the provinces to the central institutions of the financial system, the Bank of England and the London banks. The wartime boom in banking over-extended the banking system and the return of peace inevitably led to the weeding out of the weaker businesses: the years of expansion clearly belong to the period 1797–1821 during which the Bank of England suspended cash payments on its notes (Table 32). But there was certainly no flight from the banks after the war. As the cheque began to rival the bill of exchange (towards the end of this period) for the settlement of internal debts the modern banking habit may be said to have arrived.

The Industrial Revolution owed a great deal to the fall in interest rates which began in the eighteenth century (see T. S. Ashton, *The Industrial Revolution 1760–1830*, pp. 7–10). The

Usury Laws forbade a rate above 5 per cent and it was not until this ceiling was removed in 1833 that the Bank of England could raise its 'rate' above 5 per cent. As the business of discounting was tied to the Bank Rate it was difficult, in a period of crisis or failing confidence, to apply any sensible monetary brake to the economy other than by actually rationing funds. After 1833 the Bank was able to adjust its rate to check the supply of credit but, in general, it continued to follow rather than lead events. Long-term interest rates are, of course, more relevant to large-scale investment. Perhaps the best measure of long-term interest rates is given by the yield on Consols (Table 33). Lending to the state lost its terrors and became popular among the wealthy at the end of the seventeenth century. From the 1690s loans were secured against Bank of England stock. In 1756 the various issues of Bank stock were fused into a single 'consolidated' stock at 3 per cent. Apart from the two periods of war the '3 per cent Consols' remained markedly stable in value between 1760 and 1850 (as the price of £100 of stock falls under par so the interest rate rises, falls may occur in any period of insecurity but are sharpest in wartime). 'Gilt-edged' stock became as acceptable a possession as land or other property and this, in itself, encouraged new habits of investment. Without this development it is difficult to see how the funds needed for public utilities could have been raised in the eighteenth century. At 3 per cent an investment of £100 would be returned in about 30 years: in conditions like these roads and canals began to appear realistic investments.

[40] INVENTION

35 Number of patents sealed 1750–1850 (totals per decade)

1750–9	92	1800–9	924
1760–9	205	1810–19	1,124
1770–9	294	1820–9	1,462
1780–9	477	1830–9	2,453
1790–9	647	1840–9	4,581

Commentary

Inventiveness is a quality and impossible to 'measure'. Fortunately the state offered some protection to men with ideas and some indication of the spate of ideas in this century is given by the statistics of patents sealed. The object of invention was to make money as well as to be creative (why else patent the invention?). The figures are, therefore, a guide to the economic climate as much as an index of technical experiment and progress.

[41] PRICES AND WAGES

36 Average prices of wheat 1775–1850 (five-year averages: the price is per imperial quarter)

	s	d		s	d
1775	48	7	1815	84	11
1780	41	11	1820	65	11
1785	46	0	1825	60	8
1790	49	1	1830	63	0
1795	61	9	1835	48	6
1800	84	11	1840	64	7
1805	72	11	1845	55	3
1810	101	3	1850	42	10

37 Two price indices

a *An extract from the Schumpeter–Gilboy Prices Indices 1661–1823*

These are annual indices but are shown here as five-year averages. 1701 = 100.

	Consumers' goods	Producers' goods
1750	94	87
1755	95	90
1760	98	101
1765	105	100
1770	106	95
1775	114	100

	Consumers' goods	Producers' goods
1780	114	111
1785	122	111
1790	121	109
1795	143	129
1800	184	145
1805	175	
1810	213	
1815	201	
1820	162	

Consumers' goods = barley, beans, biscuits, bread, flour, oats, peas, rye, wheat, beef for salting, butter, cheese, pork, ale, beer, cider, hops, malt, pepper, raisins, sugar, tea, tallow candles, coal, broadcloth, hair, felt hats, kersey, leather backs, Brussels linen, Irish linen, blue yarn stockings.

Producers' goods = bricks, coal, lead, pantiles, plain tiles, hemp (to 1794), leather backs (to 1793), train oil (to 1783), tallow (to 1780), lime (to 1779), glue (to 1778) and copper (to 1776).

b *The Gayer, Rostow and Schwartz Commodity Price Indices 1790–1850*

This series includes both domestic and imported commodities, but only the indices for *combined* domestic and imported commodities are shown here.

1790–4	92·4
1795–9	113·9
1800–4	135·3
1805–9	140·0
1810–14	157·0
1815–20	127·1
1821–5	100·0
1826–30	97·2
1831–5	89·3
1836–40	98·8
1841–5	86·1
1846–50	82·4

Composition of the indices. The indices are based on the prices of 24 domestic commodities and 52 imported commodities. Each commodity is given a weighting.

38 Indices of average wages, U.K., 1790–1850 (Phyllis Deane and W. A. Cole, *British Economic Growth*, p. 23) (at intervals)

1840=100

1790	70	1824	105
1795	82	1831	101
1800	95	1840	100
1805	109	1845	98
1810	124	1850	100
1816	117		
1820	110		

39 A Manchester budget in 1833 and some Examples of earnings at Samuel Greg's mill at Styal, Cheshire, in 1831

a *The Manchester budget*

Income. This family disclosed its circumstances to one of the investigators of the Royal Commission on the Employment of Children in Factories, 1833. There were seven in the family but only two at work, the father, who was a fine spinner, and one daughter, aged 14 who had been working for three years, and was a piecer for her father. Together father and daughter brought home 25/– a week, but the investigator clearly felt that the man was not bringing *all* his wages home.

Expenditure	s	d
Butter, 1½ lb at 10d	1	3
Tea, 1½ oz		4½
Bread; i.e. 24 lb flour, barm, salt, and baking	4	6
Half a peck of oatmeal		6½
Bacon 1½ lb		9
Potatoes, two score a week at 8d a score	1	4
Milk, a quart a day, at 3d a quart	1	9
Flesh meat for Sunday		7
Sugar, 1½ lb a week at 6d		9
Pepper, mustard, salt, etc.		3
Soap and candles	1	0
Coals	1	6
Rent of house per week	3	6
	18	1

Leaves for clothing, sickness of seven persons, schooling, etc.   6   11

1d a week for each child was subscribed to a 'funeral society' and two children went to school for 3d a week each. A full extract from the Report on this family is given in E. Royston Pike, *The Human Documents of the Industrial Revolution*, pp. 52–4.

b Wages at Styal, 1831. Eight weeks in May and June

Family	Number	Sex and probable age	Occupation	Average weekly income
				£ s d
Bailey	9	Man, 2 youths, 4 women, 2 children	Odd hand, 2 saddlers, 2 spinners, carder, reeler, 2 winders	2 16 4
Johnson	7	Man, 3 women, youth, 2 children	Maker up, picker, 2 spinners, winder, carding room	1 18 10
Venables	6	Man, 2 youths 2 women, boy	Mechanic, maker up, picker, 2 spinners, winder carding room	1 15 11
Gleave	5	Man, woman, 3 children	Overlooker of carding room, picker, children in carding room	1 10 11½
Leigh	5	Woman, youth, 2 girls, child	Picker, others in carding room	18 0
Pepper	4	2 men, 2 women	Mechanic, carder, spinner, reeler	1 19 1
Coppack	4	2 women, 2 youths	Odd hand, reeler, carding room	1 2 6
Tongue	3	Man, 2 women	Overlooker, reeling room, picker reeler	1 9 6
Heath	3	Man, 2 children	Overlooker of spinning room, 2 doffers	1 13 4½
Goodier	3	Woman, 2 youths	Spinner, carding room	17 9

(From Frances Collier, *The Family Economy of the Working Classes in the Cotton Industry, 1784–1833*, Appendix A, p. 54, Manchester University Press, 1964)

40 Expenditure on poor relief 1748–1850, England and Wales (in £ thousand)

1748–50 (av.)	690
1783–5 (av.)	2,004
1813	6,656
1820 (av. of 1818–22)	7,207
1830 (five-year av.)	6,659
1840 „ „ „	4,556
1850 „ „ „	5,446

Commentary

The history of prices between 1750 and 1850 centres on the great inflation of the war years. The causes of wartime inflation were heavy expenditure on armaments and the armed forces together with rapid growth in the supply of credit. This situation benefited at least two groups. The first consisted of industrialists who won contracts, British or foreign, for the supply of war materials or those who found that their export markets remained buoyant. The diversion of manpower and resources into industry and war also brought about high farm prices. Money incomes did not really keep pace with rising prices: one sign of this was the sharp increase in the cost of poor relief as parish overseers adopted the practice of supplementing wages by cash allowances. But it is important to remember that the fortunes of the working class are imperfectly revealed by price and wage indices.

Clearly food purchases, especially of bread or flour, were the main items in the labourer's budget. When harvests were poor and bread prices rose his narrow margin of surplus income quickly disappeared (Table 39a). Over the long period of the wars high farm prices had the effect of pushing up all wages, but in periods of scarcity caused by a 'normal' bad harvest wages remained 'sticky' and living standards dropped. Even so this situation is difficult to reconstruct in detail. This is because wages ought to be interpreted in terms of *family* income and, secondly, because money wages themselves may tell only part of the story. Much of the agricultural distress of the early nineteenth century can be attributed to the lack of permanent employment on the land for women and children. The spread of domestic industry improved the prospects for family incomes and the advantage of the early factories, where wage *rates* were not necessarily high, was that they offered work to whole families (Table 39b). At Styal, and other industrial communities like it, employment for all members of the family could be achieved without breaking up the family as a single working unit. Greg recruited much of his labour through the poor law authorities and, as Styal itself was in an agricultural district, his workers had cause to appreciate the differential between industrial and agricultural earnings. They were also provided with good houses, large gardens, and reasonably priced fresh food from Greg's own farm. The strictly *urban* working class certainly did not enjoy these advantages.

What most families could spend on 'industrial products' was determined by current food prices. Soap, candles, coal, and clothing were the products of industry with which most people were familiar. The prices of these commodities followed the general price trends for the period, but the prices of industrial goods seldom rose with quite the same zest as foodstuffs and they show a marked downward movement in the second quarter of the nineteenth century. Transport improvement cut the cost of coal and the technical revolution in the cotton industry caused, as might be expected, a continuous fall in the price of cotton yarn and cloth from 1800 (see Table 22). But there is little sign in the nineteenth century of any significant increase in the purchasing power of wages for the majority. While incomes were, of necessity, spent primarily on food the importance of a fall in the price of industrial products was only marginal. As money incomes and agricultural output had risen in the eighteenth century there had been a substantial increase in living standards. In the nineteenth century population pressure was more acute, food prices showed very little inclination to fall after the 1820s, and a feature of the period was the growth of *aggregate* rather than *per capita* demand.

Years of high food prices caused acute distress when they were superimposed upon shrinking international markets. The textile industry as a whole was likely to suffer when money which might have been spent upon clothes went instead to buy bread. Often prolonged unemployment in the textile trades, combined with scarcity prices for food, gave the 1830s and 1840s their special character. Average wage indices give no indication of the problems faced by the unemployed. But there were groups within the working class whose fortunes were better than 'average' in this period. In printing, in shipbuilding and engineering, and in building money wages in the 1840s were as high, or higher, than they had been during the wartime inflation. Perhaps a majority of these men were skilled. They owed their relative prosperity to heavy investment in capital goods in the second quarter of the nineteenth century.

PART VI
Looking at the Industrial
Revolution

The object of this chapter is to survey, however briefly, the
visible remains of the Industrial Revolution and to show what
may be seen *today* at some of the well known sites of British
Industrial history. No one who is studying this subject for the
first time should attempt to do so for very long without wanting
to see what a textile mill or a weaver's cottage was like. But it
would, of course, require a great many photographs to do justice
to every industry and industrial region. The photographs
presented here are only a very small selection from sites which
may be seen and photographed with comparative ease. Because
the selection is small they have been used less to give a detailed
account of the sites in question than to illustrate a number of
general themes in the history of the Industrial Revolution.

It may be asked how the value of studying industrial buildings
compares with that of other types of evidence. Has it, in fact,
extended our knowledge? This is still not an easy question to
answer. Careful regional surveys of industrial sites are providing
an additional source of quantitative evidence about the cause
and progress of the Industrial Revolution. Once this work is
complete it may be possible to discuss industrial investment
much more accurately. But this does not mean that surviving
buildings are relevant to the economic argument on the Industrial Revolution. To take only one example: it is unnecessary to
look at the new dock installations of this period in order to
establish that there was a growth of international trade. The
importance of 'archaeological' evidence is obviously not the
same for a period in which there is adequate documentation as

for one in which it is deficient or unobtainable. Even so buildings can teach us a great deal. They are a sharp point of reference against which to try our generalizations. And because they may be seen and experienced they add a new dimension to an understanding of the life and environment of the first century of industrial revolution.

[42] FOUR FACES OF THE INDUSTRIAL REVOLUTION

Transport

Successive improvements in transport facilities were essential to the Industrial Revolution. The necessary investment was often huge by industrial standards and required the formal public backing of a parliamentary Act of incorporation or the direct action of new bodies like dock commissioners who were empowered to borrow on a large scale. The surviving structures of the great ages of canal and railway construction are the best known and, perhaps, the most impressive monuments of the Industrial Revolution. At a time when industrial investment came largely from retained profits canal and railway companies built and engineered their concerns with remarkable extravagance. Of course it is also true that the railways needed large and often novel buildings; nothing like the great terminus station or the large roundhouse had ever been built before. The engineering works, the viaducts, embankments, cuttings, and bridges are equally dramatic reminders of the transport revolution and many of them are fortunately in no danger of demolition.

Transport improvements fulfilled more than one function in the Industrial Revolution. They cut production costs and increased the demand for industrial goods. They assisted the concentration of population and industry. Investment in transport generated new incomes as well as stimulating the growth of key industries like iron. The better roads, the river navigations and

1 Section of cast iron wagonway: Coalbrookdale Museum

2 The iron bridge, 1779, at Ironbridge, Shropshire

3 Warehouse, Albert Dock, Liverpool

4 Cast iron water-wheel, Loxley Valley, Sheffield

5 Tilt-hammers, Abbeydale Industrial Hamlet, Sheffield

6 Abbeydale Hamlet, an eighteenth-century scythe works

7 Quarry Bank Mill, Styal, Cheshire

8 Akroyd Mill, Copley, near Halifax

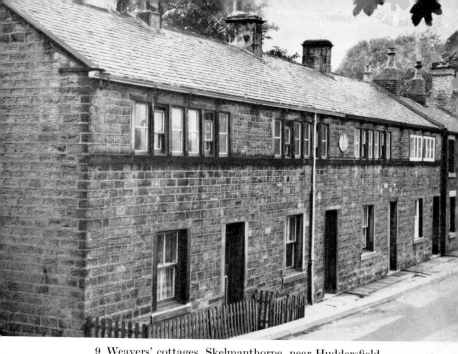

9 Weavers' cottages, Skelmanthorpe, near Huddersfield

10 Nineteenth-century lockshop at Willenhall, Staffordshire

11 Old furnace at Coalbrookdale

12 Modern dayhole, Flockton, Yorkshire

13 Coopers' shop, Ram Brewery, Wandsworth

14 Beverley Bank, 1861

15 Cottages at Belmont, near Bolton

16 Model dwellings, Kennington Common, 1851

new canals and, finally, the railways all helped to make Britain a more efficient country; the higher 'productivity' of the transport industry was one of the genuinely revolutionary changes of the period. But not every industry made the same demands upon the transport system. The need to find a good head of water often drove the early millowners to build well away from good roads or canals. Neither the raw materials nor the finished product of the textile industries were sufficiently bulky or heavy to make transport facilities a vital consideration.

Cheap and improved transport was, however, crucial to the growth of the coal and iron trades. The canals were responsible for the first age of cheap coal, and industrial users of coal, like the potters, were quick to appreciate the value of canal-side sites. The coal industry was, of course, equally instrumental in promoting the development of the railway. Wagonways running down to riverside staithes on the Tyne, Wear, and Tees were an old feature of the North-East coalfield and it was out of this environment that both the modern railway track and the steam locomotive were evolved. In thinking about the role of transport in the Industrial Revolution it is as well to remember that the successful industrial region depended as much upon its own system of 'internal' communications as upon linkages to national routes.

The industrial history of Shropshire illustrates very well the dual importance of a complex system of local communications and a region's access to national routes. Industrial Shropshire did not possess the resources to rival major centres like the West Riding, South Lancashire, or Clydeside. It was largely confined to the hills north and south of the Severn between Wellington and Wenlock. But this was an ancient industrial area; coal and iron had been worked here in the Middle Ages and the activities of the great ironmasters, the Darbys of Coalbrookdale, William Reynolds of Ketley, and John Wilkinson of Willey, are more than sufficient to assure Shropshire a place in the history of the Industrial Revolution. Apart from iron ore the region was rich in a variety of clays which lay along the edges of the coal measures, some of which outcropped on the Severn. Iron and coal were the major industries, but there were numerous brick and tile works and a well known porcelain factory was opened at Coalport on the Severn at the beginning of the nineteenth century.

The great age of the Shropshire iron industry was undoubtedly the late eighteenth and early nineteenth century. By 1796 there were at least nine large firms operating in the area and over twenty furnaces in blast. Iron had first been smelted with coke at Coalbrookdale early in the eighteenth century and it was upon the close proximity of coal and iron that the region's fortunes were based. The brick and tile works were also industrial users of coal. The ironmasters, in fact, often extended their activities into mining and into exploiting brick and fire clay close to their works. All of this called for countless short hauls of raw material and finished products. The ironmasters answered this problem by the construction of tram or wagonways. Unlike the roads and tracks of the time, the wagonway – using wooden or iron rails – did not become impassable to heavy loads during wet weather. By 1757 Coalbrookdale was linked by a wagonway, through Horsehay, to Ketley, a distance of about five miles. Cast iron rails seem to have been manufactured at Coalbrookdale itself in 1767; these were of an L-shaped pattern, the wagon wheels themselves were flangeless (see plate 1). Experiments with a steam locomotive were surely predictable in this environment. In 1802 the Cornish engineer, Richard Trevithick, came to Coalbrookdale where he supervised the construction of an engine to run on rails.

Iron track prepared the wagonway for its further evolution into the railway. If this step does not belong to Shropshire its ironmasters were certainly pioneers in the application of iron to the needs of other forms of transport. Abraham Darby III cast the components for an iron bridge over the Severn in 1779 (see plate 2). The bridge became a popular tourist attraction as well as a useful local amenity and the small town of Ironbridge grew up at its northern end. Eight years later John Wilkinson was to launch the first iron boat, *The Trial*, on the Severn. In the eighteenth century the river was the most important link between industrial Shropshire and its markets. At the mid-century the river was navigable for 260 kilometres (160 miles) from its mouth and it was worked extensively by sailing barges and the larger Severn 'trows' carrying coal from Shropshire to Worcester and other riverside towns. The traffic in coal as a domestic fuel was almost as important to this region as it was to the North-East. Yet despite the advantages of access to the Severn the river traffic posed its problems. Eighteenth-century efforts to improve the river as a waterway met with mixed success: the Severn boatmen were particularly stubborn defenders of their own interests. Above all, until the river was linked to a national system of communications its value to an expanding industrial district was limited.

The coming of the canals saw a further improvement in the internal communications of industrial Shropshire as well as linking it with other major centres. From 1772 the Staffordshire and Worcestershire Canal joined the Severn to the Midlands and major through-routes like the Grand Trunk. Shropshire itself had its own canal network and, by 1830, the newly opened Birmingham and Liverpool Canal gave the region direct access to a trunk route. The hilly countryside of Shropshire often made it impracticable to bring a canal to ironworks or colliery. Even so short extensions, like the Ketley Canal, or the Donnington Wood, were valuable improvements to local communications. At Ketley a partner of the Darbys, William Reynolds, constructed in 1778 the famous 'inclined plane' up which barges carrying ore, coal, were pulled on rollers right into the works. Canals were, of course, a better proposition in some areas than others. Branch lines were more of an undertaking than their later railway counterparts and, for the short haul of raw materials, the canal was very slow and cumbersome when compared with the railway.

By the nineteenth century communications in Britain were the admiration of Europe. This applied to roads as much as to the canals. The eighteenth-century turnpike trusts had promoted a renaissance of road making. Industrial Shropshire was adjacent to Telford's Holyhead road for which Parliament had been willing to grant money because of the political importance of the route between London and Dublin. Another aspect of the transport system which called for public action was the improvement of the docks. The growth of overseas trade had outrun the harbour and dock facilities of most British ports by the opening of the nineteenth century. Government was, of course, particularly interested in the provision of secure warehouses for the storage of goods which paid a high rate of duty. Equally important was the construction of enclosed docks, dependent upon an entrance lock, to replace old riverside quays. This made it possible to load and unload ships all round the clock. The engineering techniques which needed to be employed in the construction of new docks were similar to those used for canals and some engineers worked on both types of project.

Most British ports were the scene of major dock improvements at some time between 1750 and 1850. At London the chaos which existed on the old 'legal' quays and sufferance wharves was gradually removed as the dock companies extended their empires downstream on both the north and south banks of the Thames. By 1850 five dock companies were operating in the port and London had certainly kept pace with the demands being made upon it as a port. At Liverpool the development of 'wet docks' began earlier in the eighteenth century and new work was extensive in the 1840s – when, in fact, the creation of Birkenhead docks was only just beginning. Liverpool was the port which grew most rapidly throughout this period; five new docks were opened between 1753 and 1796, and four docks were opened in each of the last decades of this century (the docks opened in the 1840s included the first at Birkenhead across the Mersey). The success of Liverpool was based upon the growth of the Atlantic trade and the phenomenal expansion of the cotton industry. Raw cotton, grain, timber, East and West Indian products were its main imports but these were dwarfed by its exports of cottons and other manufactured goods.

The Albert Dock, Liverpool, of 1846 (plate 3) is a late example of the type of improved dock and warehouse layout which first appeared in Britain at the turn of the century. The warehouses

are ranged around the dock basin, the upper storeys flush with
the quayside while the ground floor is opened up by a continuous
arcade of immense iron pillars and broken at intervals by ellipti-
cal arches. Hand cranes stand in the arches and cast iron hoists
were provided for loading onto carts and drays which approached
via a perimeter road. By 1850 the docks were not yet integrated
with the railway system. At Liverpool goods were carted from
the docks to railway warehouses. The use of cast iron was a
common feature of the dock building of this period and this
itself indicates one way in which the benefits of overseas trade
were fed back into industry. Wigan's collieries and ironworks
had been linked to Liverpool by the Leeds and Liverpool Canal
and much of the ironwork of the Albert Dock was supplied by
the Wigan Iron and Coal Company. Twenty years earlier the
profusion of ironwork in the Liverpool Docks had caught the
attention of a French visitor, Baron Dupin, and he had no doubt
that this was to be attributed to the cheapness of iron in Britain.

Power

Water power was widely used all over Europe by the middle of
the eighteenth century. Most mills were, as their name implied,
corn mills and it is as well to remember that there were already
over 5,500 of them in England at the time of the Domesday
survey. However, the water-wheel had been put to other purposes; water-driven trip-hammers were used in ironworks, in
fulling mills, and for mashing rag in paper mills. Less commonly
the water-wheel was also used for either pumping drinking water
or draining the deeper mine shafts. Early mills were mostly of
the 'undershot' type – the water-wheel was suspended in a fast
moving stream – and as they were of wooden construction they
required a good deal of maintenance. 'Overshot' mills were
certainly known by the later Middle Ages however, and they
were probably more efficient than their more primitive counterparts. Similarly the windmill had become almost as common as
the water-mill and it, too, had been developed for purposes other
than the grinding of corn. In the Fens and the Low Countries

the windmill was used to pump water into the dykes. Neither water nor windmills were very efficient; their average power output was probably no more than 5 h.p. They certainly did not always provide a reliable source of power because water did not always run as it should and the wind was equally fickle. But these were problems which millwrights understood. The windmill was gradually brought to make the most of the wind and skilful gearing could make something of even a slow-moving stream.

Early industrial machinery in a textile mill or an ironworks did not demand a large input of power. Later improvements in the water-wheel made it quite adequate for most industrial purposes in the eighteenth and early nineteenth centuries. Overshot wheels were now known to be more efficient and water was generally fed to the wheel from either a reservoir or a bypass which channelled water from the main stream. The flow of water was controlled by a sluicegate and commonly dropped onto the wheel at half-way up, an arrangement usually known as a breast-wheel. The wheels themselves were now almost invariably made of cast iron. Modern installations of this kind were often quite cheap to construct and supplied a steady output of around 20 h.p. with a minimum of maintenance and bother. Many of these wheels worked tirelessly throughout the nineteenth century and even beyond. A simple wheel, like that shown in plate 4, met all the power requirements of a grinding shop in the Loxley Valley on the outskirts of Sheffield. It could equally have powered a small mill, but was especially suitable as power for the tilt hammers of the many forges of the Sheffield region (plate 5). In a scythe works like that shown in plate 5 it is worth noticing how much reliance was still being placed upon massive timbering; only the trip mechanism, the hammer head and anvil, and the bracings are of iron.

Within the Huddersfield woollen industry the transition from hand processes to the steam-powered mill was drawn out across a century. From the 1780s the 'scribbling' mill, in which the raw wool was drawn out and carded in preparation for spinning, spread steadily along the Colne and its many tributaries. Some of these mills were no more than extensions to existing fulling mills, some were even on the site of ancient corn mills, a majority were new buildings although the manufacturers themselves usually had roots in what was, of course, a traditional industry. The domestic structure of the industry survived beyond 1850, but the pattern of a factory industry began to emerge as both spinners and weavers gathered around the larger mills (some of them even working within it) and as further finishing processes, like cropping, were concentrated on the mill. The scribbling mills, and the later spinning mills, continued to supply the upland clothier whose warehouse was the focus of the domestic industry in the more remote villages. When power-loom weaving began to make progress in the woollen industry many of these old weaving centres developed important mills, partly because they had the skilled labour on the spot and, more importantly, because the coming of steam power no longer confined the mill to the valleys. In the valleys themselves the competition for a good water supply was often bitter and protracted; the beck was often incapable of meeting the demands now being made upon it. As a result steam power was adopted by some mills early in the nineteenth century. The spread of steam power in the Huddersfield region has also to be attributed to the existence of easily worked local coal. Extensive outcrop and 'day-hole' (plate 12) mining were well known before the advent of the steam engine; coal had long been used to heat the vats in the dyehouse. The small collieries of this area (e.g. along the Holme Valley) did not survive the nineteenth century but they did serve to allow steam power to make a very special contribution to the Huddersfield woollen industry, first to supplement water power and, then, to make it possible for some of the upland villages to foster large mills.

The Huddersfield example shows how water and steam power dictated the evolution of an established domestic industry. In this area power requirements, although growing, remained modest. In the early 1830s the township of Golcar and Lock-wood, on the lower Colne near Huddersfield, contained 12 water wheels delivering 170 h.p. altogether and 3 steam engines supplying between them 57 h.p. But more powerful steam engines were on their way. At the mill of John Brooke & Sons at Armitage Bridge a 40 h.p. engine was installed in 1832 and four years later this mill took delivery of its first power looms. The steam engine in general use for industrial purposes throughout this period was the beam engine. This had been developed primarily as a pumping engine for collieries but, with the addition of crankshaft and flywheel, was capable of adaptation for much wider use. By 1850 the horizontal engine was beginning to become more popular in industry; it was cheaper to instal, reached higher speeds, and was capable of more accurate control (one of its commonest uses was to be for colliery winding gear). An example of a small horizontal engine can be seen in plate 6. This engine was used to provide power when the water-wheel faltered, an illustration of the way in which the steam engine and the water-wheel were as much partners as rivals. Of course the steam engine did draw industry into the town and favoured the growth of large-scale operations: the Sheffield trades were clearly moving from the old country forges into the town itself by 1850.

Both water and steam power made work more efficient. Neither was the invention of this period; it was their continual improvement and widespread application which was revolutionary. Neither did this mean, in its turn, that the importance of the work done by animal power or human muscles was any the less. The horse had long been important in industry, not only for haulage, but for powering machinery of one kind or another. By working the horse on fixed tramways or on canals the animal's efficiency was greatly increased. If there were not many improvements in the manhandling of goods during this period there does seem to be a great increase in the number of cranes and hoists in use: both the steam crane and the travelling crane at least made their appearance now even if they did not come into general use until after 1850. But it is worth remembering that in building the railways the navvies had no more than the spade, the pick, the wheelbarrow, and the hand crane, all of which had been in use in Europe in the Middle Ages.

Workplace

A glance at the surviving industrial plant of this period shows immense variety both in the scale of activity and in the type of work and the conditions under which it was performed. By 1850 the advantages of size were obvious enough. Even in those industries which had pioneered large-scale production the future pointed towards still larger mills or works. The drift towards large-scale operation did not only occur in manufacturing industry where its progress was, of course, linked to the spread of power-driven machinery. Thomas Cubitt's great building firm was employing over 1,000 by the 1820s; he had extensive workshops in the Gray's Inn Road where he employed craftsmen on a permanent basis – something which was almost unknown in the trade. A similarly large labour force was to be employed by the railway contractors and was already being employed in the docks. Work of this kind, frequently organized by the gang, was often cruelly casual from the labourer's point of view but it needs to be set in the context of the rise of large-scale enterprise quite as much as the appearance of the factory population.

The growth of large-scale production is naturally very evident in the textile industries. Samuel Greg's Quarry Bank Mill (plate 7), opened in 1784, and one of the first generation of cotton spinning mills, is dwarfed by the gigantic Akroyd worsted mill at Copley, outside Halifax, opened in the late 1840s (plate 8). These great textile mills were characterized by their power-driven machinery and their workforce of factory operatives; the women and children who worked at Quarry Bank in the late eighteenth century were already machine-minders, their work bound to the rhythm of the water-frame. In the cotton industry the workers were almost all factory operatives by 1850. In the woollen and worsted industries the early mills contained only a few machine-minders; a majority continued to work at their traditional handicraft and their trade was still dominated by domestic outwork. Benjamin Gott's Mill in Leeds, opened in 1793 and only recently demolished, at first contained hand spinners working their jennies and weavers their hand-looms.

Only scribbling and fulling were mechanized activities. What Gott showed was that there were advantages to be won from more centralized management and production in a still essentially outwork industry. By the end of this period the mill was still one of the showpieces of Leeds but it was now a fully mechanized woollen mill and its workers were factory operatives.

Domestic outwork is such a persistent feature of this period that it is as well to emphasize its many forms. Steam spinning engendered a race of outworkers who were also townspeople. But in the West Riding of Yorkshire the survival of the upland villages as manufacturing centres meant that the transformation from rural outworker to factory operative was extremely gradual. The row of weavers' cottages at Skelmanthorpe (plate 9) dates from 1825. They are clearly purpose-built, illustrating the steady expansion of the woollen industry in its old centres. In the major valleys and larger villages the demand for weavers' accommodation was so pressing that the houses were built to three or four storeys. Until 1850 the firm of Richard Field of Greenside, Skelmanthorpe, was still putting all its weaving out to the cottages. Only the decision to switch to shawl-making, which required larger looms than the cottages could hold, brought the weavers into the mill and, even here, they continued to work at hand-looms into the late 1880s. For a majority of hand-loom weavers life was much less rural than this in the nineteenth century.

In the silk industry, as in the cotton, hand-loom weaving was a largely urban occupation. Unlike cotton most silks were still being woven on the hand-loom in 1850. In London the silk trade had settled in Spitalfields in the early seventeenth century and the silk weavers remained a distinct and fairly prosperous section of the city's working population until the mid-1820s. Silk throwing was mechanized in the eighteenth century and in the course of time it was inevitable that the weaving communities would gather around the throwing mills, as they were to do at Macclesfield. In Spitalfields the weavers lived either in two-storeyed terraced houses, with a characteristically long upper window against which the loom was set, or in the converted garrets of once substantial town houses which had now fallen into the hands of the silk merchants. Some examples of this type of accommodation may still be seen in Spitalfields. In Macclesfield a good many weavers' houses from this period are still standing; they are mostly three-storeyed terraced houses, with a long three-light window at both front and back on the upper storey. This was purpose-built industrial accommodation, far removed from the garret of the city or the more distinctly rural environment of the West Riding weaver or the Nottinghamshire stockinger.

In the Midlands outwork was equally common. The nailers worked in a tiny forge behind the house. By the nineteenth century what had once been industrial villages in this area were on their way to becoming fused into continuous urban sprawl. The numerous metal-working trades of the Midlands produced a world of backyard shops and small masters, 'scarcely one of whom is sufficiently important to have his name over the door' (Royal Commission on Child Labour, 1843). These men sold their finished goods to dealers in the large towns: they were genuine employers, but only on a very small scale. The 30,000 Midland nailers were, by contrast, merely outworkers and entirely at the mercy of their 'nailmasters'. The locksmiths of Willenhall belonged to the world of small independent masters and it was to one of them that the tiny shop of plate 10 belonged. The ground floor contained the forge (the lock-maker was, in origin, a smith) and the benches on which the lock components were cut and filed into shape before being assembled in the tiny loft (whose blocked-off window can be seen at the top of the photograph). Mechanized lockmaking depended upon the development of specialized machine tools and this was only at an early stage in the 1830s. The small lockshop was to hold its own for most of the nineteenth century. Around Sheffield, another region of old established handicraft in metal, the small rural works, like that at Abbeydale (plates 5 and 6), were beginning to decline by 1850. It was the Bessemer revolution which was to destroy the rural pattern of the Sheffield trades. In the 1830s there were some 500 rural works, still making their crucible steel from imported Swedish bar iron. In the next decade there were evident signs of change with the opening of large concerns, like Johnson and Cammell's Cyclops Works or Thomas Firth's Norfolk Works, on convenient new sites in Sheffield itself where they had ready access to the Midland Railway. Steam power was responsible for the rise of the big firm. So was the demand for new products like the locomotive springs made at the Cyclops Works. Despite all this the traditions of the small masters were to die hard and their small shops remained a characteristic of the Sheffield trades.

Iron manufacture was big business. The plant was extensive. This applied either to the works which concentrated on the production of cast iron or to that which was engaged in the manufacture of the various types of wrought iron. In the first case the centrepiece was the blast furnace or furnaces: in the second it was the puddling furnace and its associated slitting and rolling mills. The raw materials of the iron industry were bulky and valuable and most ironmasters were keenly interested in transport costs. Equally important were economies in fuel consumption and improvement in the quality of the final product. By raising the temperature of the furnace, and by fuelling it with coke instead of charcoal, the eighteenth-century ironmasters were able to cast molten iron before the furnace. They were also able to go in for longer production runs, because coke, unlike charcoal, was relatively plentiful, and they were now capable of building larger furnaces because coke would bear a heavier charge of ore. The result was the creation of what was virtually a new commodity and it was this fact that the ironmasters drove home to the public by the casting of bridges, boats, coffins, and the columns used in the building industry. Their success not only reshaped the market for iron but it gave a continuous incentive to large-scale production, and further technical experiment, within the industry.

The Old Furnace at Coalbrookdale (plate 11) stands on the site of the first furnace here, built in 1638. It was in this furnace that Abraham Darby first smelted iron with coke in 1709 and it was from this same furnace, after repairs in 1777, that Abraham Darby II cast the components of the Iron Bridge (plate 2). The blast to the furnace was supplied by water-powered bellows which entered the furnace through the recess on the left-hand side. The furnace was charged by hand, barrow loads of coke and ore being tipped into the furnace through its throat (open top). This was heavy work and, by the end of the eighteenth century, the materials were usually hauled up to the throat by steam power: but it remained common to use old methods, where, as at Coalbrookdale, the furnace was placed in a hollow and the platform to the throat could, at least, be built on something like a level. The molten iron was tapped from the furnace entrance onto the moulding floor. At Coalbrookdale this had gone on since the early eighteenth century; Abraham Darby I had patented his technique for casting hollow ware (like pots) in sand in 1707. What is impressive about the furnace is its massive construction. This itself was a highly skilled task. An adjoining furnace of 1792 proved unsatisfactory and never went into production. Furnace building relied primarily upon experience and instinct and ironmasters were extremely cautious in taking up new ideas. Only in the 1830s was there to be convincing demonstration that the round-hearth furnace was more efficient than the traditional square-hearth and even in the face of Neilson's successful work with the hot blast there were those who argued that cold blast made better iron.

The ironmasters had reason to be cautious, just as they had the incentive to innovate. Their plant was extremely costly. Apart from the blast or puddling furnaces, they required either effective water power or steam engines. Warehouses and offices, and often houses for the workers, were as necessary as the tramways or other transport installations (plate 1). Wherever one looks at the iron industry in this period there are signs of that attempt to make better use of capital (furnaces) and resources (raw materials) which is the secret of efficient production. Equally obvious is the effort which the ironmasters put into their search for markets; their businesses were ones which had most to lose from fluctuating demand and most to gain from spiralling demand.

Although ironworking required skill its real demands were for

physical strength and dexterity. The ironworkers were a group
as isolated and distinct as the miners. Neither were townsmen
and neither had much to do with the established artisan trades.
The miner's work was unusually dangerous. As mines were sunk
deeper the danger of exploding gases became more acute. One
answer to this problem was the safety lamp. Unfortunately the
early lamps gave a poor light and the hewers, who were paid by
results, continued using candles. Pit ventilation was still rudimentary. Probably the commonest device was to place a venti-
lating furnace at the bottom of a shaft; in this way air was
circulated through the colliery, drawn in through one or more
other shafts and forced out through the 'upcast' shaft. As the
shaft was also used for access to the mine the descent was very
uncomfortable! Ventilation by fans was only just beginning to
make progress by 1850. All ventilation was costly (it represented
part of the price which had to be paid for deeper workings) and
the need for it was often ignored; not until 1862 were one-shaft
mines made illegal. Even so the incidence of mining accidents
had been reduced by the 1840s. In the North-East the deeper
nineteenth-century pits had been more liable to explosions and
definite progress had been made here. Roof-falls were another
hazard and as yet little could be done to protect the miner from
them; danger was an everyday feature of his work. (See P. E. H.
Hair, 'Mortality from Violence in British Coal Mines, 1800–50',
Economic History Review, Vol. XXI, 3, December 1968.)

Mining is a nomadic industry and, after a pit has been abandoned, little remains to be seen but broken ground and the
outline of the old slag tips (which do give, however, some guide
to the importance of the mine). Although the deepest and most
productive pits of 1850 went at least to 300 metres (1,000 feet),
this type of working was not yet predominant. Most pits were
shallower and probably every coalfield could show examples of
the simplest mining technique, the working of 'drifts', i.e. cutting
a level from the point of outcrop back into the seam. In the early
1840s this type of mine was said to be commoner in South Wales
than the vertical pit. In Yorkshire the level was known as a
'dayhole'. Plate 12 shows the entrance and tramway of a modern

dayhole at Flockton in Yorkshire. This mine, opened in the early 1850s as 'Billy Swift's Dayhole', continued to be worked until very recently. At its peak the mine produced over 5,000 tons a year: about 10 men worked underground and 4 on the surface. The tubs were pushed by hand to a pick-up point and were then drawn out of the mine by cable. The men used pneumatic drills at the face but they mostly worked alone in 'stalls'. This is reminiscent of the 'pillar-and-stall' technique which was widely used in early collieries; here the seam was hewn open at intervals but sufficient was left standing (the pillars) to support the roof. The 'longwall' system, by which the miners worked at a continuous coal face and supported the roof by pit props, was generally only used on thin seams at this date; to use on the thicker seams (which usually meant in deeper mines) involved problems of drainage and ventilation which had not yet been overcome. Of course the pillar-and-stall system was wasteful of coal and its disadvantages were under much discussion by 1850. If this little mine at Flockton is itself of no antiquity it does show very clearly the persistence of what was once a common method of operation and its scale is certainly a reminder of the profusion of tiny mines which were a feature of every coalfield during the Industrial Revolution.

The man who worked in one of the traditionally skilled trades had little in common with the ironworker, the miner, or the factory operative (who was often a girl or woman!). His trade had to be learnt by a long apprenticeship and was usually practised under stringent rules. No one was quicker to defend his privileges and status than the craftsman and his trade society was a highly effective, as well as sometimes eccentric, organization. This was certainly true of the coopers, who were one of the several important woodworking trades of the period. 20,000 coopers were enumerated in 1851 and of these probably a fifth worked in London. The barrel was widely used as a packing case but it was of major importance in the drink trade. The brewers were the largest employers of coopers. Not only was the beer distributed in barrels but the storage containers were nothing more than huge barrels. Plate 13 shows a corner of the coopers' shop at Young and Co's Ram Brewery, Wandsworth. Most of the work in this shop is now confined to repairing barrels, but it is still necessary to make new staves, or the discs which close the barrel at top and bottom. Out of the picture to the right is a small forge on which the iron hoops are heated before being placed over the staves. Brewers, of course, needed 'wet' or 'tight' cooperage as their barrels had to contain liquid and this was the most skilled section of the trade. Barrels used as 'dry' containers required less skill in construction; so too did pails or churns – which were also coopers' products.

Behind the improvements in agriculture and transport, as well as the progress of manufacturing industry, went the steady growth of Britain's financial institutions. The workpeople here belonged to the growing army of clerks. The Census of 1851 distinguished four important regiments within this army; the 'commercial clerks' (43,760), the civil servants (30,963), not all of whom were clerks in the strict sense, the 'law clerks' (16,590), and the rising class of railway clerks (10,948), which also included station masters. Most clerks no doubt worked in very small offices; the Census enumerated 13,256 solicitors and attorneys, which suggests that a law office rarely contained more than one or two clerks. A large commercial office, like that in *Dombey and Son*, had, perhaps, upwards of half a dozen clerks – including a boy and a messenger. In industry accounting was primitive and only the larger firms bothered with a counting house and clerks. The bigger textile mills almost certainly had an office and one of these can be seen at Samuel Greg's Quarry Bank Mill at Styal.

Two or three clerks is certainly all that can have been employed at the Beverley Bank (plate 14) in 1861 when this photograph was taken. Beverley Bank was a fairly typical country bank serving the prosperous East Riding of Yorkshire. It was founded in 1790 by Sir Christopher Sykes, a prominent local landowner, and was linked to branches at Malton and Hull. Sykes retained control of the Bank until 1805 when it was taken over by a new partner, Robert Raikes. In 1808 Raikes went into partnership with the old-established London firm of Currie but they too sold out to Messrs Bower and Duesbery in 1811 and this firm was still working the Bank in 1861. The activities of the Beverley Bank, like those of many other country banks, had few direct links with industry. It lent money to turnpike trusts, to the East Riding authorities for a new house of correction (in 1820) and to a variety of local traders, including corn merchants. Sir Christopher Sykes used the bank to finance enclosures and other improvements on his Sledmore estate. This was useful work and clearly related to the overall pattern of economic progress in this period. In the nineteenth century the bank regularly kept some £3,000 on deposit with its London agent, Glyn, Mills & Co. From 1808 to 1811, for which full accounts of the East Riding Bank (i.e. Hull, Malton, Beverley together) have survived, the Beverley branch was keeping upwards of £50,000 to over £100,000 to its credit at Hull. This money was certainly being used to finance trade out of Hull. (See L. S. Pressnell, *Country Banking in the Industrial Revolution*: the accounts of Raikes, Currie & Co for 1808–13 appear in Appendix 11, pp. 526–7.) It was in ways like this that the country banks were to make their contribution to the Industrial Revolution. Early bank buildings are not all that common today and this is probably a field in which drawings or early photographs are much more important than surviving buildings; this photograph was found in the Priest's Room of St Mary's Church, Beverley.

Homes

Next to work, and the means to buy the first necessities, food and clothing, nothing matters more than house and home. Most families rented their house in this period but this did not prevent them becoming passionately attached to their home. Perhaps the focusing of a powerful public emotion on the 'Englishman's home' is really a Victorian phenomenon; it was certainly a sentiment diffused well beyond the frontiers of the middle class. The idea of home as a refuge has an obvious relevance for generations which have known rapid change and frequent migration. For many the creation of a stable home was a life-long task and one that often had its setbacks and failures. In every nineteenth-century town the hundreds, if not thousands, of homeless were a constant reminder of the basic misery – to be without a home at all. Of all the injustices against which working men strove in this period none aroused more bitterness than the ruling of the Poor Law authorities after 1834 that a family had to sacrifice its home before it could claim relief.

How good a home a family could make depended upon how much they could afford in rent and, almost as important, what their money bought in terms of accommodation. Despite the obvious importance of space there were still many families living in single-room houses or tenements throughout this period. This was partly a matter of regional tradition; in Scotland and the North-East the one-roomed household was the norm. Elsewhere it was the poorest – the Irish almost inevitably – who lived in one room and this type of accommodation was common in most large cities. The tiny rents which these families could manage encouraged landlords to cut up properties into tenements. The result was usually horror and often, although not always, a fat profit for the landlord. As one slum landlord, an undertaker, explained to Octavia Hill in the 1860s:

Yes Miss, there are plenty of bad debts. It's not the rents I look to; but the deaths I get out of the houses!

These conditions aside, most English families, and this included the working class, hoped to have their homes to themselves and that home was expected to be a house. They didn't always succeed; families often had to take lodgers and a recent analysis of the 1851 Census returns for York suggests that between 6 and 10 per cent of labourers' houses were shared with others.

There were considerable variations in the size of house built for the majority during the Industrial Revolution. Two-roomed houses were a feature of most industrial areas throughout the period but they were increasingly built with the scullery forming an additional room and, by the nineteenth century, it was usual to divide the upstairs into two bedrooms. Bedroom space was a highly prized amenity: even for middle-class houses bedroom space was often a higher priority than, say, efficient water supply or proper drainage. The model cottages which Prince Albert had designed for the Great Exhibition were most remarkable for including three bedrooms – as well as an internal w.c. (plate 16 and figure 1). The Potteries (see Chapter 35) was an area of extremely rapid growth in the early nineteenth century. But there was plenty of building land here and this meant better

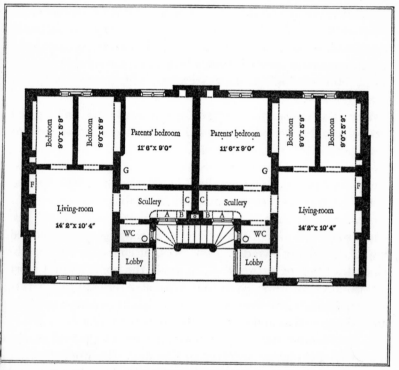

Figure 1 Model cottages designed by Henry Roberts for the Great Exhibition of 1851

housing for the potters. In 1829 it was noticed that there were 'many wide and spacious new streets of dwelling houses' throughout the Potteries, and the four-roomed, one-family house was reported as typical of the area in the mid-1840s. The two house plans in figure 2 certainly suggest a movement towards more generous standards in the nineteenth century. By contrast the

greater density of population, and higher land values, made
Birmingham a town of cramped, back-to-back courtyard, housing of the type illustrated in figure 2. But however many rooms
the house possessed its construction standards and amenities
were highly significant. Average-sized houses which were damp,
or poorly provided with water or privies, were usually the first
to begin the descent from meanness into irretrievable squalor.
And apart from the essentials few houses built for working people
before 1850 made any appeal to the eye. Some perpetuated sound
local building tradition. In London a little stucco might be used
to lighten even a humble terrace but there was no sign, as yet,
of the bow window or other Victorian embellishments to the
terraced house.

What the house itself offered could easily be endangered
throughout this period by a hostile environment. Local government was often either powerless or inactive. The workman
necessarily had to live near his work and put up with the industrial pollution which this entailed. In the town the fight against
dirt must have been continuous and no doubt called for fervent
effort. And for many households the home was also a workplace
where some member of the family, or perhaps several, followed
one of the outwork trades. There was, of course, a long established tradition of outwork which made the home seem a most
natural place for work. Even so it was a step forward to separate
work and home. The weavers' houses at Skelmanthorpe (plate 9)
surely improved as homes when the looms went into the mill?

A considerable quantity of housing from the period of the
Industrial Revolution survives to this day. The worst has, for
the most part, been demolished in the twentieth century and
much of the very worst went even before 1900. What remains is
extremely various. The best places to find it are in the smaller
industrial towns, which have not had the housing problems of
the very large city, the early industrial, and especially, textile
villages, and in the type of industrialized countryside which is,
perhaps, best represented by the West Riding of Yorkshire.
Some of the most interesting sites are those in which the housing
was originally the work of a great employer who used a supply

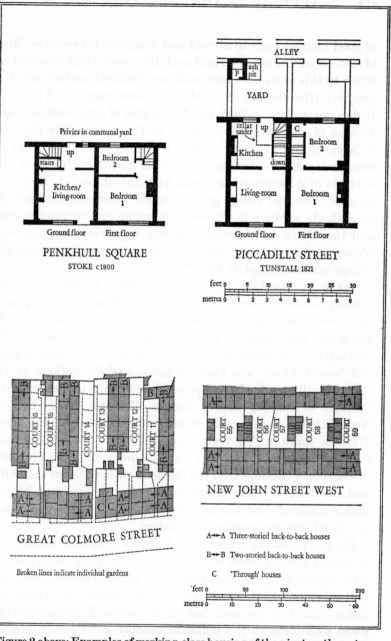

Figure 2 above: Examples of working-class housing of the nineteenth century
in the Potteries
below: Mid-nineteenth-century back-to-back houses in Birmingham

of good housing both to attract and discipline his workers. Most of the communities are rural and they owe their survival as much to this as to the exercise of firm landlord control over the property (the absence of which, in a town, might well cause it to deteriorate into a slum). Good examples of eighteenth-century villages of this type are at Styal in Cheshire and in the mill villages of the Derwent Valley in Derbyshire. This kind of community did not disappear in the nineteenth century and new variants of it continued to occur. At Belmont, outside Bolton, a sizeable industrial village grew up in the nineteenth century, its inhabitants working in the local bleaching and weaving works, and their lives and housing carefully supervised by their employers and by the local squires – after whose country house the village was named (plate 15).

Yet it is true that the urban employer in the nineteenth century was rarely concerned with the supply of houses, although there are spectacular exceptions both before, and after, 1850. In the town housebuilding was an expensive operation and the employer was disinclined to tie up funds in it. The estate of some 150 houses which was built to accommodate workers at the Akroyd mill at suburban Copley (plate 8) was, in fact, an early example of building society finance. The first houses built at New Swindon in the early 1840s were provided by the Great Western Railway. They are tiny, but they were substantially built of Bath stone, and they survive today. But the Company discontinued building after the financial stringencies of the 1840s, and the discovery that Brunel's costs for the line were heavily underestimated, and the later houses at Swindon were built in the usual way by speculative builders.

By the 1840s the more acute features of urban housing had attracted the attention of philanthropists. They were particularly appalled by the foul conditions of the London 'rookeries' and other notorious slums. These were scarcely the product of industrialization as such but they provoked solutions which owed something to the uniform, soundly constructed, housing which had been built in some industrial communities. Their differences were that this had to be high-density housing, because land values were high, and it had to be built by the cheapest methods. If there was to be a typical response to this situation it was to be found in the gaunt block of model tenements, now often horrifying in prospect, a sad comment on the narrowness of the Victorian vision but, equally, an indication of the immense problems with which it had to contend. Prince Albert instructed H. Roberts, who was to specialize in this kind of work, to design two cottages for the Great Exhibition to show what might be done on a slender philanthropic budget and these were later reerected on Kennington Common (plate 16). Four small flats, contained in a simple, unfussy and unattractive shell, was the answer. The drainage was correct, the staircase in the central niche met the problem of access in an ingenious and economical way; these cottages are a foretaste of industrialized building, their austerity pointing to a future in which many people were to have better homes provided for them – but not always the homes which they would have chosen had the choice been theirs.

Further Study and Reading

Important examples of early machinery are preserved in the great national collections, like the Science Museum in London and the Royal Scottish Museum in Edinburgh. Local museums often have valuable collections, especially where they serve the area of a major industry, like the Tolson Memorial Museum, Huddersfield. Transport history is well covered by the museums at Clapham, York, and Swindon (for railways), and by the British Waterways Museum at Stoke Bruern. Unfortunately very few historic industrial sites have been preserved for exhibition in this country. Something is now being done about this. Allied Ironfounders Ltd have preserved Abraham Darby's furnace and opened a museum at the Coalbrookdale Works to illustrate its history. The Council for the Conservation of Sheffield Antiquities, acting with the Sheffield Corporation, have put a small grinding works, Shepherd Wheel, in working order, and have restored the Abbeydale Industrial Hamlet, which comprises an eighteenth-century scythe works and workmen's cottages. Samuel Greg's Quarry Bank Mill at Styal in Cheshire is now in the possession of the National Trust.

Although very few industrial buildings have been carefully restored in this way, a great many do, in fact, survive. There are many remarkable examples of continuity in the use of industrial premises. Much, of course, has been destroyed. The urgent need to preserve at least an accurate record of these buildings, their equipment and accounts, has led to the rapid development of industrial archaeology in the last few years. An introduction to this subject was published in 1963, Kenneth Hudson, *Industrial Archaeology* (John Baker). The first in a series of detailed regional studies have now been published by David and Charles and these are the best guides to use in the field; particularly useful are Frank Nixon, *The Industrial Archaeology of Derbyshire*; David M. Smith, *The East Midlands*; Owen Ashmore, *Lancashire*; and John Butt, *Scotland*. Most regions display a diversity of industrial activity but a study in depth of a single industry has as much to offer. W. K. V. Gale, *Iron and Steel* (Longmans, 1969) is an excellent short history of the technical development of a major industry. These books are well illustrated but they are primarily studies in depth. As an introduction to industrial history W. H. Chaloner and A. E. Musson, *Industry and Technology* (Vista Books, 1963) makes very effective use of its 238 plates: there is a profusion of line drawings, based upon contemporary sources, in T. K. Derry and T. I. Williams, *The Shorter Oxford History of Technology* (Oxford University Press, 1960), and this is the most convenient reference book on every aspect of technological history. A very wide collection of contemporary drawings and paintings of industrial scenes are reproduced in F. D. Klingender, *Art and the Industrial Revolution* (Evelyn, Adams, Mackay, 1968).

Looking at industrial buildings helps to explain the environment of work in the Industrial Revolution. But it does not, in itself, explain all we should like to know about working life in this period. Hardship and hard work make their mark on the mind and the body. Bent backs and twisted limbs were the physiological signs of the Industrial Revolution; the psychological impact is less certain but no less real. In both areas there was no doubt gain as well as loss. In this connection something can be learnt from folk song, some of it now available on record. Although not all the songs belong to this period the following records are both moving and valuable: *Along the Coaly Tyne*, Topic Records, 12T189; *The Iron Muse*, Topic, 12T86, and *Deep Lancashire*, Topic, 12T188.

INDEX

INDEX

nosophobic – fear of disease?